European Economic Prehistory

A new approach

European Economic Prehistory
A new approach

Robin Dennell

Department of Prehistory and Archaeology
University of Sheffield, Sheffield, UK

1983

ACADEMIC PRESS

A Subsidiary of Harcourt Brace Jovanovich, Publishers

London · New York
Paris · San Diego · San Francisco · São Paulo
Sydney · Tokyo · Toronto

ACADEMIC PRESS INC. (LONDON) LTD.
24/28 Oval Road
London NW1

United States Edition published by
ACADEMIC PRESS INC.
111 Fifth Avenue
New York, New York 10003

British Library Cataloguing in Publication Data

Dennell, Robin
    European economic prehistory.
    1. Man, Prehistoric — Europe — Economic aspects
    I. Title
    330.94   GN803

    ISBN 0-12-209180-9

Phototypeset by Dobbie Typesetting Service, Plymouth, Devon.
Printed by St. Edmundsbury Press, Bury St. Edmunds, Suffolk.

To
Pogg, Grendel and Min

Preface

In advance, it is as well to say what this book is, and is not, supposed to be. It is primarily intended to be a sketch-map of a continent, rather than a detailed compendium of every landmark and curiosity. Whilst it may well be read by those unfortunate souls who have to sit university examinations in prehistoric archaeology, it is not designed to be a source of reference. Instead, I hope that it will help people to view European prehistory through a different pair of spectacles from those designed in the last century, and also to regard economic prehistory as more than the study of faunal assemblages and lists of plant remains. Whilst these are useful sources of data, they should not exclude other types of evidence: in recent years there has been an unfortunate tendency amongst economic prehistorians to approach their subject matter as simply the study of man as a bipedal stomach ingesting anything worth eating within a hour's forage of his settlement. Because I wanted to write a book that encompassed a large part of European prehistory, yet was sufficiently brief to be read in a short time, I have assumed that readers are already familiar with terms such as Acheulean, Neanderthal or *Bandkeramik*, or sites like Olduvai, Kostienki, Star Carr and Karanovo. The bibliography is intended to be selective rather than exhaustive.

The pressures on prehistorians to specialize in an area and period have perhaps never been stronger than today. For my part, I have always found it impossible to decide between the study of early hominids or the origins of food production, and have thus tried to maintain over the years a somewhat bigamous relationship. What has united them for me is an underlying interest in prehistoric subsistence, whether based upon the extraction or the production of food resources, and I hope that this theme will help readers to follow a common thread from the emergence of hominids to the development of cereal cultivation and sheep husbandry several million years later.

Inevitably, a book such as this is never the sole product of the author, and there are several who should be thanked. The idea behind this book stemmed from a suggestion by Norman Hammond three years ago, who deserves thanks for his guidance in its initial stages. I owe much to those stalwart students at Sheffield who have stoically accepted my inability or refusal to give them answers to the problems on which they have had to write examination essays, and to Nic Ralph, who has been an invaluable sparring partner over the years. Sue Stallibrass and Val Kinsler coped heroically with unravelling my spaghetti-like prose, as did the library staff at Sheffield, when faced by my voracious appetite for photocopying, and for articles from the British Library and from overseas. Gill Stroud and Liz Ayres wrestled manfully with the typescript and drawings. I have also benefited greatly from conversations with many people, especially Lewis Binford, John Cherry, Roland Fletcher, Clive Gamble, Roger Jacobi and Val Shelton-Bunn; needless to say, they are not to blame for anything that I have written.

Sheffield, January 1983

Contents

List of Figures and Tables

Introduction

This book attempts a new framework of European prehistory up to the time when cereals and sheep were used as food resources by most of its inhabitants. In my opinion, a new structure is long overdue. The main divisions of the Stone Age—the Lower, Middle and Upper Palaeolithic, the Mesolithic and Neolithic—were drawn up over a century ago in terms of those artefacts that could be most usefully employed in constructing a chronological framework. Gradually, these periods became encrusted with social and economic accretions. By the 1870s, the Palaeolithic and Mesolithic had become firmly equated with hunting and gathering, and with "savagery", that ferocious and unrestrained way of life that the Victorians found so repulsive yet curiously appealing, and the Neolithic with barbarism, agriculture, food-production and sedentism (see Westropp, 1872). In time, it became clear that these periods were not "epochs", as used by geologists, but were variegated spatially as well as chronologically, and so they became subdivided into a plethora of cultures, each defined by various artefacts and styles. As data and specialists proliferated, units of study became smaller and smaller, and what had previously been summarized in a paragraph was often expanded into a lengthy monograph. This profusion of detailed local studies has long obscured the main features of the periods they are trying to elucidate, and has often impeded communication between pre-historians. A weighty tome on, for example, the perforated nose-plugs of South East Liechtenstein in the Late Middle Bronze Age may constitute impressive scholarship, but is hardly likely to initiate a stampede to the nearest bookshop.

Like old soldiers, archaeological periods do not die but simply fade away (in most cases, all too slowly). Today, the archaeological periods constructed in the nineteenth century can still be discerned behind the facade of twentieth century renovations. Syntheses of European

1

prehistory often attempt a more modern appearance by renaming some of the main periods, or by adding a few morsels of the "New Archaeology" to an otherwise traditional fare of the "Old Prehistory". Thus the Upper Palaeolithic may be renamed as an age of advanced hunters, the Mesolithic as early holocene hunter–gatherers, or the Neolithic as the first farmers. These terms may pay lip-service to the shift of interest over the last 20 years from the technology to the subsistence of prehistoric communities, but often the evidence is shepherded into (and by) the same old pens as before.

Cosmetic alterations of this kind are rarely satisfactory, for the boundaries of the periods they perpetuate may not have been drawn in the most appropriate place. For example, it was all very well to define the beginnings of prehistory by the first appearance of tool-making when this skill was supposed to distinguish "Man the Tool-Maker" from other animals, and to have been one of our earliest characteristics. However, as work has shown over the last 15 years, man is not the only tool-maker, and hominids have spent at least half the time they have existed on this planet without making artefacts. Or again, the lumping together of all evidence for man's presence in Europe before prepared-core techniques became common into the immensity of the Lower Palaeolithic obscures the point that at some time during this period, Europe was probably permanently occupied for the first time. The replacement of mousterian by upper palaeolithic assemblages need not, as first thought, have coincided with the appearance of *Homo sapiens sapiens* and the extinction of Neanderthals. To take another example, the beginning of the Mesolithic is defined by the end of the last ice age, yet a large body of data indicates that this immensely important climatic event began earlier, in the late Palaeolithic. Food-production and agriculture are no longer regarded by many as synonymous, and neither need have begun in Europe when pottery and polished stone were first used. All these points emphasize the need for a new structure that can provide better premises for the evidence than those built a century earlier.

This is especially necessary because Europe is no longer the only continent to have a prehistory. With the emergence over the last 20 years or so of what can be termed a "world prehistory", many prehistorians— particularly in north-west Europe—have attempted to open channels of communication with those working in other areas by addressing topics that transcend local boundaries of time and space. The most ambitious of these attempts have tried to develop a general theoretical framework by focussing upon either prehistoric societies or archaeological data. Binford's (1965) ideas of a systemic archaeology, which comprised the study of the relationships between the technology, ideology, social organization and environment of prehistoric societies, and Clarke's (1968) *Analytical Archaeology*, which tried to arrange archaeological data into a coherent hierarchical structure, were probably the two most influential of these endeavours; certainly both contributed much to what became the "New Archaeology" on both sides of the Atlantic at the end of the 1960s. These early attempts to harness the power of General Theory to fly above the morass of local detail encouraged further flights (some more fanciful than others), and resulted in a large output of cross-cultural comparisons of features common to many prehistoric societies: the development of food-production, ranked societies or ceremonialism

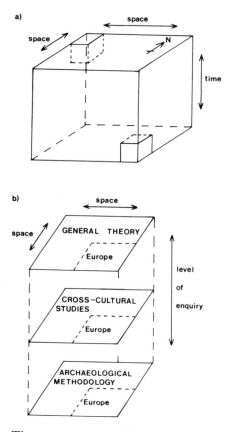

Fig. 1: The two structures of European prehistory.
The first (a) is the traditional one, and based on regional studies of specific periods. In the last 20 years, a different one (b) has developed alongside it, and is more concerned with general topics than with specific areas or periods.

are convenient examples. Another type of cross-cultural study has been the investigation of prehistoric societies in the same kind of environment, such as arctic, desert or maritime. All these studies have been less concerned with how a *particular* area developed through time than with elucidating *general* processes of adaptation and change. Finally, methodological studies have been important in opening up new avenues for communication by exploring how the archaeological record was created, and how best to sample, analyse and interpret it.

As a result of the development of these thematic studies, we now have two structures within European prehistoric research (see Fig. 1). The "traditional" structure may be likened to village life: a researcher working on a period and area will be best informed about the activities of his neighbours, but know much less about the research being undertaken elsewhere. In contrast, the newer structure resembles more the craftsmen's guilds of medieval northern Europe: those working in, for example, the Worshipful Company of Faunal Analysts may well be aware of what their fellow faunal analysts are doing, but be largely in ignorance about other types of research. In practice, of course, many prehistorians have a dual identity and try to tap both networks to remain informed of regional as well as thematic developments.

What seems very doubtful is that the existing framework, devised generations ago in terms of technological change, is the most appropriate way of studying themes of general interest. For the earlier periods of European prehistory, these include the behaviour of early hominids, the ways that late pleistocene hunter–gatherers responded to conditions of extreme coldness and aridity, and later to the onset of interglacial conditions, the origins of food-production, and the relationships between hunter–gatherers and agriculturalists. All these topics are areas of widespread and fruitful interest, and there is no reason why the terms of reference for their study should be predetermined by minor aspects of material culture.

1. Towards a New Framework

Abstract

This chapter proposes that the study of prehistoric subsistence, of whatever period, should comprise three components: the physical and social environments of prehistoric societies, and their competitors. Societies can be divided into two basic units: the subsistence group, concerned primarily with day-to-day food procurement, and the reproductive network to which each belonged. Food resources are classed as traditional or novel, to highlight the importance of sheep and cereals in post-glacial Europe but to avoid the problems of how to distinguish wild from domestic plants and animals.

The main focus of this book is prehistoric subsistence. Although the major aspect of this topic is food, the importance of other commodities — notably fuel and raw materials such as wood, bone, antler, hides, furs, fibres, clay, metal and stone — should not be ignored. The reason why we should treat subsistence as a central theme in prehistoric studies is simply that it is an essential and universal human need, irrespective of social and chronological context. Ideally, its study should comprise three main components.

The first is the one given the most attention in recent years, and concerns the relationships between human groups and their *physical* environment. This type of enquiry largely involves identifying the food resources in a given area and period; with establishing their relative importance, probable distribution and abundance; and with suggesting how these factors affected the size of human groups, their annual movements, and the location of their settlements. Since climate directly affects the type, distribution and abundance of the resources used by man, the effects of climatic change on human populations also figure prominently in this type of study. This is especially true for studies of human groups during the Pleistocene, the climate of which has frequently alternated between glacial and interglacial conditions. As the recent drought in the Sahel showed so cruelly, even minor perturbations of temperature and precipitation can have far-reaching consequences upon human societies, and so should not be overlooked when discussing archaeological data that span only a few millennia or even centuries. Fortunately for the prehistorian, our knowledge of the climatic changes that occurred during the time-span of human evolution has improved out of all recognition in the last few years, and now offers excellent opportunities for investigating the ways that prehistoric communities were affected by at least the most marked of these changes, especially at the end of the last glaciation.

However important climate and food resources are to our understanding of prehistoric subsistence, other factors should not be forgotten, and economic prehistorians should be interested in more than just the interactions between human groups and their resources. In the first place, we are unlikely to be dealing with what can be caricatured as "economic man": that is to say, with human (or proto-human) groups whose size, distribution and annual activities were determined solely by the distribution and abundance of their food resources, or even with groups that were preoccupied solely by the quest for food. Still less can we assume that they operated with a perfect knowledge of their environment and neighbours which allowed them to obtain their food in the most efficient way imaginable, or to maintain a precise balance between their numbers and the productivity of their resources. Rather, we have to take into account as a second topic the *social* environment of prehistoric groups. Particularly important here are the ways that they *organized* the procurement and distribution of food, as well as information about the environment in which they lived. No less important are the mechanisms they employed to ensure that individual groups were incorporated into a viable reproductive network which would allow them to persist from generation to generation.

At present, the social environment of prehistoric groups is less well understood than their physical environment. Not surprisingly, economic prehistorians have tended to give most (and perhaps too much?)

emphasis to the more tangible and quantifiable data on resources, settlement patterns and palaeo-environments. Although the ways prehistoric societies organized themselves are less immediately accessible to present archaeological expertise, they deserve more attention than they have received. One recent and neat example that illustrates the importance of social factors in influencing the success or failure of subsistence economies is provided by the fate of the Norse settlements on Greenland that lasted from the eleventh to the fifteenth centuries A.D. Whilst the weather conditions of the "little ice age" during the fifteenth century undoubtedly had adverse repercussions upon them, climatic factors alone cannot be held responsible for their collapse. One has to explain why it was the Norse settlements that foundered, whilst the local Inuit populations survived. What seems to have happened is that the Norse leadership was ultra-conservative, and refused to allow their communities to adapt to new conditions by, for example, imitating the ways of their heathen Inuit neighbours. Moreover, the church, which dominated the Norse leadership, had probably done much to weaken the local economy by appropriating the best lands and investing most surplus wealth in prestige items such as stained-glass windows instead of in more mundane but practical directions. Both climatic and social factors were thus responsible (McGovern, 1980).

The third theme that should be incorporated into discussions on prehistoric subsistence is again one that has received less attention than it merits. This concerns the relationships between man and his *competitors*. The importance of this topic stems simply from the point that man would not have been the only species interested in his food resources. Instead, a considerable proportion of his potential diet is likely to have been appropriated by a wide range of species, ranging from large carnivores to intestinal bacteria, before man was to simplify many of his food chains in recent centuries by the (often indiscriminate) use of fire-arms, traps and pesticides. In the case of pleistocene economies, we should not be blinded into regarding hunting as a matter that concerned only man and his quarry simply because man was the only carnivore that happened to make stone tools. Animals such as lion, hyaena, wolf and their ancestors would have competed with man for all but the largest herbivores; given the speed, strength and stamina of many of these predators, it is unlikely that they would have had only a marginal impact on the amount of game that man could kill and eat. To put this point in perspective, it is useful to contrast the dozen or so reindeer that Sturdy (1975) estimated were the minimum needed to maintain one person for a year in the late glacial with the annual total of around 30 that a wolf takes from modern caribou herds (Reimers and Klein, 1979). Nor should we ignore the possibility that many a human and proto-human life was terminated by carnivores. Even in modern agricultural communities, predators can take a significant portion of each year's newly-born livestock; in this context, the domestication of the dog perhaps affords us our earliest example of man reducing the effect of competitors by the use of biological control.

Plant resources are also likely to have been sought after by species other than man. This point is nicely illustrated in a recent study of the competitive interactions between man and deer for acorns in aboriginal California (Gage, 1979). In this instance, the biomass of acorns and deer, if calculated separately and then added together, could have supported a much larger human population than appears to have been the case. However, acorns were staple resources of both man and deer, and so the numbers of deer that could be eaten depended in part upon the amount of acorns that man harvested for himself. When this triangular relationship is borne in mind, the actual aboriginal population levels appear more reasonable. Much the same type of competition occurs in agricultural communities.

One form that is especially recurrent is between man and his livestock for the crop resources. More livestock produce more manure, and so higher crop yields can be obtained; however, the livestock then require more winter feed; if they are fed with part of the crops, there will then be less available for human consumption. If, on the other hand, man consumes most of the crops, there will be less available for livestock; fewer livestock results in a smaller production of manure which in turn can cause crop yields to fall, and thus less grain will be available to man. This particular vicious circle was certainly a major weakness of many medieval European farms (e.g. Slicher van Bath, 1963) and is likely to have been as critical in prehistoric times as well. Another important form of competition whose significance is often underestimated is between man and rodents for crops. Here, competition can often be heavily weighted in favour of the latter. It has, for example, been suggested that the elimination of the rat from India could have such an effect on net grain production as to turn that country into a major grain exporter (Pirie, 1969). Finally, there is still a wide field of enquiry yet to be undertaken into the intestinal parasites that can consume much of what man eats with no benefit to him. How these are likely to have changed as man shifted his diet in the Holocene towards plant foods, and in later periods of prehistory began to live in larger, more permanent but probably less hygenic settlements, provide some disgustingly enthralling topics for future research (see e.g. Greig, 1981).

If these are our main themes, we have to be able to treat them in a way that satisfies two basic conditions. The first is that we must take full account of the peculiar nature of the archaeological record. When prehistorians try to monitor changes in human behaviour through long periods of time, they can do so only by observing a record that is made up of innumerable short and usually widely spaced events—such as the butchery of an animal, the knapping of a few flint tools, or the construction of a shelter. Before comparisons can be drawn between samples of different ages, the human (or proto-human) behaviour represented by each of these events has first to be established, for otherwise we might find ourselves comparing, for example, the flint-knapping site of one period with a hunting camp of another. One way in which we may infer past behaviour from archaeological assemblages is by studying how similar assemblages are formed today in ethnographic or experimental situations. However, some of the behavioural patterns that led to the formation of past assemblages may no longer exist, and ethnographic studies need not exhaust the full range of explanations of how pleistocene ones were created. Similarly, ethnographers can only observe the formation of the archaeological record over very short periods, rather like a series of snap-shots; in contrast, pleistocene archaeologists observe a record that is "a massive palimpsest of derivatives from many separate episodes" (Binford, 1981:197), formed over a much longer period. For instance, an archaeologist might be studying faunal assemblages from a series of cave deposits, but one might represent the debris of several activities performed in summer, whilst another might have resulted from one activity carried out in winter, whilst a third might be a mixture of both, containing also the remains of other carnivores' meals. To treat all three assemblages as though they resulted from one uniform pattern of behaviour would obviously lead to highly spurious conclusions.

Establishing sample comparability is probably the most daunting methodological problem currently facing economic prehistorians. The problem can be broken down into three components. First, one has to decide how representative an excavated area is of the rest of the site, and whether the excavated site is representative of others in the same region or of the same period. Secondly, the possibility that excavation techniques have biased the composition of samples has to be considered. Next, the natural and human agencies that may have modified the original composition of the sample before excavation have to be investigated. Only then can one try to establish how the sample was created in the first place. Each of these topics has generated a large volume of literature in recent years that would fully justify another book. For the moment, it is enough to emphasize that much of our present

evidence on European prehistoric subsistence is not sufficiently well
controlled for us to recognize how it was created. Consequently, it is
often difficult for us to discern trends in subsistence patterns through
time as confidently as we would like. As will emerge in this book, we are
often in the uncomfortable position of knowing enough to realize that
much of our material is less useful than was once thought, but not yet
having the quality of data that is required.

The second condition that has to be met is that our conceptual
framework is sufficiently precise to allow us to discuss both the physical
and social environments of prehistoric populations, yet flexible enough
to be applicable to the entire range of human societies that inhabited
Europe up to when cereals, sheep and goat were used as food resources.
We need also a way of classifying the resources used by all these societies
that can highlight the importance of the changes brought about by the
adoption of cereals and caprovines without becoming bogged down in the
troublesome mire of how we can distinguish wild from domestic
resources in the archaeological record.

First, a look at the units we might use to discuss prehistoric societies.

I. PREHISTORIC SOCIETIES

Much prehistoric research over the last 20 years has been devoted to
dismantling and rebuilding a prehistoric famework that had been
constructed of archaeological "cultures". These, defined originally as a
set of regularly associated traits (Childe, 1929:v–vi), were regarded as the
manifestations of different "peoples" who shared the same customs,
subsistence and technology. By noting styles and artefacts shared by
adjacent cultures, prehistorians were able to build a relative chronological framework for Europe by assuming that major innovations such
as agriculture and metallurgy were first developed in the Near East, and
then spread across Europe by the processes of diffusion and migration.
Once absolute dating techniques (particularly ^{14}C) had been developed,
cultures lost their primary function as chronological devices, and
attention moved on to examining the spatial distribution of different
types of artefacts. Studies of pottery and metal products often brought
home the point that what had previously been regarded as a neatly
defined culture was probably better explained in terms of exchange
networks or the products of hierarchically organized societies.
Subsequently, cultures have also lost almost all their former ethnic
connotations in studies of the later periods of prehistory.

The concept of the archaeological culture, as originally defined by
Childe, has also largely atrophied in palaeolithic and mesolithic research,

although for different reasons. The most critical was that cultures—defined largely by stone tools—obscured an important element of technological variability. Because hunter-gatherers may use and discard several different tool-kits in the course of their annual activities, the presence of different contemporaneous assemblages in a region need not indicate that it was occupied by several different cultures—and thus peoples. Even where only one culture was recognized in a region, attention was frequently drawn away from the differences between assemblages; anomalous ones could be dismissed as "atypical", and the main attention focussed upon how a culture—at a regional level—was distinct from others. To many, this approach accomplished little beyond showing that certain types of assemblages were found within the area of their distribution. In order to explain how assemblages were used and discarded, and how those who made them had lived, it was necessary to consider more carefully than had often been the case the time of year that a site was occupied, the activities conducted there, and the behaviour of the resources that were used. These objectives required that the environment was seen as more than a convenient backcloth against which a culture had whiled away its time on the stage of human development.

Finally, those prehistorians interested in very early periods found it difficult to accept that an entity such as the acheulean culture, distributed over a vast tract of time and space, could ever have been the product of one "people". Instead, some preferred the safe vagueness of labels such as simply "the Acheulean"; others attempted more precise terms such as "industries" or "techno-complexes" that were devoid of any ethnic connotations.

Finding units of study that can replace the archaeological culture in ways acceptable to prehistorians working on the Palaeolithic and Mesolithic, and to those interested in later periods, has proved difficult. In recent years, there seems to have been a consensus of opinion towards thinking about prehistoric "societies" rather than "cultures", and these have been classified in a number of ways. One is in terms of their social complexity, ranging from "simple" to "complex"; another is Service's (1962) well-known tripartite scheme, based on social organization, of band, tribe and chiefdom. Others have classified societies in terms of their subsistence base; three recent attempts have drawn contrasts between mobile and sedentary economies (Vita-Finzi and Higgs, 1970), generalized versus specialized ones (Gamble, 1978), or between foragers and collectors (Binford, 1980a).

Although all these schemes are useful, they encounter at least one of the following three criticisms. The first is that the term "society" is so vague as to be almost meaningless at times, since it can be applied with equal validity to population units ranging from "European bronze age society" to "a society in bronze age Wessex". Secondly, simple bi- or tripartite classifications of economies or societies are usually frustrated by the subsequent discovery of anomalous examples, whose inclusion is often at the expense of the coherence of the original scheme. Thirdly, it has proved extremely difficult to devise a framework that would be equally useful to those prehistorians studying the European Palaeolithic and Mesolithic, and those interested in later periods. To some extent, this point is academic, given the profound indifference with which each usually regards the other. However, as this state of affairs probably owes more to the way that prehistoric archaeology has developed over the last century than to the ways that late mesolithic and early neolithic groups regarded each other, some common ground would be desirable.

What we shall use here are two demographic units. The first is the *subsistence group*. This can be defined as a group of people habitually associated with each other throughout at least part of the year for the procurement of those resources necessary for their physiological well-being, and for the rearing of young and caring for the old and sick. Both functions probably emerged at a very early stage of hominid evolution as the most effective way of solving the problems of exploiting seasonally and spatially dispersed resources, and rearing offspring that were helpless for a long period after birth and whose survival depended upon cooperative behaviour. The size of subsistence groups does not have to remain constant throughout the year, but may change as members form smaller sub-units; for example, a hunting band might split into smaller groups at some times of the year to exploit dispersed resources, or part of an agricultural community may transhume to seasonal pasture with the flocks. Nor does its membership have to remain constant, since members may leave to join another group and be replaced by others. However, at any given time of the year, its size should remain roughly the same from year to year. A subsistence group should also be associated with an annual territory: that is to say, with an area that it and neighbouring groups will recognize as containing its food resources.

Six examples of subsistence groups are shown in Fig. 2. The first two represent hunter–gatherers. As the figure shows, foragers may use several camps during the year, and will remain at one until the resources are depleted, at which point they will move to another. In the case of collectors, group members may split into smaller units to obtain resources that are in season at the same time but located in different places. The next two examples are of agriculturalists. The fourth example, of a group of shifting cultivators who move their settlement every 5 years or so when crop yields drop to a point they consider

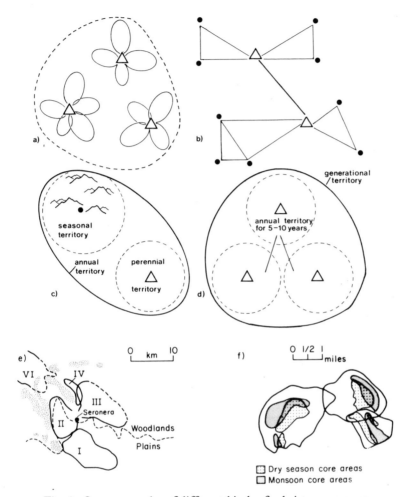

Fig. 2: Some examples of different kinds of subsistence groups.
(a) foragers; (b) logistic hunting-gathering; (c) crop agriculturalists who utilise an adjacent area of upland grazing in the summer; (d) shifting cultivators; (e) lion prides; (f) a langur group. (From Dolhinous, 1972, pp.181-238)

unacceptable, makes the point that the annual territory may be considerably smaller in some cases than the decadal one. The final examples are of a lion pride and a langur group. The point of these examples is that on a pleistocene time-scale, we need an analytical unit that can be applied to early hominids as well as to *Homo sapiens sapiens*. Because our proto-human ancestors should be studied as extinct primates rather than merely as simpler versions of ourselves, some bridge is needed to link the study of man to that of other animals. Of these, the most important for understanding early human behaviour are the other higher primates from which we diverged, and those carnivores which live in groups and prey upon the same type of animals as did our ancestors.

In recent years, prehistoric subsistence groups have received considerable attention, and there has been much progress in modelling at least their general features. Greater emphasis than before is being given to recovering dietary and environmental evidence, with establishing the time of year that a site was occupied and the activities that were performed there: Star Carr (Clark, 1954) is no longer an isolated example of the kind of information that can be obtained from these types of evidence. The technique of catchment analysis (Vita-Finzi and Higgs, 1970) has also proved useful as a way of evaluating the type and abundance of the food resources that could have been used, and why particular locations may have been chosen for settlement.

Despite this progress, two problems have remained depressingly stubborn. The first is how to assess the dietary importance of prehistoric plant foods when these are much less likely to be preserved than animal remains, particularly in non-agricultural contexts. The second is that the *function* of many archaeological sites—particularly palaeolithic ones— is unclear. One especially worrying point is that many are assumed to have been base camps—and thus the main foci of settlement—but may have served other functions, such as food-processing stations, or have been occupied for only short periods under highly exceptional circumstances. This latter possibility may well be true of cave sites, from which most of our evidence for pleistocene subsistence is derived. As recent hunter-gatherers seem to have lived in caves only very rarely (see Binford, 1978a:489; Jennings, 1979), most of our evidence of palaeolithic subsistence may relate to very atypical events in the lives of these peoples. As we shall see later, these two problems frustrate the interpretation of much of our dietary and settlement data on subsistence during the Pleistocene.

As a demographic unit, the subsistence group is usually too small to provide its members with an adequate range of potential mates. For this reason, we need to recognize a larger unit which can be called the *reproductive group*. This comprises a set of subsistence groups within which the members of any one unit will tend to find a mating partner; it is, in effect, the regional breeding population that ensures the long term viability of each subsistence group. Since it functions both by encounters between and within groups, it also serves as an information network that can provide each subsistence group with knowledge about their neighbours and their regional—as opposed to local—environment. This latter function is vital, as it lessens the probability that a group will compete for resources with neighbouring groups; knowledge of the regional environment also helps local groups to respond better to periodic fluctuations in food supply.

Reproductive networks are not yet part of the conceptual repertoire of prehistoric archaeology. They are, however, well documented ethnographically: two good examples are the breeding networks of the !Kung bushmen (Howell, 1980) and Alaskan Eskimo (Wilmsen, 1973). Pleistocene mating networks have also been the subject of an important simulation study by Wobst (1974) which showed very clearly the constraints that regulated the spacing of subsistence groups within their mating network: if subsistence groups are too close to each other, they will compete for food resources, and so the energy costs of obtaining food will rise; if too far apart, communication between each becomes difficult, and the mating network is in danger of fragmenting. When groups are too large, resources may become locally depleted; however, once they become too small, there may not be enough members to undertake all the necessary tasks, and so aggregation with another group may be required.

To date, there have been few attempts to identify prehistoric mating networks from archaeological data, and the problems of so doing are substantial. The most promising line of enquiry seems at present in improving our ability to recognize regional styles in artefact and artistic production that stemmed from the movements of individuals between subsistence groups. Clark (1975), for example, has claimed different "social territories" of early holocene populations in the Baltic region, and Close (1978) has defined stylistic territories in the late Palaeolithic of the Sudan. Another recent study (Conkey, 1980), this time of the styles used in palaeolithic cave art in northern Spain, indicated that some of these caves may have served as "aggregation sites" where members of subsistence groups within a mating network regularly convened.

II. RESOURCES

For a very long time now, European prehistorians have drawn an important distinction between the supposedly hunter-gatherer societies of the Palaeolithic and Mesolithic, and the supposedly agricultural ones of the Neolithic and later periods. In recent years, what seemed at first a crisp contrast between the two has become very blurred, and much confusion has arisen over how to distinguish food-extraction from food-production in the archaeological record.

One reason has been that recent ethnographic data, collected more assiduously than in the eighteenth and nineteenth centuries, do not show such a clear dichotomy between hunters and farmers as once thought. As the influential *Man the Hunter* (Lee and DeVore, 1968) symposium showed, many alleged hunters rely mainly upon plant foods, and the few hunter-gatherer societies left today are so varied as to frustrate any easy way of defining the hunting-gathering way of life. Australian data on aboriginal subsistence has been especially important here in showing how food-production—including the sowing, transplanting, protection, reaping and storage of plants, and the construction of channels to breed eel (Allen, 1974; Lourandos, 1980)—features in societies traditionally regarded as exemplary hunter-gatherers.

A second range of problems has arisen from archaeological data. An early casualty was the neatly-wrapped package of prehistoric behaviour, whereby the social organization and subsistence inside each parcel could be inferred from the technological label on its wrapping-paper. For example, the occurrence of pottery has often been taken as evidence of food-production, and the occasional find of mesolithic pottery associated with what seemed to be wild animals was taken as no more than interesting exceptions to a general rule. This assumption was rudely shaken by the discovery in the Near East of the "aceramic Neolithic"; although this concept was as preposterously contradictory as that of a slumbering insomniac, it brought home the point that large settled communities, and possibly food-production, may have arisen before the invention of such items as pottery which had originally been used to define the Neolithic. These neat packages further disintegrated when metal and morphologically wild resources were found in neolithic contexts, and polished stone, substantial settlements and domesticated dogs in pre-neolithic ones. As these discoveries accumulated, pre-historians came to emphasize that the most important aspect of the mesolithic–neolithic boundary lay in the replacement of hunting and gathering by food-production. Consequently, they attached more weight to biological data and less to artefactual criteria.

Unfortunately, the criteria for distinguishing wild from domestic resources in the archaeological record have become severely weakened over the last decade.

A. Animal domestication

The most important criteria that have been used to show animal domestication in Europe and the Near East have been (i) changes in the distribution of an animal to beyond its "natural" (i.e. early holocene) environment; (ii) the type of animal; (iii) a reduction in body size; (iv) changes in morphology and sexual dimorphism and (v) differences between the faunal assemblages created by hunters and farmers.

Of these, the first is of little use for identifying *local* domestication, as may have happened with pig, cattle and dog; in the case of sheep and goat, it is difficult to decide whether changes in their distribution occurred naturally or through human agencies (see Chapter 8). The second criterion rests upon the somewhat Orwellian assumption that all animals were once wild, but some were more wild than others; thus the presence of red deer, elk or gazelle in faunal assemblages was taken as automatically indicative of hunting, on the grounds that these animals were inherently unsuitable for domestication. This view is seriously undermined by the ease with which these can be, and have been, domesticated in recent years (see Wilkinson, 1972).

Evidence that the body size of animals, particularly cattle and pig, became smaller is one criterion for recognizing prehistoric animal domestication that is particularly problematic. In the first place, the size of many animals well beyond the pale of human economies also decreased in the post-glacial (Jarman and Wilkinson, 1972), and so post-glacial dwarfing in cattle and pig need not have occurred entirely because of human factors. In cases where the faunal record of an area is well calibrated and extends back into the late Pleistocene, it may be possible to discriminate between a reduction in body size caused by man, and that caused by changing environmental circumstances (see e.g. Davis, 1981). Often, however, this type of study cannot be undertaken with the data currently available, and thus the fact that neolithic livestock are often smaller than their mesolithic counterparts is not an unambiguous indicator of domestication. A second problem is that of sexual dimorphism. For example, Grigson (1978) has argued that the size of *Bos primigenius* in northern Europe did *not* decrease in the early post-glacial; instead, she attributed the size differences between early and later post-glacial aurochsen in these areas to the differences in size between males and females. In addition, it is often difficult to distinguish female *Bos primigenius* remains from those of male *Bos tauros*, and so the status of many neolithic cattle in Europe is uncertain. Increased morphological variability and sexual dimorphism (criterion iv) are also problematic. Whilst these may increase as a result of domestication, they need not have been apparent in its early stages. Furthermore, it is often difficult to assess these features when, as is so often the case, faunal material from prehistoric sites is badly fragmented.

The fifth criterion, of differences between the faunal assemblages of hunter-gatherers and farmers, was used because zoologists in effect passed the problem of recognizing domestic animals back to archaeologists and ethnographers and asked for differences in the way that hunters and farmers exploited their environments. A clear contrast was drawn between the two: hunters killed their prey at random and with no thought of conserving their resources, and thus created faunal assemblages that showed no preference for any one type of animal, age or sex group. In contrast, farmers specialized upon a few species only, and safeguarded their resource base by culling only those animals surplus to breeding requirements—namely most of the immature males, and those animals too old for further use.

This was unfortunately a gross over-simplification, for the type of clustering thought to characterize only neolithic and later faunal assemblages was found in many earlier ones. That is not to say, as some have claimed (e.g. M. Jarman, 1972), that domestication thus extends back into the Palaeolithic. Instead, it is more likely that similar faunal assemblages could have been produced in several different ways. For example, Wilkinson (1976) showed that the type of faunal patterning which Barker (1975a) cautiously explained as evidence for selective herding in Italy during the last glaciation could have resulted from a "catch-as-catch-can" strategy. It is also worth noting that predators such as lion, hyaena and wolf also obtain most of their food from only a few species, and often kill mainly young or very old animals. In doing so, they seem to be selecting those animals that are easiest to kill, rather than conserving their resources for the sake of cubs as yet unborn.

At present there is no general agreement over which criteria should be used to distinguish prehistoric wild from domestic animals, or indeed whether they should be so distinguished. Some have argued (e.g. Higgs and Jarman, 1972) that there is such a wide spectrum of man-animal relationships between random hunting and systematic breeding that a clear unequivocal line cannot be drawn between wild and domestic resources, and so the term "husbandry" should be used to cover both. This point of view effectively strips the mesolithic-neolithic transition of any changes in subsistence strategies, and is not a view acceptable to most. The majority would tend to argue that although a simple division between "wild" and "domestic" is not sufficient to describe adequately the diversity of man-animal relationships seen today and in prehistory, important changes nevertheless did occur in many parts of Europe during the Neolithic, and thus the term domestication, however faulty, should be retained. Whether it can be salvaged by defining several types of domestication, as Brothwell (1975) has proposed, seems uncertain, judging from the lack of attempts to do so.

B. Plants

The difficulties of distinguishing wild from domestic plants are no less problematic, but arise for different reasons. One is that there is so little data on pre-neolithic plant foods that the notion of pre-neolithic gathering is largely a matter of faith, and our ideas on what the wild ancestors of modern cultigens were like is still a matter of conjecture. A second problem is that the seeds or grains of many plants do not always change on domestication. This is particularly true of many legumes, and also of other plants that are today uncultivated but were in medieval times, and could have been so in the prehistoric past. For this reason, archaeobotanists have often taken the *abundance* of a plant species as indicative of whether or not it was cultivated. This leads to a third problem, namely that the abundance of a plant species depends greatly upon the domestic circumstances under which a plant was preserved; indeed, under some circumstances the commonest plant species could represent a plant that was not eaten but discarded as refuse (Dennell, 1976a).

In my opinion, the criteria commonly used for recognizing wild and domestic resources in the archaeological record are ambiguous at best, and at worst, obfuscate rather than clarify changes in prehistoric subsistence economies. That is not to say, however, that significant changes did not occur between 8000 and 5000 b.p. in many parts of Europe. Although the evidence is often appalling, we should expect that the changes around this time in the types of resources, the size and type of settlements and to a lesser extent, the technology, were associated with and initiated by major changes in the way man obtained his food.

What has often been omitted from discussions on prehistoric domestication is that it involved important relationships between man and man, as well as between man and resource. In modern hunting societies, a group may have communal ownership over the animals or plants within their territory. However, an individual animal is owned by an individual hunter only when killed, and not whilst alive. If the animal killed is female and has young, the person who killed it has no particular property rights over the young. By contrast, such rights do exist amongst pastoralists. Individual animals can be stolen, and ownership of a female also carries with it similar rights over the offspring. This important feature embodies within it opportunities for investment, and for deliberately increasing the size of the herd or flock (see Ingold, 1980). Much the same features apply to gatherers and farmers. The former may have communal rights over the plant resources in their territory, and will harvest and consume them on a communal basis; farmers, on the other hand, will own specific plant resources and are not obliged to cooperate in obtaining and processing them. This too brings opportunities for investment in the way of fields, drainage/irrigation canals and manuring.

Unfortunately, it is the social dimension of domestication that is the most elusive in the archaeological record. Although evidence for byres and stalls, household storage and food-processing areas can sometimes indicate that resources were managed on household lines, their absence need not indicate that there was no individual or household ownership of resources. Social criteria cannot yet be applied as a way of distinguishing the origins of food-production over prehistoric Europe.

What I shall do here is to sidestep the thorny issues raised so far, and use instead a simple contrast between subsistence economies based on *traditional* resources and those reliant upon *novel* ones. These terms need defining in terms of space and time. For example, a historian would regard maize, tomatoes and potatoes as novel resources in Europe since they were not introduced until the sixteenth century, when they were grown in addition to traditional crops such as wheat and barley. A prehistorian interested in the last 10 000 years might regard the latter as novel, since they first appeared well into the Holocene and replaced local traditional resources. The last-mentioned might in turn be viewed as novel from the point of view of a plant geographer, since they did not colonize northern Europe until the end of the last glaciation.

For the purposes of this book, resources will be classed as novel if their usage increased from an insignificant to a significant level over a third of the continent in less than three millennia. Although unashamedly arbitrary, this definition is useful in highlighting the dramatic expansion of wheat, barley, legumes and sheep over much of Europe within a blink of the pleistocene eye after 8000 radiocarbon years ago. In contrast, animals such as reindeer, red deer, horse, pig and aurochs, may have greatly and rapidly expanded their area of distribution in times of abrupt climatic change, but had long been important features of human subsistence. Other species may also have changed their distribution as dramatically as sheep and cereals, but remained unimportant sources of food. This distinction between novel and traditional resources also avoids the troublesome problem of whether cereals and caprovines were introduced to Europe from the Near East or had been present in parts of Europe during the early Holocene and even the Pleistocene. As we shall see later, these resources may well have been present before their dramatic expansion after 8000 years ago, but do not seem to have been important. By contrasting traditional with novel resources in the way suggested, we also circumvent the (presently insoluble) debate of whether some traditional resources (such as cattle, pig and reindeer) were domesticated before the expansion of novel ones.

2. Europe: the Empty Continent?

Abstract

This and the next chapter are concerned with the European archaeological record prior to 100 000 years ago. Here, we look at the climatic background to human evolution, the evidence for early hominid evolution and behaviour, and the sparse evidence for hominids in Europe before a half million or so years ago. This sparseness may result from the rate at which archaeological evidence has been destroyed over the last million years, but is more likely to indicate that Europe was not permanently occupied until fairly late in man's history. Some environmental and behavioural reasons why this might have been so are suggested.

Although the antiquity of man was first demonstrated in Europe well over a century ago, it is in Africa that most of the evidence for his evolution has been discovered. To explain why this should be so, we need to consider first, the climatic background to human evolution and secondly, the fossil and archaeological evidence from outside Europe.

I. THE CLIMATIC BACKGROUND TO HUMAN EVOLUTION

As has long been realized, we evolved under climatic conditions that have been atypical of this planet's history in two ways. Firstly, the earth's climate cooled to the point where large areas of the oceans and land masses were covered by ice. Secondly, these predominantly glacial conditions were frequently interrupted by short episodes of interglacial climate such as that which prevails today.

Why the earth's climate has been unusually cool in recent geological time may be attributed to two main factors. The first and major one was changes in the circulation of deep-water currents in the oceans that led to the flow of cold water from around the poles into equatorial regions. Particularly important here was the isolation of Antarctica, and the formation of a circumpolar Antarctic Ocean as Australia gradually drifted northwards to its present position between 60 and 30 Myr ago, and the opening of connections between the Arctic and neighbouring oceans by 5 Myr ago. These increases in the strength of *longitudinal* current were accompanied by a weakening of *latitudinal* flow within the tropics. Here, the formation of the Panama Isthmus some 3·5 Myr ago prevented the flow of water between the Atlantic and Pacific; whilst the closure of the eastern end of the Tethys Sea some 16 Myr ago stopped water from flowing between the Indian and Atlantic Oceans and created what is now the Mediterranean. Secondly, the formation of high mountain chains such as the Andes, Rockies and Himalayas trapped moisture over land masses, and facilitated the growth of land-based glaciers.

Two types of explanation have recently been offered as to why interglacials have often punctuated the predominantly glacial climate of the last 3 Myr. The first is that they are caused by variations in the earth's orbit, and can thus be modelled in a *deterministic* manner. In what became a highly influential paper, Hays *et al.* (1976) argued that variations in the earth's orbit, its tilt and the precession of the equinoxes (the time of year when a given part of the earth is nearest the sun) over cycles of 100 000, 42 000 and 23 000 years respectively accounted for most of the climatic change over the last 700 000 years. However, the fit between the climatic record over the last half million years and models based wholly upon orbital variations is not a perfect one (see Imbrie and Imbrie, 1980) and for this reason some researchers have explored stochastic models that explain climatic change as the result of instabilities inherent in the earth's climate. One suggestion along these lines is that ice sheets may grow to a point at which they become unstable, and collapse until they grow again (see e.g. Bowen, 1980; Oerlmans, 1980).

At present, the most continuous and detailed record of the climatic background to our evolution comes from analyses of deep-sea cores (see Box 1). The general trends of the last 60 Myr are clear from cores taken in the Antarctic Ocean (Kennett, 1980). As Fig. 3 shows, surface ocean temperatures fell from 20°C in the early Eocene to only 7°C in the early Oligocene, some 35 Myr ago, when substantial Antarctic sea-ice began to

---

Box 1: Deep-sea cores

Much of the ocean floor is covered by sediments that have often accumulated over millions of years, and which contain the remains of microscopic creatures called foraminifera. When alive, these live at varying depths above the ocean bottom, and absorb into their shells the prevailing isotopic composition of the sea water. This consists of two types—a lighter H_2O^{16} and a heavier H_2O^{18}—and the ratio of one to the other depends upon the prevailing salinity. When fresh water is extracted from the oceans and locked up on land as ice or snow, the proportion of the heavier ^{18}O in the oceans increases. Thus changes in the ratio of $^{16}O:^{18}O$ provide a direct indication of past global ice volumes, and thus of sea-levels. In addition to providing a record of past climatic change that is more continuous, sensitive and unambiguous than that obtainable from terrestrial sources of evidence, these cores can also be calibrated by noting how magnetic particles in them were orientated whilst sediments were accumulating. This is because these particles orientate themselves relative to the prevailing magnetic field of the earth. This field has reversed several times in the earth's recent history at times that have been dated from volcanic deposits on land.

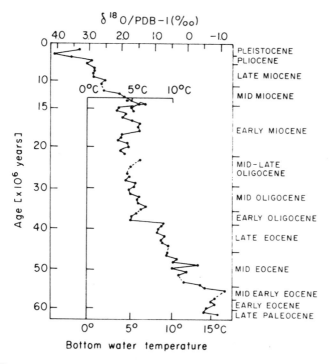

Fig. 3: Temperature trends of the last 60 million years (from Kennett, 1980).

form. The Antarctic ice-cap first developed between 16 and 13 Myr ago, and has remained much the same size over the last 10 million years (Kerr, 1981). In the late Miocene, between 4·5 and 4·3 Myr ago, its volume may have been up to 50% larger than today. Thereafter, it shrank and was fairly stable throughout the so-called "pre-glacial Pliocene" until it grew again around 2·6 Myr ago.

It is around this time that the glaciation of the northern hemisphere began. Although ice-rafted debris was being transported into the Arctic Ocean 4·5 Myr ago, it became much more abundant around 2·5 Myr ago (Margolis and Herman, 1980). Analysis of core V28-179 from the Equatorial Pacific shows that the climate was already fluctuating from glacial to interglacial conditions by 3·2 Myr ago, but especially after 2·5 Myr ago when ice sheets became established in the northern hemisphere (Shackleton and Opdyke, 1977). A similar pattern of cooling after 3·1 Myr ago is indicated in the Mediterranean (see Thunell, 1979a).

The main climatic features of the last 2 Myr are well illustrated by core V28-239 (Shackleton and Opdyke, 1976), taken from a depth of 3500 m off the Pacific Ocean floor. Although the lower parts of this core are not as finely resolved as the upper sections, at least nine glacial–interglacial cycles are indicated between 2 million and 700 000 years ago. Eight further cycles are shown in greater detail by the upper part of this core, and also from core V28-238 (Shackleton and Opdyke, 1973). Perennial ice cover has persisted over the Arctic Ocean throughout this time (Herman and Hopkins, 1980), and interglacials have often been 100 000 years apart. Because the isotopic composition of the oceans changed by roughly the same amount during each glaciation, each was probably of similar intensity (Shackleton and Opdyke, 1976), and resulted in a lowering of world sea levels by 90–130 m. Although terrestrial data generally lack the continuity and clarity of oceanic evidence, they nevertheless confirm these trends. Multiple glacial–interglacial cycles, far more complex than those once encompassed within the simple four-stage Alpine sequence of Günz, Mindel, Riss and Würm, have now been established from studies of vegetation (e.g. Zagwijn, 1974), fossil soils (Fink and Kukla, 1977) and raised beaches (Butzer, 1975).

Two conspicuous features to emerge from recent studies of pleistocene climate are that interglacials appear to have been short, and to have ended as abruptly as they began. Judging from the present calibration of deep-sea cores, interglacials may have characterized only 10% of the Pleistocene; indeed, their total duration over the last 2 million years is now less than the 250 000 years once ascribed to the "Great" or Mindel-Riss interglacial, an interlude that has now shrunk to a mere 15 000–16 000 years (Flohn, 1979). At least four and probably seven glacial episodes of the last 700 000 years ended swiftly (Shackleton and Opdyke, 1976:453), and interglacials may also have ended as abruptly. This last point may have important implications for how we explain the paucity of evidence for European hominids before a half million years ago (see p.37 ff.).

II. HOMINID EVOLUTION

In both pleistocene archaeology and polite society it is far safer to discuss the weather than our origins. Whilst our knowledge of the climatic background to human evolution is now fairly coherent, no topic has aroused greater controversy than how we evolved. Although (or because!) the number of fossil hominids more than doubled during the 1970s, there is little consensus as to how this evidence should be interpreted. Fortunately however, there is at least some agreement as to where the main arguments lie (see e.g. Cronin *et al.*, 1981).

The emergence of the hominoids that were the ancestors of ourselves (the Hominidae) and the gorilla, chimpanzee and orangutan (the Pongidae) was probably closely related to the climatic changes of the Tertiary that have just been outlined. As the climate became cooler and drier, seasonal contrasts would have become more pronounced and tropical forests less uniform, supplemented by a mosaic of grass and woodland habitats. Cachel (1979) has suggested that the trend towards lower temperatures may have resulted in an increase in the body size of early hominoids, and this in turn may have led to a reduction in the number of offspring per litter. The growth of more open and diverse vegetational communities may also have encouraged early hominoids to utilize a wider variety of seasonally and spatially distinct plant foods, to develop facilities for moving in both terrestrial and arboreal environments, and to use their hands and teeth for grasping and cutting leaves, fruits and hard-coated seeds. Tooth enamel may also have become thicker to cope with these harder foodstuffs. Although the fossil evidence is meagre in the extreme, these features may have been present in some of the Old World late oligocene hominids (for example, *Apidium* and *Aegyptopithecus*) of some 30 Myr ago.

By 14 Myr ago, in the mid-Miocene, hominids may already have diverged from the ancestors of the modern great apes. The evidence is sadly very poor, and much hinges upon the tooth and jaw fragments assigned to the genus *Ramapithecus*. Specimens have so far been found in Africa, Asia and perhaps Europe. The Fort Ternan specimen from Kenya of *R. wickeri* was found in deposits 12·5-14 Myr old (Simons, 1969), whereas those of *R. punjabicus* from the Siwaliks in Pakistan are younger, and date from 12·5 to perhaps 8 Myr ago (Pilbeam *et al.*, 1977;

Tauxe, 1979). It is unclear whether *Ramapithecus* is represented in European localities. Simons (1977) considered that the 11 Myr old specimen of *Rudapithecus hungaricus* (Kretzoi, 1975) and the 9 Myr old find of *Graecopithecus freyburgii* were in fact examples of *Ramapithecus* that were incorrectly classified when first discovered, but this claim does not appear to have been upheld (see Pilbeam, 1979).

The evolutionary status of *Ramapithecus* is very contentious. A few years ago, there seemed a reasonably plausible case for regarding this creature as the earliest hominid, and as distinct from *Sivapithecus*, another miocene primate that was thought to have been ancestral to modern pongids. However, the hominid features of the dentition of *Ramapithecus* are not unequivocal, and recent discoveries have shown that the generic distinctions between *Ramapithecus* and *Sivapithecus* are not as clear as once thought (e.g. Andrews and Tekkaya, 1980; Greenfield, 1979). The latest discoveries of miocene hominoid fossils from deposits 8-12 Myr old in Pakistan (Pilbeam, 1982) seem to indicate that the *Ramapithecus-Sivapithecus* complex was related more to the ancestors of the orang-utan than of man, chimpanzees and gorillas. If so, the divergence between the African apes and hominids might not have occurred until after 8 Myr ago (Andrews, 1982).

This view is one that can be supported by advocates of the so-called "molecular clock", who argue that hominids and pongids diverged only 5-6 Myr ago. This line of reasoning is based upon the biochemical similarities in serum between the great apes and ourselves; dissimilarities are assumed to have arisen at a constant rate, and this in turn is extrapolated from the rates at which other better documented and less controversial lineages diverged (Sarich and Cronin, 1977). However, these biochemical studies have often given results that are markedly at odds with the fossil record and should perhaps be treated with caution (see Jacobs and Pilbeam, 1980) for the moment.

Between 8 and 4 Myr ago, hominid fossils are virtually non-existent. The only finds so far consist of a molar some 6·5 Myr old from Lukeino, a mandible fragment perhaps 5-5·5 Myr old from Lothagam and part of a distal humerus some 4-4·5 Myr old from Kanapoi (see Tobias, 1980). None of these East African finds are very informative. The first-mentioned tooth shares many features found in modern chimpanzee molars, whilst the latter has attributes intermediate between those in modern pongids and late pliocene hominids (McHenry and Corruccini, 1980). This scant evidence does not contradict the view that hominids and pongids had already diverged by the beginning of the Pliocene.

Thanks to recent discoveries at Laetolil and Hadar in East Africa, we now have two excellent well-dated fossil samples from between 4 and 3

Myr ago. This evidence includes the spectacular finds at Hadar of "Lucy", represented by 40% of the skeleton, and find Number 333 of 19 individuals (Johanson and Edey, 1981), as well as the stunning trail of hominid footprints at Laetolil (Leakey and Hay, 1979). Other material from this time-range may include some of the South African finds referred to as *Australopithecus*. Unfortunately, the uncertainties over their dating plague most discussions of hominid evolution. Estimates of the age of the oldest specimens range from as much as 3·7 Myr (Partridge, 1973) to less than 1·5 Myr old (Vrba, 1974); many of the arguments over whether hominid evolution featured two or three lineages depends largely upon which dating is preferred (Pilbeam, 1980). Meanwhile, no account of human evolution is complete without the South African evidence, or wholly convincing with it.

So far, there is little unanimity of opinion over this group of pliocene hominids. Initial assessments of the Hadar material suggested that two genera were represented—the larger one, *Homo* and the smaller, *Australopithecus* (Johanson and Taieb, 1976). Later, a more detailed evaluation (Johanson *et al.*, 1978) concluded that only one, sexually dimorphic hominid was present, and that it was sufficiently distinct to be assigned to a new species of *Australopithecus*, *A. afarensis*. Johanson and White (1979) have since claimed that all the hominid material from Laetolil also belonged to this taxon, even though its discoverers have suggested that it included specimens of both *Homo* and *Australopithecus* (Leakey *et al.*, 1976). Whilst other researchers (e.g. Boaz, 1979a; Tobias, 1980) are prepared to accept that there is no evidence for *Homo* before 2 Myr ago, they seem less willing to agree that *Australopithecus afarensis* is significantly different from *A. africanus*.

Until this phylogenetic free-for-all is resolved, little can be said with confidence about our pliocene ancestors. If Johanson and White's claims are upheld, there was only one type of hominid at this time, and it was small, sexually dimorphic and bipedal. This last point is the most significant: as demonstrated both by post-cranial fragments and the footprints at Laetolil, our ancestors were bipedal 3·5 Myr ago (Charteris *et al.*, 1981; White, 1980), at least 1·5 Myr before any significant enlargement of the brain, and at least 1 million years before the earliest evidence for tool-making (see below). However, as is obvious from riding a bicycle, it is considerably more difficult to remain stationary than to move forward. Whilst we know that Lucy could, in White's words (Johanson and Edey, 1981:163) have beaten you to a hamburger, we do not yet know if she could have stood and waited for one. Evidence at how successful our pliocene ancestors were in living bipedally may in future relate more to the small but momentous changes in the balancing mechanisms in their ears than to the more robust evidence of their knees and footprints. More discoveries are needed like the australopithecine ear ossicle some 1·5 Myr old from Sterkfontein in South Africa (Rak and Clarke, 1979).

Around 2 Myr ago, the hominid lineage appears to have split into two. One, the australopithecine, continued as a small, bipedal and small-brained hominid, with a body weight of *ca.* 35-50 kg (Steudel, 1980) and a cranial capacity of *ca.* 440-530 cc (McHenry, 1976). The australopithecine lineage probably includes "Nutcracker Man" from Bed I at Olduvai, as well as the finds of *Paranthropus* from South Africa and Koobi Fora. Two types of australopithecine are recognized: a small, gracile one, known mainly from South African sites, and a more robust version represented in both East and South Africa. Whether these differences represent one (Swedlund, 1974) or two (Wolpoff, 1976) sexually dimorphic and polytypic species, or indicate allometric developments in which an increase in body size was accompanied by changes in the proportions of different parts of the body (Pilbeam and Gould, 1974) is still unclear, and will remain so until the South African finds are firmly dated.

The other lineage is classed as *Homo* and is chiefly marked by a larger body and by a cranium that had a capacity of *ca.* 600-700 cc (Holloway, 1973; but see Wolpoff, 1981), and which was more lightly constructed than the australopithecine one. At present, the earliest representatives of our genus are those finds from Bed I at Olduvai that are *ca.* 1·8 Myr old and classed as *Homo habilis*. Similarly dated finds from Member E at Shungura and the specimen from Koobi Fora, known only by its catalogue number (KNMER-1470), may also belong to this lineage. (For the controversies over the Koobi Fora dating, see Hay (1980) and included references.) Another early example of *H. habilis* might be the finds from Java, originally called *Pithecanthropus modjokertensis*, that have recently been dated to *ca.* 1·9 Myr b.p. (Ninkovitch and Burckle, 1978). The earliest examples of *H. erectus*, whose cranial capacity was *ca.* 1100 cc, are dated to around 1·5 Myr ago and come from Koobi Fora (Walker and Leakey, 1978). As the youngest specimens of *H. erectus* at Olduvai are perhaps only 600-800 000 years old (Rightmire, 1979a), little anatomical change appears to have occurred for the 800 000 years or so after its first appearance.

The length of time for which *Australopithecus* and *Homo* coexisted remains uncertain, and hinges upon the dating of the australopithecine specimens from Chesowanja in East Africa and Taung in South Africa. The former, dated originally to *ca.* 1·1-1·2 Myr b.p. (Carney *et al.*, 1971) has now been redated to > 1·4 Myr (Hooker and Miller, 1979). Taung may be the youngest of the South African australopithecine sites (Butzer, 1974), even if one discounts Partridge's (1973) estimates that the cave was formed only 0·9 Myr b.p. (see De Swardt, 1974). The confusion over this site has been exacerbated still further by Tobias' (1973) suggestion that the type specimen of *Australopithecus africanus* may in fact have been a young *A. robustus*! Given these uncertainties, a prudent conclusion might be that *Australopithecus* and *Homo* coexisted for at least half a million years, and possibly for twice as long.

The problem of where hominids evolved is still intractable. The last two decades of discoveries seem to have firmly established Africa as the "cradle of mankind", and not Asia, as thought by many when the first discoveries of *Homo erectus* were made in Java in the 1890s, and in China in the 1930s. However, the question of an Asian origin for man is perhaps best left open at present (see Campbell and Bernor, 1976; Todaro, 1980), especially if the date of 1·9 Myr for the hominid remains from Java is confirmed. The notion of an African origin for man may reflect as much our ignorance of the Pliocene in China, India and Pakistan as our knowledge about East and South Africa at this time.

III. EARLY HOMINID BEHAVIOUR

Not surprisingly, given the meagre scraps of evidence upon which prehistorians feed, there is a wide divergence of opinion over the dietary and social behaviour of early hominids. Although the discovery of what may have been their camps and butchery sites has considerably improved the quality of our data, the evidence is still sufficiently tenuous to be compatible with a wide variety of models.

So far as can be inferred from the distribution of early hominid sites, lakesides and streams were preferred locations for settlement (Boaz, 1977; Peters, 1979); besides the obvious need for drinking water, such places would also have provided shade, shelter and locally high densities of small game and plant foods. The earliest forms of *Homo* are assumed to have been fully terrestrial, living either under trees — as perhaps at the KBS site at Koobi Fora (Isaac, 1978) — or in crude huts, as at Olduvai Bed I (Leakey, 1971). However, our evidence will show an inevitable bias towards lakes and rivers for the simple reason that these are also environments where sediments accumulate in a manner conducive to the preservation of archaeological material (see e.g. Gifford and Behrensmeyer, 1977).

Studies of the composition of late pliocene and lower pleistocene fossil assemblages from East Africa suggest that hominids were uncommon and, judging from modern analogues, may have lived at densities as low as 8 to 170/1000 km^2 (Boaz, 1979b). As hominids probably lived in small groups, these figures would imply either that the links between subsistence groups in the same mating networks were very tenuous, or that large areas were unoccupied.

Such is the poor quality of evidence on the diet of early hominids that they have been portrayed as anything from blood-thirsty bone-crunching flesh-eaters to peaceful, plant-collecting vegetarians that ate the occasional morsel of meat. According to which ethological data are preferred, one can make a plausible case that predation developed after (Jolly, 1970), alongside (Teleki, 1975) or before (Szalay, 1975) a vegetarian way of life. Studies of modern gatherer-hunters in very arid regions, notably the Bushmen, have also been incorporated into many arguments for the role of plant foods in the diet of early hominids, even though these lived mostly in moister areas where animal resources may have been more abundant.

The most conclusive evidence for early hominid meat-eating should be the animal bones found in the same deposits as stone tools and hominid remains. However, it is often doubtful whether these animals were killed and eaten by early hominids. The point is nicely illustrated by the South African cave deposits containing the remains of ungulates and austra-lopithecines. At first, these assemblages were interpreted as evidence of hunting by australopithecines. Yet, as Brain's (1981) work has shown, it is more likely that the australopithecines were hunted rather than hunters, and played no significant role in causing the deaths of other animals in these deposits. Even when animal remains and stone tools have been found together in open-air "living floors" and "butchery sites", as in East Africa, the association between the two may be purely fortuitous; as Binford (1977) has reminded us, these sites may be simply "hydraulic jumbles" of material deposited and mixed together by stream action. For this reason, attention has to focus upon the faunal and lithic material incorporated into fine-grained sediments, as at Koobi Fora, where fluvial jumbling was minimal. Here, the cut marks and pattern of bone breakage are important in showing that at least some of the faunal remains were modified by hominids. The fact that in at least one case a cut mark was *under* a carnivore tooth-mark implies that it was the carnivore that scavenged what was left by the hominid, and not vice versa (Bunn, 1981; Gamble, 1981; Potts and Shipman, 1981). Even in such cases, the evidence indicates only that meat was eaten, but not that animals were hunted. One possibility worth considering is that early hominids exploited the wastefulness of their predator competitors by extracting the marrow from the bones of freshly-killed animals, and only seldom killed prey themselves.

As the remains of the plant foods they may have eaten have not survived, indirect sources of evidence have to be used. At present, the clearest is that the wear on some of the tools 1·5 Myr old from Koobi Fora probably resulted from the working of plant material (Keeley and Toth, 1981). Analysis of the strontium content of hominid skeletal material has so far proved inconclusive in showing the proportion of plant food in early hominid diet (Elias, 1980) but analyses of carbon isotope ratios may be more fruitful if the technique can be refined (see Ericson *et al.*, 1981). The contents of coprolites may also prove informative if their hominid origin can be demonstrated by parasitological analysis (Boaz, 1977:53), as might the attrition and wear of tooth enamel. Perhaps the most compelling argument in favour of plant foods being a major part of early hominid diet is that predation is a high risk strategy: wolves kill on only 10% of their attempts (Mech, 1970) and even the lion fails more often than not (Schaller, 1972). A small, slow hominid may therefore have relied upon a steady intake of low-risk plant foods for most of his diet, and scavenged or hunted for the rest. One intriguing recent suggestion is that early hominids may have occupied the niche filled by bear and pig in higher latitudes by exploiting roots and tubers, and thus avoided competition with other animals (Hatley and Kappelman, 1980).

As far as social organization is concerned, early hominids almost certainly lived in groups (see Lovejoy, 1981). The main advantage of communal living is that it improves the chances of survival for the young before they are able to fend for themselves. Wild dog, for example, feed lactating mothers and their pups in their dens by regurgitating food down their throats (Lamprecht, 1981); the transport of food to infants at a home base may well have been one of the earliest features of hominid society. Group behaviour can also be advantageous to a carnivore in enabling it to hunt more effectively. Wolf (Mech, 1970), hyaena (Kruuk, 1972) and lion (Schaller, 1972) have a higher success rate and waste less of the carcass when hunting in groups than when alone. Whether group behaviour developed in some of the large carnivores and early hominids in order for them to predate more effectively is perhaps dubious. As Lamprecht (1981) has pointed out, the advantages of communal hunting may have emerged as side-effects of other factors, such as competition for females and territory, and the need to defend kills against other predators.

Circumstantial evidence that early hominids lived in groups comes from the incredible find of 19 hominids who all died together some 3·5 Myr ago at Hadar (Johanson and Edey, 1981); and from the trails of footprints that a pair of hominids made whilst walking alongside each other at Laetolil (Leakey and Hay, 1979). Even allowing for the problems of interpreting archaeological sites that are more than 1 Myr old, at least some of those in East Africa were probably "home bases" where groups lived to rear their young and to procure food (Isaac, 1978). Given that such cooperative behaviour probably existed, there are several ways in which it could have been organized. One possibility is that males hunted, and females gathered (Isaac, 1978), as in many modern hunter-gatherer societies. This somewhat traditional view of "Man the Hunter" is open to criticism and may indicate only that most modern hunters (and palaeolithic archaeologists) have been male. As female lions (Schaller, 1972) obtain more meat than do males, an alternative scenario is that it was the female early hominids who hunted to feed themselves and the young, whilst males gathered and devoted most of their energies to defending their harem against other males, or trying to gain control of one. Another possibility, of course, is that both sexes, either singly or cooperatively, obtained vegetable foods and the occasional meat (Isaac and Crader, 1981) and brought some food back to a home base where it could be processed and shared. In all these cases, it is likely that much of the food was consumed on the spot whilst foraging, judging from the present behaviour of gatherer-hunters, apes and carnivores.

So far as early hominid technology is concerned, there is now good evidence for the making of several types and sizes of stone tools and for the transportation of stone "manuports" so that tools could be made when needed. At present, it is customary to ascribe all tool-making to *Homo* and to regard *Australopithecus* as, at most, a tool-user. However, given the ability of chimpanzees (McGrew *et al.*, 1979; Sabater, 1974) and orang-utans (Wright, 1972) to make tools, there need not have been any "cerebral Rubicon" to cross before a small-brained hominid could do the same. What may have been more important than the size of the brain was its internal organization. In this context, one particularly critical aspect may have been the emergence of laterality, whereby right or left-handedness developed, which enabled one hand to keep an object such as a stone immobile, and the other to modify it by percussion (see Frost, 1980). We need not, therefore, be unduly surprised if the tools found recently at Hadar and dated to 2·5 Myr b.p. (Lewin, 1981) were made by a small-brained australopithecine-type of hominid, and not by one with a larger cranium. In this context, it is interesting that the operational procedures for making the stone tools at Olduvai appear to have been very simple indeed (Wynn, 1981). If australopithecines were capable of making stone tools, it would be surprising if they stopped this practice as soon as *Homo habilis* appeared around 2 Myr ago, and prehistorians may have to face the somewhat awesome prospect that much of the lower pleistocene archaeological record was the product of two types of hominid.

One recent and, if confirmed, immensely important discovery at Chesowanja in East Africa is that fire was already used some 1·5 Myr ago (Gowlett *et al.*, 1981). As fire has long been regarded as a Eurasian discovery of only the last half million years, many views on the colonization of temperate latitudes may need revision.

At present, there is no firm evidence for any major changes in hominid behaviour between 2 and 1 Myr ago. This may largely be because our present sample is too small to allow detailed comparisons between sites and assemblages formed under the same conditions but at different periods. However, the fossil record does not show any significant changes either (Rightmire, 1981), and so a long period of stasis may be implied.

IV. THE EUROPEAN EVIDENCE FOR HOMINIDS BEFORE 0·5 MYR AGO

Although the evidence that hominids inhabited Europe before a half or even a quarter of a million years ago is frankly atrocious, it at least hints of their presence (Fig. 4). If we leave aside as grossly suspect a claimed — and subsequently lost! — polyhedron from St Vallier in France that may have come from a layer possibly 2·3–2·5 Myr old (Bordes and Thibbault, 1977:120), there are a few European localities, mostly in the Massif Central of France, that might contain artefacts more than 1·5 Myr old. One of these is La Roche Lambert, where a concentration of broken bones was found associated with some indeterminate pieces of flint and quartz; as these raw materials are not thought to have been locally derived, they may have been carried there by hominids (Bordes and Thibbault, 1977:120). At Sandalja I in Yugoslavia a "pebble-tool" and hominid incisor were associated with a faunal assemblage like that from Senèze in France which is probably more than 1·6 Myr old (Valoch, 1975). This evidence is more convincing than that from Chilhac, also in France, where "pebble-tools" were found in very dubious association with a mid-villafranchian fauna (Delporte, 1976:803).

Archaeological evidence from the latter part of the Lower Pleistocene (*ca.* 1·5 to 0·7 Myr b.p.) is only slightly more convincing. Sinzelle, another French locality, has a late villafranchian fauna possibly *ca.* 1 Myr old and a slight suggestion of hominid activities. Although no artefacts were found, Delporte (1976:803) suggested that the striations and fractures on some of the bones may have resulted from hominid causes. Whilst this is possible, it needs to be demonstrated in the same way as at Koobi Fora (see Bunn, 1981; Potts and Shipman, 1981). Vallonet (de Lumley *et al.*, 1963) is perhaps one of the least ambiguous lower pleistocene sites in Europe, and contains artefacts which are probably associated with a late villafranchian fauna. Dating this site has proved

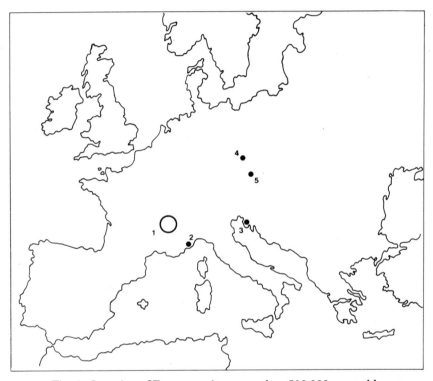

Fig. 4: Location of European sites more than 500 000 years old.
Key: 1 Massif Central sites; 2 Vallonet; 3 Sandalja; 4 Prezletice; 5 Prbice.

difficult. Its initial placing within a "Donau-Günz" interglacial is now more or less meaningless since the status of these glacials is highly dubious. Palaeomagnetic studies showed that the layer containing the tools had a normal polarity which could correspond with the Jaramillo Event, *ca.* 0·9-0·95 Myr b.p. However, Bonifay (1975:206) has pointed out that the faunal assemblage contains some later components, so that the palaeomagnetic reading could indicate the Brunhes period; if so, the site may be less than 0·7 Myr old. Material from Prezletice in Czechoslovakia (Fejfar, 1969) may be of comparable antiquity. Here, crude tools and a disputed hominid tooth fragment were found with a cromerian fauna formerly correlated with a Günz-Mindel interglacial.

The relevant layer has a reversed magnetic polarity that might fall between the Jaramillo Event and the Brunhes-Matuyama boundary; in other words, between 0·9 and 0·7 Myr b.p. (Valoch, 1976). The site of Prbice, another Czechoslovak site, may also lie in this time range (Valoch *et al.*, 1978). Finally, artefacts have been found in layers dated to around 700 000 years old in the lower and middle pleistocene site at Isernia in Italy (Bidduttu *et al.*, 1979). It is not yet clear if these are *in situ* and associated directly with the faunal remains.

The archaeological record for the first half of the Middle Pleistocene continues in as patchy a manner as before. At St Estève-Janson, traces of fire and broken bone were found well into the interior of a cave; although no stone tools were present, it seems difficult to explain this evidence without invoking some kind of hominid activity. At La Romieu, artefacts were found associated with an early middle pleistocene fauna, but both were probably derived from further upslope. Outside France, the site of Stranska Skala (Bordes and Thibbault, 1977) contains stone tools and an early middle pleistocene fauna. The important hominid site of Vertesszöllös in Hungary (Kretzoi and Vertes, 1965) may also belong to this period; the absolute date for this site of 0·37 Myr b.p. (see Table 1) is probably its minimum age.

V. WHY IS THE AFRICAN DATA BETTER?

The contrasts between the African and European evidence for early man are profound indeed. Europe has no equivalents of Olduvai Gorge, Koobi Fora, Hadar or Laetolil, and it is not until well into the Middle Pleistocene that its archaeological record is of comparable quality to the African. Why this should be so is a problem that has two facets. The first is why the European evidence is so much sparser than the African until the last half or so million years; in the next chapter, we can ask why the quality of the European data should improve after this time.

At this stage, we can examine two explanations for the differences between the archaeological record in Africa and Europe.

A. Geological accident?

The notion that Africa was the "cradle of mankind", whilst Europe was an empty cot, could simply reflect geological accident. Europe has no equivalent of the Rift Valley, where fossil and artefactual material was often buried shortly after death or discard under gently deposited fluviatile and aeolian sediments that thereafter remained largely undisturbed until re-exposure in recent times (see e.g. Bunn *et al.*, 1980).

Table 1: Age determinations of some European lower and middle pleistocene archaeological sites.

Site	Dating technique	Date b.p.	Comments	Source
Isernia	K/A	680 000 ± 60 000 730 000 ± 70 000	Dates layer with bones and artefacts	Sevink et al., 1981
Prezletice	Palaeomagnetic	750-890 000	Reversed polarity	Valoch, 1976
Petralona	ESR U/Th ESR	340 000 ± 30 000 > 350 000 160-240 000	Stalagmite above skull Stalagmite above skull Dating of skull	Ikeya, 1978 Ikeya, 1978 Hennig et al., 1981
Swanscombe	U/Th	326 000 + 99 000 − 54 000	Sample from upper middle gravel with acheulean artefacts	Szabo and Collins, 1975
Clacton	U/Th	245 000 + 35 000 − 25 000	Sample from gravel with clactonian assemblage	Szabo and Collins, 1975
Brundon	U/Th	174 000 ± 30 000	Sample from layer with hand-axes and prepared cores	Szabo and Collins, 1975
Stutton	U/Th	125 000 ± 20 000	Probably dates last interglacial	Szabo and Collins, 1975
Victoria Cave	U/Th	120 000 ± 6 000	Dates Ipswichian (last interglacial)	Gascoyne et al., 1981
Terra Amata	TL	230 000 ± 40 000	Sample of burnt flint; age much younger than estimate of excavator	Wintle and Aitken, 1977
Vertesszöllös	U/Th	> 370 000	Minimum age of site	Butzer and Isaac, 1975:895
Pontnewydd	U/Th	180 000 ± 20 000	Dates Lower Breccia containing bulk of archaeological finds	Green et al., 1981
	TL	200 000 ± 25 000	On burnt flint; dates use of fire and the human tooth found	Green et al., 1981
Abri Bourgeois-Delauney	U/Th	185 000 ± 30 000	Dates early Neanderthal mandible	Schwarcz, 1980

In Europe, conditions have been much less favourable for preserving traces of early man: rivers have recut their channels too often, and successive glaciations have eroded deposits, destroyed much of their archaeological contents and dispersed the remainder. In the case of caves, many of these have been scoured out and emptied of their deposits, as appears to have happened in northern Spain (Butzer, 1981).

If hominids lived at densities as low as has been suggested (see above), the chances of retrieving the remains of those that happened to be incorporated into sediments favourable for their preservation over the next 2 million years or more are slight, even in East Africa. For example, the sample of *ca.* 120 individuals recovered from deposits spanning perhaps a million years at Koobi Fora may represent only one forty-thousandth of the original population (Walker and Leakey, 1978). In Europe, the taphonomic shredder may have been so thorough that virtually all traces of early man have been destroyed.

B. Did early hominids manage to colonize Europe?

An alternative explanation for why there is so little evidence of hominids in Europe before half a million years ago may simply be that its successful occupation lay beyond their ability. There are several reasons why this might have been so.

The first are two simple latitudinal factors. To date, all hominid remains more than a million years old have been found within 35° of the equator; that is, within a zone in which the shortest day is *ca.* 10 h long. One factor that may have discouraged early hominids from extending their range into areas such as Central Europe (40-45°N) may have been that the length of daylight during the winter was too short for them to procure and process their foods. Secondly, seasonal contrasts in the availability of foods—especially plant ones—become increasingly pronounced with higher latitudes, and may have deterred hominids lacking the ability to hibernate or to store foods for several months of the year.

Seasonal contrasts in the availability of plant foods would have become accentuated as the earth's climate cooled after 10 Myr and especially after 3 Myr ago. Whether southern Europe was too cold for hominids after this time is perhaps debatable in view of their ability to tolerate winter conditions 1500 m above sea level around Sterkfontein and Makapansgat in southern Africa at the same latitude south of the equator as southern Europe is to the north. What may have been of greater importance than the coldness of the European climate was its instability. As noted above, the "switch" from glacial to interglacial climates appears to have been very rapid, and even warm episodes may have been suddenly interrupted by reversals to colder conditons (see e.g. Flohn, 1979). The adverse effects that such fluctuations may have had upon early hominid populations in temperate regions such as Europe can be illustrated by the following example.

We can suppose that early hominids lived in a loose reproductive network formed of small subsistence groups, as suggested by Isaac (1972). If the climate suddenly worsened, food resources would have become more dispersed and less abundant, and so hominids would have had to forage more widely. Consequently, subsistence groups would have become more widely spaced, and thus more isolated from each other. Under such conditions, individual groups would have been less able to maintain contact with their neighbours, and so the mating networks to which they belonged would have become endangered. The paucity of evidence for hominids in Europe before a half million years ago might therefore be attributed at least as much to short-term climatic factors as to the longer-term average trend to lower temperatures.

Argument so far has been based heavily upon the supposition that early hominids were largely vegetarian, and that Europe was by and large deficient in the type of plant foods they could utilize. However, they ate at least some meat, and Europe was undoubtedly rich in animal resources. It could thus be argued that early hominids were omnivorous and could have simply increased the proportion of meat in their diet when plant foods were scarce. For reasons that will become evident in the next chapter, the strategies needed for exploiting a landscape in which plant foods are scarce are very different from those necessary if they are abundant, and may have required an organizational ability beyond the level of early hominids until fairly recently.

One other factor that may have been important is that early hominids were scarce, even in Africa: the Ethiopian highlands, for example, were probably not colonized until perhaps only one million years ago (Clark and Kurashina, 1979). If early hominids lived at densities as low as has been suggested, colonization of other areas from small founding populations would have been a very slow process.

One other clue that might help explain the meagre and possibly intermittent character of the European record before 0·5 Myr b.p. comes from the fossil record of other animals. Now that pleistocene faunal sequences can be calibrated, it seems that several animals may have extended their distribution in a series of short "pulses" rather than in a continuous manner. During the Pliocene, for example, there were three major "dispersal events" at around 3·7, 2·6 and 1·9 Myr ago; the ancestors of the horse and elephant colonized Europe during the second of these (Lindsay *et al.*, 1980). Other similar pulses occurred around 1·0 and 0·5 Myr ago (Bonifay, 1980). If, as Lindsay (1980) suggests, these dispersals were triggered by climatic and geological events, they may also have affected early hominids. An important point here may be that Europe is difficult to colonize from the south, since its main connections with Asia are the Dardenelles, and with Africa, the Straits of Gibraltar. The former would often have been dry land, whilst the latter has probably been open throughout the entire Pleistocene, although often narrower than today. Evidence for land bridges across the Mediterranean is so far unconvincing (see e.g. Conchon, 1976). One implication of these data is that once animal populations (including early hominids) colonized Europe, they may have become isolated, and if they foundered, recolonization might not have been possible for long periods. Early hominids might therefore have colonized perhaps the southern parts of Europe several times during the Lower Pleistocene, but unsuccessfully; for most of man's history, Europe may have been only intermittently occupied, and empty for long periods.

3. The Colonization of Europe

Abstract

In this chapter, the archaeological evidence from between 100 000 and 500 000 years ago in Europe is reviewed. It is suggested that at some point during this period, Europe was successfully colonized on a permanent basis. The main developments that enabled this to happen were primarily conceptual rather than technological. Of particular importance was the ability to occupy landscapes in which the food resources were primarily mobile and whose locations were thus unpredictable and constantly changing, as were those of neighbouring subsistence groups in the same mating network.

At some time after a half, or perhaps only a quarter, of a million years ago, the archaeological evidence from Europe improves markedly. First, it is much more abundant, even if we discount the thousands upon thousands of hand-axes that have been intermittently recovered over the last century from river deposits in western Europe. Secondly, the lithic industries are more clearly definable in terms of regional and chronological variants such as Acheulean, Clactonian or Levallois, even if their significance is often obscure. Finally, there are some open-air sites of comparable quality to those from much older contexts in East Africa, even if they are pitifully few. Three problems underlie any attempts at dealing with these data.

I. CHRONOLOGICAL NEUROSES

The present evidence gives rise to two chronological anxieties. The first (and less intractable) is determining when these changes occurred; in other words, whether we are dealing with a "long" or a "short" chronology. These uncertainties can be attributed to two factors. The first is that the techniques for dating material older than 35 000 years (beyond which standard ^{14}C techniques become unreliable) and younger than 500 000 years old (the younger limit of K/A dating) are still being developed. Because of this, there are only a few absolute dates of between 100 and 500 kyr, and often these are better treated as possibilities than as established points in time until confirmed by other methods. Some of the more reliable of these dates are listed in Table 1.

The second cause for uncertainty is that middle pleistocene specialists are still in the awkward stage of shedding one set of chronological clothes for another. As was evident even 30 years ago, the climatic changes of the Middle Pleistocene involved far more than the three glacials separated by two interglacials which Penck and Bruckner recognized in the Alpine foothills in the early years of this century. The more it became necessary to subdivide the Günz, Mindel and Riss glacials (and their regional equivalents), as well as the intervening interglacials, the more difficult it became to correlate deposits in a convincing biostratigraphical manner. Ultimately, a reliable chronological framework for the Middle Pleistocene will emerge only when terrestrial sequences are firmly dated, and tied to the oceanic record.

Some sites have already been correlated in this manner, although with varying success. Two of the best examples are the sites of Bilzingsleben in East Germany (Harmon *et al.*, 1980) and Pontnewydd in North Wales (Green *et al.*, 1981) (see Fig. 5). In each case, archaeological evidence has been dated, correlated with independently dated climatic stages shown in marine cores, and the correlations then checked by palaeoclimatic evidence. These examples are far more convincing than the attempt to correlate three undated palaeosols at the highly important open-air site of Terra Amata (southern France) with stages 11, 13 and 15 of the marine record (dated to *ca.* 380, 480 and 550 kyr (de Lumley, 1976)). Significantly perhaps, the only absolute date from this site implies that the site could be considerably younger than the 380–450 000 years assigned to it by the principal investigator.

Meanwhile, however, the chronological discipline over most of the middle pleistocene evidence from Europe is appallingly lax; for example, the elephants at Torralba in Spain (Butzer, 1965; Freeman and Butzer, 1966), which probably died within a few seasons, are currently able to

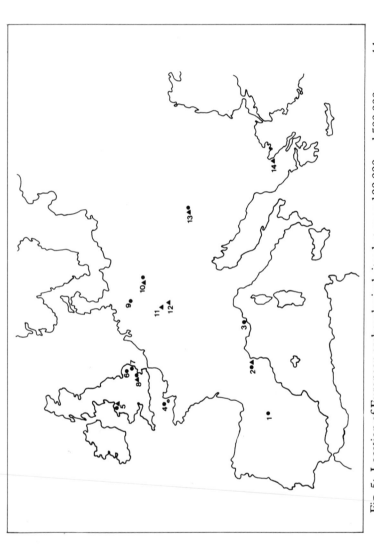

Fig. 5: Location of European archaeological sites between 100 000 and 500 000 years old.

Key: 1 Torralba; 2 Arago; 3 Terra Amata; 4 La Cotte de la St Brelade; 5 Pontnewydd; 6 Hoxne; 7 Clacton; 8 Swanscombe; 9 Lehringen; 10 Bilzingsleben; 11 Mauer; 12 Steinheim; 13 Vertesszöllös; 14 Petralona.

Circles: archaeological sites; Triangles: hominid finds.

rampage through 300 000 years of the Pleistocene, and may be anything between 300 and 600 kyr old.

The other chronological neurosis is less easy to resolve: are the changes in the character of the archaeological record after a half million years ago real or apparent, sudden or gradual? At present, most absolute dates for early man sites in Europe tend to be less than 400 000 years old. This patterning may indicate that man was scarcer before this time, or simply that contexts containing evidence of his activities and more than 400 000 years old are rare. There is at present little hope of demonstrating whether changes in the density and continuity of human settlement in Europe was gradual or sudden, and the chronological accordion can be compressed or extended to play a variety of tunes. Some of these are shown in Fig. 6. In the first model, the evidence from the later part of the Middle Pleistocene is seen as no different from that of earlier periods; the only reason why it is more abundant is that a smaller proportion of the data has been destroyed. All the other models show a real change in the density and continuity of human settlement in Europe at some point

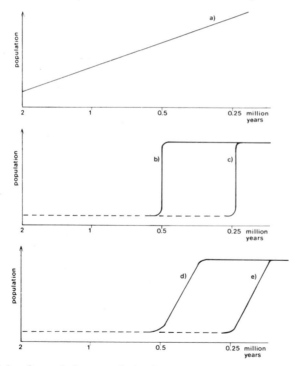

Fig. 6: Models of population trends in the Lower and Middle Pleistocene of Europe.

during the Middle Pleistocene, notwithstanding the effects of the taphonomic shredder upon the preservation of earlier evidence.

These imponderables aside, my own feeling is that a real change occurred between 500 000 and 250 000 years ago. The reasons behind this view will emerge later, but are based largely upon the argument that the effective colonization of Europe required a considerably different and more complex mode of behaviour than seems to have prevailed during the Lower Pleistocene in Africa.

II. SITE INTERPRETATION

As with the problems of calibrating the Middle Pleistocene, we are again in the midst of an uncomfortable change-over in attitude. Whilst much has been learnt in recent years about the processes which affect the preservation of different types of pleistocene archaeological sites and their contents, we are all too often ignorant about the role which each may have played in individual cases.

By far the commonest type of middle pleistocene archaeological evidence from Europe are collections of cores and flakes from fluviatile deposits. The assemblages to which these tools originally belonged have been sorted to varying degrees by the stream action which resulted in their eventual deposition further down-stream. Thus the size, shape and frequency of each tool type in these samples will reflect not only the activities and traditions of those who made them, but also the type of natural processes that resulted in their preservation. The same point applies equally well to the faunal remains that are often associated with stone tools in river deposits. As several recent articles have shown, the frequency with which an animal (or part of it) is represented in fluviatile deposits depends greatly upon the type of stream current and channel bed. In the case of many medium-sized mammals, small compact bones, such as phalanges and carpals, and teeth, are the most easily transported (Voorhies, 1969; Wolff, 1973); however, under some conditions it is the skull that is the most likely part of a human skeleton to be carried the furthest (Boaz and Behrensmeyer, 1976). Modelling bones or stone tools as sedimentary particles in order to determine the extent to which they have been sorted by stream action is a complex process (see e.g. Behrensmeyer and Hill, 1979; Shackley, 1978), and rests heavily upon detailed contextual information of a kind often lacking from earlier investigations. Given these uncertainties, it is perhaps debatable whether the amount of attention lavished on European lower palaeolithic artefacts from river channels has been fully rewarded.

The tiny handful of sites that are sufficiently well-preserved to have been called living or kill sites are potentially our most informative class of data, but present serious problems of interpretation. The first is determining the activities carried out by their occupants. In some cases, this might be done by looking at the proportions of bone to chipped stone: Isaac (1971), for example, made an early attempt to identify living, butchery and workshop sites from such criteria. An alternative and preferable approach is to rely upon the spatial patterning of material within a thin, well-defined horizon. At Terra Amata, for example, cooking and tool-working areas were identified within the confines of some kind of shelter (de Lumley, 1969). Unfortunately, it is often difficult to exclude the possibility that material was dispersed after man had left the vicinity. An example here might be one of the elephants that had been butchered at Torralba some time during the "Mindel" glaciation: as the untouched side lay uppermost, the carcass must have been rolled over, probably by stream action as it was found in a coarsely-sorted gravel (see Freeman and Butzer, 1966).

The second problem is that subsistence strategies of this period almost certainly involved the use of several sites throughout the year, so no single site, however well preserved or excavated, can provide more than a partial account of the subsistence system to which it belonged. Establishing the function of stone age sites requires a quality of data rarely encountered in studies of middle pleistocene Europe. One basic piece of information that is required in this context is the time of year when a site was occupied. Sometimes one can make a reasonable guess from the general location of a site. For example, the butchery sites of Torralba and La Cotte de la St Brelade (Scott, 1980) were probably visited in the spring or summer, as neither locality would be attractive in winter during a glacial; the former, because of its altitude (1100 m above sea level) and the latter, because of its position on the northern edge of a peninsula facing a glacial Atlantic. Ideally, seasonality should be established from direct evidence, such as the bones of migratory birds, deer antler, or $^{18\text{-}16}$O analysis of shellfish (see Shackleton, 1973). Such attempts have so far proved unsuccessful; unfortunately, the suggestion that Terra Amata was occupied during the summer (de Lumley, 1969) must now be in doubt, since the pollen which supposedly indicated occupation at that time of year was not derived, as first thought, from human coprolites but from limestone nodules (Trevor-Deutsch and Bryant, 1978).

III. TEMPORAL CHANGE AND SPATIAL VARIABILITY

One of the greatest problems in dealing with archaeological material of this time range is how to explain the differences between samples from different periods and areas. We can consider first the more serious problem of discerning temporal change.

It is understandably tempting but dangerous to conclude that the differences between two or more samples of the same type of material and from the same area, but of different ages, are the result of gradual cultural change. Suppose, for example, that the mean length of hand-axes in one assemblage was 300 mm, and that in another of some 100 000 years later only 200 mm. To conclude that the mean length had decreased by 100 mm as the result of gradual and continuous cultural change would imply an annual rate of reduction of only 0·001 mm. Since there is no conceivable way that 4000 generations of hand-axe makers could have exercised this degree of control, this proposition is clearly nonsensical. The same point is true of the following example, this time of two faunal assemblages from a cave deposit:

Sample 1	Red deer	30%	Penultimate glacial; *ca.* 130 kyr
Sample 2	Red deer	60%	Last interglacial; *ca.* 100 kyr

In this case, a gradual increase in the importance of red deer of 30% over 30 000 years implies a mean annual rate of increase of only 1% every millennium. Again, it is impossible to envisage how a group of hunters could have increased their intake of venison in so miserly yet consistent a fashion. Long-term changes — whether in the size and shape of tools, or the percentage of different types of prey — cannot be explained as the outcome of gradual and continuous processes, since it is not possible to explain how such minor incremental changes could have occurred consistently over such long periods.

The point is made clearer if we look briefly at the study of long-term processes in biology and geology. Evolutionary trends over long periods of time in, for example, the size of human teeth can be explained in terms of genetic processes and environmental pressures that combine to produce a gradual directional change. Similarly, the accumulation of several hundreds of metres of sediments can be easily accounted for as the result of innumerable tiny increments. However, behavioural change is unlikely to occur in this way. Artefacts do not clone themselves or have sex lives; nor do they hybridize, mutate, or pass on their acquired characteristics to their offspring; likewise, the proportions of animals in faunal assemblages do not shrink or expand of their own accord like some kind of pulsating jellyfish. Rather, they are the outcome of a wide variety of short-term circumstances. Those who created them may, of course, have done so with their own cultural preconceptions in mind, but probably changed these (either deliberately or unintentionally) over short periods of time. White and Thomas (1972), for example, noted changes in the sizes and shape of axes made over a matter of weeks by New Guinea highlanders. At any point in time, the size and shape of tools and the composition of tool-kits are likely to have varied considerably, depending on the type of raw material (e.g. Jones, P., 1979) and the intended duration and type of usage of the assemblage (e.g. Binford, 1979, 1980a). In like manner, the composition of a faunal assemblage is likely to have depended upon immediate circumstances, such as the length, type and seasonality of occupation of a site, but not upon the inexorable but imperceptible pressure of a long-term dietary trend. Unless the full range of variation in tool use and diet at any point in time is known, the differences between lithic and faunal samples of different ages cannot be safely attributed to the workings of a nebulous process of long-term cultural change. Consequently, when dealing with long time-periods that are sampled very imperfectly, prehistorians may have to forfeit the aim of studying human behaviour as something that changed in a gradual and continuous manner. Instead they may have to treat the evidence from different geological periods as different facets of the same behavioural system. Whilst it is possible to contrast the subsistence strategies of, for example, Neanderthals and early *Homo sapiens sapiens* during the last glaciation, it is unlikely that we can infer how each cultural system changed over periods as short as 5 or 10 thousand years.

Inter-regional comparisons also encounter similar problems of inadequate sampling. One that is important stems from the likelihood that pleistocene hunter-gatherers used several tool-kits throughout the year. Because of this, an assortment of lithic assemblages from the same time-range could have resulted from a variety of activities, or represent different traditions of manufacture. This problem of functional variability will rear its ugly head in the next chapter, but has already impinged itself on the significance of the differences between acheulean and clactonian assemblages. These have traditionally been regarded as the product of two cultural traditions, in which the former used bifacial implements whilst the latter relied entirely upon flake tools. Ohel (1979), however, has recently suggested that the clactonian industry represents merely the preliminary stages in the preparation of some of the tools found in acheulean assemblages. Whilst this proposal has been treated sympathetically by some European workers (e.g. Bordes, 1979), those most familiar with British clactonian assemblages and similar ones in the eastern part of Europe (e.g. Müller-Beck, 1978) are inclined to regard these as the products of a tradition separate from the Acheulean. Thus the absence of hand-axes in the Clactonian and in eastern Europe has been explained in ecological terms by the suggestion that these were used for wood-working; in the drier and more continental conditions of eastern Europe, there were few trees and hand-axes were thus not used.

This controversy underscores the point that all too little is known about the function of palaeolithic stone tools. This ignorance also vitiates many attempts to establish the function of sites and hence elucidate what subsistence activities were performed. Morphological classifications, based upon the shape of a tool, are dubious since they can often foist our own (western) concepts of tool-use upon the past. Just because we might tend to hold an acheulean biface between our hands to use it as an axe is no guarantee that it was ever used as a hand-axe except by archaeologists (see Kleindienst and Keller, 1976).

Functional classifications are obviously preferable. Here, an objective that would greatly aid the study of middle pleistocene subsistence patterns would be the recognition of those sets of tools which hunter-gatherers would have needed most often: projectiles for killing animals, tools for butchering carcasses, for working wood, for processing plant foods and for carrying (Isaac, 1980). Although many tools were undoubtedly made of wood, these are preserved only exceptionally, as at Lehringen, where a wooden spear was found (Movius, 1950) and Stoke Newington, from where some sharpened birch stakes (Roe, 1981:175) were recovered. Identifying the use of stone tools from the microwear on their edges is laborious but within the range of current research techniques (Keeley, 1980). At present it seems unlikely that there was a close relationship between the shape and function of lower palaeolithic stone tools: the same type of tool could have been used for different purposes, and the same purpose accomplished with different tools. Binford (1979) has further suggested that the type of tool made for a specific purpose will depend upon the context of its use; for example, an expedient tool, made as a "one-off" for one purpose only, will tend to be more hastily made than one required for the same purpose but made in anticipation of that usage.

In view of these difficulties, it might be legitimate to conclude that once archaeologists interested in the European Middle Pleistocene have described and dated the material at their disposal, they can thereafter do little until blessed with sites of the quality of Koobi Fora or Olduvai. A similar course of action could be recommended to those studying the subsistence of this time. Despite Hawkes' assertion that subsistence was one of the prehistorian's easier objectives, our evidence for this in the Middle Pleistocene is depressingly pitiful. Whilst we have a fair idea of the potential range of mammal resources (Kurtén, 1968), we have virtually no direct data on which of these were exploited, still less on what age or sex classes were culled, how they were butchered or on how food was distributed within subsistence groups. As depressing is our complete ignorance as to what plant resources (if any) were used.

However, a more positive attitude is also justified. A few pieces of evidence do stand out with some clarity in the otherwise impenetrable fog, and even though fog is by its nature murky, its extent at least gives some indications of prevailing atmospheric conditions. One useful way of approaching the data of this period is along the lines suggested by Isaac (1981), who suggested that we can structure the archaeological evidence for hunter-gatherers hierarchically in a way analogous to physics. Our smallest unit—or "particle"—is an individual artefact or bone fragment. When taken individually, these are generally uninformative, but may prove more useful if studied collectively in terms of their spatial location across a landscape (see e.g. Foley, 1981). In this instance, we can take the general distribution of the great mass of artefacts roughly assigned to the later part of the Middle Pleistocene as indicating that large areas of Europe were inhabited as far north as North Wales and North Germany, and as far east as Roumania and Poland. Secondly, we can take the fact that these artefacts can often be grouped into regional traditions as implying some continuity in the occupation of an area. Thirdly, they provide some evidence that the techniques for detaching regular flakes from stone nodules improved; on current estimates, prepared-core techniques were used by 200 000–180 000 years ago in Africa (Wendorf *et al.*, 1975) and Europe (Table 1). So, whilst no individual particle is particularly informative, they collectively demonstrate man's presence in these temperate latitudes and the range of environments he was able to colonize.

The next unit can be regarded as "atoms", or sets of particles making up an indivisible event, such as a set of conjoining stone or bone fragments. Perhaps the most famous example from middle pleistocene Europe of this type of unit is the flint nodule that Worthington Smith reconstructed from 13 flakes at Caddington in the last century (see Roe, 1981:196). However, most of the data from occupation sites are "molecules", or compounds of these, in that they represent composites of different activities that have somehow to be decoded by breaking them down into their constituent parts of atoms. In a few cases, such decoding has been possible; for example, the "precise moment in time" recorded in level 5 at La Cotte, where 5 mammoths and a rhino plunged to their deaths, most probably with some assistance from man.

At this stage, some further pieces of evidence are worth mentioning.

A. Human skeletal evidence

This forms an important but problematic source of evidence on the middle pleistocene occupation of Europe. The sample is small, and amounts to an average of only one find each decade over the last century; or, if put another way, to only one individual for every 20 000 years of the time-span that the sample probably covers. Although the specimens are poorly dated, most can be placed in chronological context relative to the two best-known finds from Swanscombe and Steinheim which are usually assigned to the "Mindel-Riss"—an interglacial that is probably composite, however. These are probably in the same time-range as the remains from the recently re-investigated and highly important site of Bilzingsleben in East Germany (Mania, 1979a), dated to *ca.* 225 000 b.p. This group of finds is younger than the jaw from Mauer in Germany and the occipital fragment from Vertesszöllös in Hungary, but older than the skull fragments from Arago in France, dated to the "Riss" glaciation and probably between 150 000 and 200 000 years old (Day, 1977). Tragically, the best-preserved find, of a complete skull from the cave of Petralona in Greece, is also the worst-dated, since its stratigraphic relationship to a long sequence of deposits dating from the last glaciation to the early Middle Pleistocene is unknown. The most detailed investigation of this find assigns it a provisional age of *ca.* 360 000 years, an estimate which may place it in the same time-range as the finds from Mauer and Vertesszöllös (Stringer *et al.*, 1979); however, a recent absolute date implies that it may be younger (see Table 1).

Assigning these finds to a particular species of *Homo* has not proved easy. This is partly because the sample is too small to show the extent to which the differences between specimens should be attributed to individual and sexual variation, and to geographical and chronological factors. Another reason is simply that the Linnéan system of classification was not designed with evolution in mind, and is inappropriate for classifying individuals drawn from an evolving population. Because labels play such an important role in the way we view the world, we should be wary about the way we use them. If, for example, all these finds are classed as *Homo erectus*, we are implying that anatomically they were essentially like individuals represented by East African finds that are a million years earlier. From there, it is but a short step to arguing that human behaviour changed little over this period. On the other hand, if we class them as *H. sapiens*, there are then the dangers of arguing first that the permanent colonization of Europe occurred simply because *H. sapiens* had evolved, and secondly that hominid behaviour 250 000 years ago can be modelled along exactly the same lines as present-day hunter-gatherers. Calling some specimens *H. erectus* and others *H. sapiens* can be equally unsatisfactory, in that it can over-emphasize the importance of minor features, and create additional (and perhaps superfluous) problems. Vlček (1978), for example, proposed that the Bilzingsleben specimens belonged to *H. erectus*, unlike the Swanscombe and Steinheim finds, which he classed as *H. sapiens*. Acceptance of this view could then entail an unnecessary exercise in explaining how these two types of meat-eating, tool-making hominids coexisted, and why one then died out.

These problems of classification are perhaps seen better in a wider context. At present, the earliest examples of *H. erectus* are from East African contexts more than 1·5 Myr old (Rightmire, 1979a). Not surprisingly, these finds are considerably different from those found in contexts at least a million years younger at Choukoutien in China, even though these too were once classed as *H. erectus*. In the light of these recent discoveries of very early examples of *H. erectus* in Africa, the differences between the specimens from Choukoutien, Swanscombe and Steinheim are much less than once seemed. What some (e.g. Bilsborough, 1976; Wolpoff, 1980) have suggested is that the taxon *H. erectus* should be reserved for the earlier African examples, and that definition of *H. sapiens* should be relaxed to include the Choukoutien specimens as well as all the European middle pleistocene finds, possibly by subdividing these into various "grades" (see Stringer *et al.*, 1979).

This approach has the merits of avoiding a proliferation of species and subspecies, and of being sufficiently flexible to accommodate a high degree of variation within the same evolutionary continuum. By stressing that these finds are intermediate between *H. erectus* and modern *H. sapiens sapiens*, it also cautions us against assuming that the behaviour of these individuals was exactly like that of *H. sapiens* now, but allows for the possibility that it was different from that of earlier hominids.

B. Technological evidence

Although the notion of human progress was deeply enshrined in prehistorians' minds in the last century, it has been notoriously hard to verify (or refute) for the immense span of the Lower and Middle Pleistocene. However, a few hints are at least suggestive that behaviour had become more complex by 250 000 years ago.

First, there is the suggestion by Wynn (1979) that the operational procedures used to make hand-axes 300 kyr ago in East Africa were considerably more complicated than those employed during the Lower Pleistocene. Next, the hut at Terra Amata (de Lumley, 1969) may be rudimentary, but nevertheless represents a more complex set of concepts than the small, circular structure built at Olduvai almost 2 million years ago. The use of internal space is more clearly differentiated, with distinct areas for working raw materials and cooking. Whilst on Parkinsonian principles work can expand to fill the available space, it is equally arguable in this instance that the structure was built in anticipation of these (and possibly other) activities, and thus denotes a more complex type of planning.

Until the discovery of burnt clay at Chesowanja showed that fire was used in East Africa over 1·5 Myr ago, fire was seen as one of the principal innovations that helped man to colonize northern latitudes a million years later. To some extent, this may still be true, since the use(s) to which fire was put at Chesowanja remains enigmatic. It was not necessarily the possession of fire that mattered so much as the ways it was used: besides its obvious use for keeping people warm, it can of course be employed in several other ways—for cooking plant foods, joints of meat, and carcasses in their skins to retain the juices (Black, 1969); for prolonging the length of usable light each day; or outside settlements, for driving game; burning scrub to encourage the growth of new shoots (cf. the "fire-stick farming" of Australian aborigines (Gould, 1971)); as a signalling device that can be used by day or night. (It does not, however, seem to be of much use for hardening wooden projectiles, as has been suggested for the "spear" from Clacton (see Coles, 1979:168).) Whilst some of these uses are impossible to establish, the presence of charcoal at Torralba (Freeman and Butzer, 1966), Hoxne and Marks Tey (Roe, 1981:283) may indicate some kind of off-site usage of fire in middle pleistocene Europe. Although fire may prove to be one of man's oldest technologies, it may still have been used more systematically and for a wider range of purposes by 300 000 years ago. As importantly, its manufacture may have become better controlled.

C. Elephants, rhinos, hippos and kill sites

Several instances are now known of animals that were probably dismembered, and possibly killed by early hominids. As Table 2 indicates, the commonest animals are very large ones such as elephant or hippo. Most of the African "kill sites" contain the remains of only one animal, and may indicate only that a group of hominids came across an elephant or hippo that was about to die (if, for example, senile or trapped in deep mud), or had just expired (perhaps with some encouragement), and was then butchered. With the exception of Olorgesailie DE/89, the other instances of kill sites in which several species are represented may

Table 2: African and European kill and butchery sites from the Lower and Middle Pleistocene.

Site	Date (b.p.)	Comments	Source
AFRICA			
Hippo-artefact site (HAS), Koobi Fora	ca. 1·8 Myr	1 hippo skeleton and some artefacts	Isaac, 1978
Olduvai:			
— Upper Bed I FLK North	ca. 1·8 Myr	*Deinotherium* skeleton and some artefacts	Leakey, 1971
— Lower Bed II FLK North	ca. 1·7 Myr	*Deinotherium* skeleton and some artefacts	Leakey, 1971
Gadeb 8	> 0.7 Myr	1 hippo skeleton and some artefacts	Clark and Kurashina, 1979
Olorgesailie	ca. 0·4 Myr	90 baboon remains and some artefacts	Isaac, 1977; Shipman et al., 1981
Namib IV	?0·4–0·7 Myr	*Elephas recki*, some artefacts; could be a butchery site, camp or palimpsest	Shackley, 1980
Elandsfontein 10	0·2–0·4 Myr	15 mammalian species present, some artefacts. Probably result of several processes	Klein, 1978a
Duinefontein 2	0·125 Myr	12 mammalian species. Probably palimpsest	Klein, 1975
Mwanganda	Early Upper Pleistocene	1 elephant and butchery tools	Clark and Haynes, 1970
EUROPE			
Torralba	0·3–0·6 Myr	Remains of several elephants and some other species; artefacts. Some mixing by solifluction possible	Butzer, 1965; Freeman, 1981; Freeman and Butzer, 1966
La Cotte	Penultimate glaciation	5 elephants and 1 rhino	Scott, 1980
Lehringen	Last interglacial	1 elephant with wooden spear in ribs — one that got away?	Movius, 1950

represent faunal and artefactual material derived from several sources, and so the evidence for butchery here is less clear.

The two European sites of Torralba and La Cotte are different, in that several animals are present, and man seems to have played a larger part in causing the animal's death. At Torralba, for example, there are large concentrations of elephant (and other) remains; at La Cotte, the butchered remains of five elephants and a rhino lie at the base of a steep cliff (Scott, 1980). Both cases probably represent ambush sites, where animals could be stampeded either into marshy ground (as at Torralba) or over a precipice. In neither instance is there any reason to talk of specialized elephant hunting. As Freeman (1981) points out, elephants form only one third of the total number of individual animals at Torralba, and La Cotte represents the outcome of only one episode. In any case, elephants have such enormous feeding requirements (*ca.* 100 kg per day (Stanley, 1980)) that they live at low densities, and must have represented enormous but rare amounts of meat. As there is no evidence of caching, most of the carcass must have been eaten almost immediately, or wasted. Freeman's (1981) interpretation of the Torralba data seems reasonable, and applicable also to La Cotte: that groups of hunters went to localities where they expected very large game to be present and where these could be ambushed, killed what they could, removed as much meat as they could eat or carry, and moved off again.

A question that is worth asking, and which will be returned to shortly, is why middle pleistocene groups killed such large, dangerous and uncommon animals when many other smaller and less dangerous types of prey were readily available.

D. Central Asia

Finally, it is worth mentioning some recent work in Soviet Central Asia. Although archaeological exploration of this vast area has only just begun, current evidence suggests that it was colonized around 225 000 b.p. (Davis *et al.*, 1980; Ranov and Davis, 1979). If confirmed, this evidence might support the proposition that the expansion of man into the temperate and continental latitudes of Europe, beyond the Mediterranean fringe, and Central Asia occurred at roughly the same time.

IV. SUBSISTENCE AND THE COLONIZATION OF EUROPE

As noted already, direct evidence of subsistence prior to the last interglacial in Europe is meagre in the extreme. The evidence, taken as a whole, can also be interpreted in several ways: as showing a gradual increase in hominids in Europe from the late Pliocene onwards; or a gradual extension of their range from Africa into more northerly regions; or as the result of a behavioural breakthrough that enabled a comparatively rapid expansion into most of Europe and the southern parts of Central Asia. If the last mentioned is the case, we have then to explain what it was that enabled hominids to do so then, but not before, and without resorting to a circular argument based on the European fossil human remains. It explains little to argue that Europe was colonized because a more advanced type of hominid had evolved if the main case for his "advanced" behaviour is that Europe was colonized. Instead, we need to be more precise in suggesting what types of behavioural changes were needed for this continent to have been successfully colonized.

We can straightaway dispose of the idea that Europe was colonized because the climate ameliorated to the point that hominids could cope with an environment that had previously been too inhospitable. From what is now known of middle pleistocene climate, glacials were of the same intensity as the last glaciation, and punctuated by only short interglacials. As suspected even before the deep-sea evidence became available, there was no "Great" or Mindel-Riss interglacial to provide a quarter million years of Arcadian warmth in which early man might have basked. We thus have to explain what adaptations were needed for early man to live in a predominantly glacial environment, and in latitudes where the growing season and length of daylight were considerably shortened during the winter; where there was a wide range of animal resources, ranging in size from marmots to mammoths, but probably little in the way of plant foods except perhaps in short interglacial interludes.

A useful starting point is to contrast two types of subsistence strategies that early hominids may have adopted: one in an environment such as East Africa where both plant and animal resources were abundant, and the other in one lacking plant foods, such as glacial Europe.

In the first example, a significant part of the diet was obtained from a small number of staple plant foods such as seeds, nuts, fruits, roots and tubers. Each was available on a seasonal basis, and distributed across the landscape in clusters of varying size, rather than uniformly. Because these resources were static, they provided not only predictably-located sources of food, but also reference points from which a simple mental map could be made of the landscape, and used as a basis for determining the pattern of day-to-day food procurement. In terms of the time taken to locate them, these are low-cost resources; energy spent in gathering and processing them would of course raise their costs (see Hawkes and

O'Connell, 1981) but can be disregarded for the purpose of this argument, since this would apply also to animal resources.

Plant clusters of the kind described would also have been important in minimizing the costs of obtaining animal resources. That is to say, these — whether small mammals, birds or large game — would have been most commonly encountered during foraging trips to areas of plant foods, and thus could have been taken without the need for expeditions specifically undertaken for the sole purpose of obtaining meat. The advantages of acquiring meat in this way are obvious. Hunting (as judged from the failure rate of present-day hunter-gatherers and predators) is a high-risk venture that is often unsuccessful, so there are sound reasons for foraging in a way that will produce a guaranteed return in the form of plant foods and a possible bonus in the form of meat, whether a tortoise or a dying elephant. (The same point is made by Binford (1980a) in respect to collecting stone for tool-making as an activity embedded in other tasks.) Secondly, this type of foraging would have required little if any sexual or generational division of labour, since both sexes and most age groups could participate in collecting plant foods, small game, and in scavenging. It is only during the occasional and more ambitious hunting of large game that labour would need to be more rigorously organized. A third advantage is that the location of plant foods does not change appreciably from year to year, even though it may change throughout the year as different plants come into season. Because of this degree of stability in the location of staple food resources, individual groups would also have been able to predict the location of their neighbours at any time of the year, and thus to maintain without undue difficulty the ties needed to ensure that reproductive networks remained viable.

In the second example, we can explore the consequences of removing the clustered plant resources that previously served both as food sources and as topographic reference points. At first sight, it might seem that the main result would have been simply that more animal foods had to be obtained to compensate for the loss of plant resources. However, matters are unlikely to have been so simple. In the first place, the costs of locating small game would have been greatly increased. This is because they could no longer have been obtained at little or no extra expenditure of effort during foraging trips to predictable sources of plant foods, but would have to be obtained in special journeys. However, without the guaranteed return of plant foods, the proceeds from making foraging expeditions solely to obtain resources that are available in small amounts and unpredictably located are likely to have become too low to justify the effort involved. Meat-procuring trips would have become worthwhile only if the anticipated returns outweighed the predicted uncertainties of locating and obtaining them. As Schaller and Lowther (1969) have pointed out from their observations of non-human predators in the Serengeti of East Africa, early hominids are unlikely to have ever lived by scavenging alone, since there is too much competition for this source of food. Under such circumstances, it would thus have made sense for hominid groups to concentrate upon medium and large-sized game, such as deer, pig, bovids, horse and elephant.

Exploiting these types of animals as staple resources poses very different problems from those encountered in the first example. Because their seasonal movements often extend over a considerable area, any hominid group dependent upon them would also have to move over larger distances than before. Moreover, mobility is one of the main ways that herbivores can respond to short-term changes in weather and resource availability, and so their location at any time of the year is likely to change from year to year. These two points, when taken together, would affect hominid populations in three ways. First, population densities would fall because each group would have to exploit a larger annual territory than before. Secondly, because each subsistence group would have been continually responding to changes in the location of its resources, it would have had little ability to predict the precise location of its neighbours at a given point of the year. As subsistence groups became increasingly isolated, so mating networks would have been endangered unless some form of institutionalized contacts were implemented. Thirdly, because of the uncertainties over where an animal resource is likely to be located, combined with the difficulties of pursuing and killing it, a change in food-procurement techniques would have been required. What might be expected is that only part of a group (? adult males) participated in obtaining most of the food, and that the rest of a group would have been fed with meat transported back from kill sites to occupation sites.

It is important to note that these two very different kinds of subsistence strategies could have operated at exactly the same technological level. The main differences between the two are perceptual (see Binford, 1980a); in the latter example, subsistence groups could have survived only if they could map their landscapes in terms of the constantly changing locations, first of their animal resources, and secondly of neighbouring groups within the same mating network.

On the argument advanced here, Europe beyond the Mediterranean perimeter could not have been effectively colonized until these *perceptual* problems had been resolved. It is possible that these difficulties were not overcome until well into the Middle Pleistocene, and lay beyond the ability of both *H. habilis* and *H. erectus*. At this point, we can return to the role of very large mammals in the subsistence strategies of middle pleistocene Europe. Quarry as large as elephant or rhino would have provided enormous quantities of meat, far larger than one group could have consumed in a few days. On the other hand, the likelihood of a successful kill would have been greatly enhanced if several groups cooperated in stampeding or cornering them. These animals might, therefore, have provided an inadvertent social as well as dietary function in providing an incentive for groups to aggregate, and thereby reinforce the ties needed to maintain viable mating networks.

Two interesting exceptions to the argument that Europe was primarily a continent of mobile resources may be noted. The first are coastal regions, where shellfish were available in well-defined static clusters, and perhaps exploited (as hinted at by the evidence from Terra Amata). As shall be seen later, these were probably exploited in holocene times more as predictable than as staple resources, and might have served the same role as plant foods in providing spatial landmarks around which other subsistence activities could be organized. The second exception may have been the brief episodes of interglacial climate during which plant resources would have become more abundant, and enabled groups to subsist to a greater extent on a combination of plant foods and small game, supplemented by larger quarry.

4. The Mousterian Muddle

Abstract

This chapter pairs with the next one, and examines subsistence strategies during the last glaciation, from ca. 100 000 to 30 000 b.p. Here, the main concern lies with the middle to upper palaeolithic transition. It is argued that neither anatomical nor typological evidence is conclusive in showing either continuity or change in behaviour between these two periods, and thus alternative approaches need to be tried. The use of faunal data is examined, and it is concluded that recent claims for continuity in subsistence patterns between the Mousterian and the early Upper Palaeolithic are not valid. This chapter ends with a discussion of what can be safely summarized at present from this rather messy set of problems.

Between the end of the last interglacial in Europe and the start of the Upper Palaeolithic lies the Mousterian, a timescape in which there are few fixed points and many chimaeras. Establishing what kind of subsistence strategies operated in this long period, and whether or not they were different from those of the Upper Palaeolithic are abstruse problems in themselves, but are also entangled with two other equally thorny issues. The first is whether or not the European Neanderthals, with their middle palaeolithic mousterian tool-kits, were displaced by incoming populations of modern man (*Homo sapiens sapiens*), already equipped with an upper palaeolithic technology and possibly different methods for obtaining and processing food. The second is a general methodological problem of how we can recognize changes in pleistocene hunting strategies from sequences of faunal assemblages from cave deposits.

I. WHAT HAPPENED TO NEANDERTHAL MAN AND THE MOUSTERIAN?

Although human palaeontology has come a long way from when Boule first presented the Chapelle-aux-Saints Neanderthal as the typically horrible product of a dank and murky gene pool in which the earliest upper palaeolithic peoples had most wisely refused to bathe, the evolutionary status of Neanderthal Man is still far from clear. Opinion has long polarized over two diametrically opposed viewpoints: one that the European Neanderthals lay outside the mainstream of human evolution and died out; the other, that they evolved directly into *H. sapiens sapiens*.

Those favouring the first hypothesis have argued that the "ante-Neanderthals" of the last interglacial and preceding glaciation resembled ourselves more than the Neanderthals (e.g. Stringer, 1974), and that the differences between European late Neanderthals and early *H. sapiens sapiens* are too great for the former to have evolved into the latter in the short time-span available. These differences extend beyond the size and wear of the dentition (which have received a great deal of attention) and include the occipital "bun" at the back of the cranium, the enlarged nasal sinuses and protruding lower face, the robustness of the limb-bones, and differences in the hands (see Trinkhaus and Howell, 1979). We may, however, discount the claim of Lieberman and Crelin (1971) that Neanderthals lacked the same capacity for speech as ourselves, since their suggestions on how and where the Neanderthal larynx was placed have been soundly criticized (Burr, 1976; Carlisle and Siegel, 1974). Thirdly, and looking further afield, recent evidence suggests that modern types of man had emerged by 100 000 years ago in East (Day *et al.*, 1980; Kennedy, 1980) and southern (Butzer *et al.*, 1978; Rightmire, 1979b) Africa, and so modern man probably evolved outside Europe. Finally, the fact that Australia was colonized at least 40 000 years ago (Jones, R., 1979) by modern types of man whilst Neanderthals were occupying Europe must imply that modern man evolved somewhere between the two areas.

However, the case for a "Neanderthal phase" is also strong. Several researchers (e.g. Jelinek, 1980; Malez *et al.*, 1980; Sheets and Gavan,

1977; Smith and Ranyard, 1980) have claimed a considerable degree of continuity in the evolution of the face and dentition from *H. erectus* through the European Neanderthals to ourselves. Brace in particular has argued that the European Neanderthals were not the evolutionary deviants that many have claimed them to have been, and that there is no good reason why they could not have been directly ancestral to ourselves. So far as the dentition is concerned, there is certainly a great deal of continuity between them and early *H. sapiens sapiens*: mean tooth size decreased by only 5% between the end of the Mousterian and the early Upper Palaeolithic, compared with a subsequent reduction of 20% during the latter period (Brace, 1979). Additionally, it is hard to see how the West European Neanderthals could have evolved in complete genetic isolation from other European populations during the 70 000 years between the end of the last interglacial (see Fig. 7) and the advent of the Upper Palaeolithic.

II. WHERE DID THE UPPER PALAEOLITHIC ORIGINATE?

The origin of European upper palaeolithic assemblages is just as contentious a problem as that of where and how modern man originated. The classic diffusionist view argued that the upper palaeolithic of Europe represented an intrusive tradition, largely because many of the tool types were very different in shape (and possibly in function) from those of the Mousterian, and were made by different techniques. In addition, bone, antler and ivory were used much more often than before as raw materials for making tools. Other innovations associated with upper palaeolithic tool assemblages are art, the burial of the dead with grave goods (Harrold, 1980), and cobble-lined hearths that effectively conserved heat. Supposedly "transitional" assemblages that contained both middle and upper palaeolithic types of tools and debitage could be dismissed as the result of mixing, either whilst cave sediments were accumulating or during excavation.

Diffusionists can also exploit the chronological evidence to their advantage. Upper palaeolithic-type assemblages have been dated to 36–38 000 years b.p. in western Iran (Hole and Flannery, 1967), and northern (McBurney, 1968) and southern Africa (Butzer *et al.*, 1978), whereas none in Europe can be reliably dated to before *ca.* 34 000 b.p. Two age determinations, claimed to relate to very early upper palaeolithic assemblages can be dismissed as unreliable, since they lie right at the limit of ^{14}C dating. These are one of 44 000 b.p. for an aurignacian assemblage from Istallöskö in Hungary (Gábori-Csánk, 1970) (see Fig. 8) and one of 42 000 b.p. for an upper

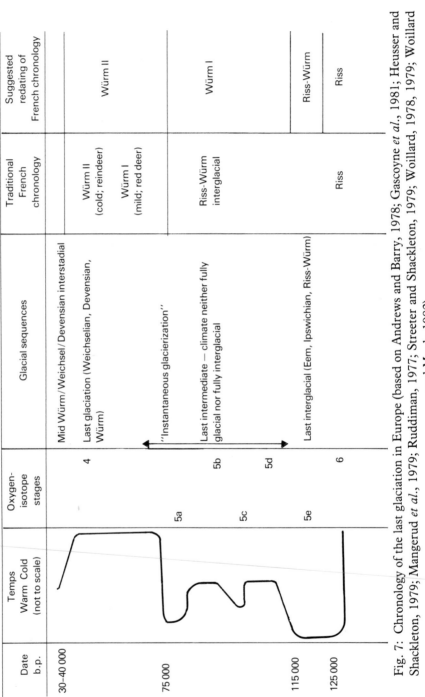

Fig. 7: Chronology of the last glaciation in Europe (based on Andrews and Barry, 1978; Gascoyne *et al.*, 1981; Heusser and Shackleton, 1979; Mangerud *et al.*, 1979; Ruddiman, 1977; Streeter and Shackleton, 1979; Woillard, 1978, 1979; Woillard and Mook, 1982).

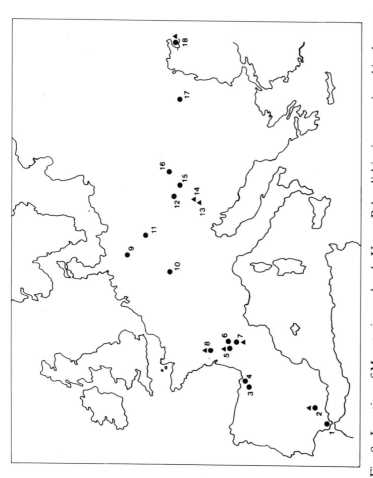

Fig. 8: Location of Mousterian and early Upper Palaeolithic sites mentioned in the text.

Key: 1 Gorham's Cave; 2 Carigüela; 3 Balinkoba; 4 Lezetxiki; 5 La Ferrassie; 6 Combe Grenal; 7 Combe Capelle; 8 St Césaire; 9 Salzgitter-Lebenstedt; 10 Stadel; 11 Königssäue; 12 Tata; 13 Krapina; 14 Veternica; 15 Erd; 16 Istallöskö; 17 Molodova; 18 Starosl'ye.

Circles: archaeological sites; Triangles: hominid finds.

palaeolithic horizon at Samulica in Bulgaria (Vogel and Waterbolk, 1972).

However, the case for a local origin of the European Upper Palaeolithic can also be championed. In the past, palaeolithic archaeologists often looked for the most idiosyncratic features of palaeolithic tool assemblages in order to draw distinctions between assemblages of different ages. This approach inevitably overlooked the features that were common to assemblages of different periods. So far as the late Mousterian and early Upper Palaeolithic is concerned, a plausible case can be made for regarding the chatelperronian and aurignacian assemblages of western and central Europe as essentially local developments from a mousterian background (Bricker, 1976; Brose and Wolpoff, 1971).

The chronological evidence can also be turned against the diffusionists, since the transition from Middle to Upper Palaeolithic cannot be firmly established until the *latest* mousterian as well as the *earliest* upper palaeolithic assemblages are reliably dated. Some of the dates for late mousterian assemblages are undoubtedly unreliable: three examples are those of 33 000 b.p. from Tata in Hungary (Gábori-Csánk, 1970: also chapter 5: 92), and those of *ca.* 30 000 b.p. from Les Cottes and La Quina in France (Vogel and Waterbolk, 1972). As unreliable are some of the earliest upper palaeolithic dates: for example, the oldest ^{14}C dates from early upper palaeolithic horizons at Yafteh in western Iran are not always from the lowest levels (Hole and Flannery, 1967:161). In many cases, mousterian assemblages are dated only vaguely by ^{14}C to somewhere beyond 40 000 b.p. As events of this age-range are at the limit of standard ^{14}C techniques as well as other radiometric ones (e.g. Th/U and K/A), dates in the range of 35 000–100 000 b.p. are often extrapolated from circumstantial evidence, such as the assumed rates at which cave sediments accumulated. As these might not have accumulated at a constant rate or even continuously, the resulting dates may be in error. In view of all these problems, it may be premature to claim that the Mousterian of western Europe ended significantly later than elsewhere (see ApSimon, 1980).

III. WHO MADE WHAT?

According to the classic diffusionist argument, Neanderthals and mousterian industries were replaced at the same time by populations of modern man and upper palaeolithic industries. Those who oppose this view maintain either that *H. sapiens sapiens* developed before the Upper Palaeolithic, or that Neanderthals made at least some upper palaeolithic assemblages. Usually such claims do not pass detailed examination.

In at least two cases where *H. sapiens sapiens* has been reported in firm association with middle palaeolithic assemblages, it is not certain that the skeletal remains *are* fully modern in appearance. One such site is Jebel Qafzeh in Palestine, where remains of *H. sapiens sapiens* were reported in association with levallois–mousterian assemblages. However, these finds have not been fully described, and most opinion tends to the view that they are neither like those of "classic" Neanderthals nor of *H. sapiens sapiens* (see Day, 1977:100). So too with the site of Carigüela in Spain, where modern types of man have been claimed from a thoroughly mousterian context (Bricker, 1976). In this instance, the frontal remains from level 9 are said to have many Neanderthal features (de Lumley and Garcia-Sanchez, 1971).

In other cases, it is the association rather than the identification of the find that seems in doubt. For example, the skull of *H. sapiens sapiens* from the mousterian layer (h) at Veternica in Yugoslavia may have been in a grave that was dug into the mousterian layers from the overlying aurignacian (f) horizon (Smith, 1976). Similarly, the *H. sapiens sapiens* child supposedly from a mousterian context at Starosl'ye was almost certainly *not* associated with that layer (see Klein, 1969b:195).

Evidence that Neanderthals made upper palaeolithic assemblages is at present intriguing but unconvincing. If the identification and association of the Neanderthal remains in a chatelperronian layer at St Césaire (Lévêque and Vandermeersch, 1980) are confirmed, it will doubtless become a powerful piece of evidence for those who regard the French Upper Palaeolithic as an indigenous phenomenon. However, those casting doubts over the Neanderthal status of this find have been quick off the mark (Wolpoff, 1981).

IV. SUMMARY

At present, the "Neanderthal problem" remains unsolved. It is unclear whether European Neanderthals evolved into or were replaced by *H. sapiens sapiens*. It is also uncertain whether the Mousterian and Upper Palaeolithic were entirely the products of Neanderthals and *H. sapiens sapiens* respectively. Whilst the earliest upper palaeolithic stone-tool assemblages may have developed from a local mousterian background, it is difficult to derive art, the elaborate ritual and the common use of bone, ivory and antler in the Upper Palaeolithic from the same source.

Finally, it is unclear whether the appearance of upper palaeolithic stone-tool assemblages was accompanied by major changes in behaviour, or represented simply a more efficient way of using flint.

These problems are largely ones of definition and dating. The first of these is particularly true of the term "Neanderthal". This has been defined chronologically, as denoting all populations after the penultimate glaciation and before 35 000 b.p.; in cultural terms, which make the Neanderthals coterminous with the Mousterian; or in morphological and metrical terms for the skeletal material. The last mentioned are preferable, given that the dating of most finds is so imprecise and that there is no reason why the Mousterian and Neanderthals should have been inextricably linked. However, the use of morphometric criteria to define Neanderthals depends heavily upon the significance attached to the facial morphology of the west European Neanderthals, which is viewed either as a functional development relating to the teeth, or an adaptation to a cold climate that affected the size of the nasal sinuses (see Stringer, 1978).

The dating of Neanderthals and the Mousterian is plagued by several problems. One is that the relative age of the key Neanderthal finds is uncertain. For example, the remains from Krapina in Yugoslavia may belong to the last interglacial, or to an interstadial perhaps 50 000 years later (Day, 1977:67); whichever is chosen considerably affects the status of the so-called "progressive" Neanderthals of eastern Europe. A second problem is the absolute age of these finds. Most have been dated indirectly from their geological context by reference to a climatic sequence which places the onset of the last glaciation to between 60 000 and 70 000 years ago. On this "short" chronology, the development of the "classic" Neanderthals is slotted into a period only 25 000–30 000 years long, which many would argue leaves too little time for them to have evolved into modern man. This view might change now that the end of the last interglacial can be put back to over 100 000 years ago (Fig. 7) and the time-span of the Neanderthals thus doubled. One effect of this new "long" chronology might be to create a long enough gap between late Neanderthal and early *H. sapiens sapiens* remains in Europe to make the idea of a gradual, continuous evolution from one to the other more acceptable to its critics. Thirdly, it is difficult at present to date precisely the end of the Middle Palaeolithic, and so it is unclear whether or not it lasted significantly longer in Europe than elsewhere. At present, there is no equivalent of the bristle-cone pine that can be used to check the accuracy of ^{14}C dates beyond 10 000 b.p., and preliminary attempts to calibrate ^{14}C dates back to 32 000 b.p. have produced conflicting results (see Barbetti and Flude, 1979; Stuiver, 1978). Some of these problems may eventually be overcome by the incoming generation of dating techniques that may allow material up to 100 000 years old to be dated reliably (see Banning and Pavlish, 1979; Stringer and Burleigh, 1981).

In view of all these uncertainties, it would be unwise to base any argument for change or continuity in human behaviour between 30 000–35 000 years ago on either anatomical or typological evidence. Recently, there have been several attempts to see if major behavioural changes occurred at this time by studying late middle and early upper palaeolithic faunal assemblages from cave deposits. These studies have consistently indicated that these assemblages are similar in composition, and it has thus been concluded that no significant changes in subsistence strategies occurred. Before we look at this evidence, we should first examine how it has been studied.

V. THE RECOGNITION OF STABILITY IN PLEISTOCENE HUNTING BEHAVIOUR

In recent years, details of the type, age and sex of prey taken by pleistocene hunters have become indispensable in providing much of the raw data upon which studies of palaeolithic subsistence are based. In these types of studies, changes in any of these attributes are assumed to indicate different hunting strategies, resulting either from environmental changes, or from changes in the ways that hunting strategies were organized and implemented. Conversely, and very importantly in the context of the middle to upper palaeolithic transition, an *absence* of change in the proportions and age of prey species in faunal assemblages is assumed to indicate that hunting strategies also remained unaltered. This assumption may be unwise, for the same general features of prey assemblages from different periods could have been produced by very different kinds of hunting strategies.

We can take as an example red deer, which was the commonest prey for several tens of millennia in many areas of Europe during the last glaciation. At some point in time, these were killed by spears hurled from spear-throwers, or with bows and arrows, instead of by stabbing. By greatly increasing the distance over which animals were killed, deer could have been killed more easily and probably more frequently. Perhaps as importantly, the hunting of deer during winter would have become easier and the supply of food throughout the year more regular. Alternatively, techniques for butchering and cooking may have improved, and resulted in a more efficient use of carcasses. Another possibility is that the introduction of technologies for conserving meat by drying and smoking would have helped to overcome seasonal shortages of food as well as providing hunting parties with field rations that would enable them to make more extensive hunting trips than before.

In addition to these *technological* innovations, important organizational changes may also have occurred in the way that food was obtained and consumed. For example, hunting strategies may have changed from a foraging to a logistic type, as defined by Binford (1980a; see also Fig. 2), and coped more successfully with seasonal fluctuations in the availability of food resources.

Another example mentioned earlier (Chapter 1: 19) is the change from hunting to herding. In this instance, the main changes affect the social relationships between man and man, as well as between man and reindeer, and can lead to a considerable increase in the numbers of animals available to a human group. Finally, changes might have occurred in the way that food was distributed between different age and sex groups within subsistence groups.

In all these cases, the type, frequency, age and sex of the meat resources represented in a series of faunal assemblages would not necessarily have changed. As Fig. 9 shows, the death of an animal is the

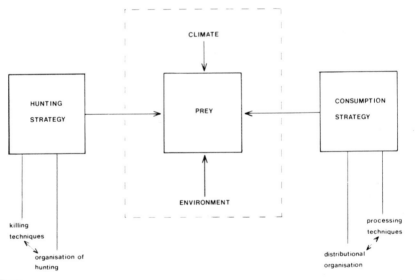

Fig. 9: Factors affecting the composition of pleistocene prey assemblages.

end point of several ways of killing it, and the starting point of a variety of ways of consuming it. Whilst these issues may have been of little interest to the prey, they are relevant to the economic prehistorian because they emphasize the need to consider faunal data within the overall context of the strategies that were used to obtain and consume food. For example, improvements in hunting techniques might be detected from artefactual data and from the variety of animals—especially small and elusive ones—that were killed. Detailed analyses of the time of year when animals were culled would show whether animals were killed year-round when required, or during one or two major kills. Storage of meat in caches might be inferred from the types of anatomical elements most commonly represented in settlement sites, and from studying the fragmentation patterns of bones to show how animals were butchered. Changes in cooking techniques require consideration of the type of hearths and ovens that were used, and finally, analyses of human skeletal material can help show if the nutritional status of subsistence groups had changed. Whilst much can be learnt from the study of pleistocene faunal assemblages, it is not enough to conclude that hunting strategies continued unchanged simply because the main types of prey remained the same as before.

With these points in mind, we can now turn to some of the mousterian and early upper palaeolithic faunal data from various parts of Europe.

VI. FAUNAL EVIDENCE FROM THE MIDDLE AND EARLY UPPER PALAEOLITHIC

Most of this evidence is very coarse-grained, and allows only the broadest of generalizations about human predation and diet. Because the numbers of bones from each site are often small, it is often necessary to combine the collections from several sites into a single regional sample. As this may include evidence from different types of site, and perhaps also the refuse of carnivores besides man, its main value is to show the types of resources available in different areas and at different periods.

Three types of animals represented in these assemblages pose special problems. The first are carnivores such as hyaena and wolf. These could represent animals that were killed by man, or which lived (and died) in caves when man was absent. If the latter, their remains could have been mixed up with human debris, particularly as cave sediments often accumulate very slowly. Because carnivores such as hyaena accumulate bones in caves (Henschel *et al.*, 1979; Sutcliffe, 1970), it is not always certain how many of the bones of the species in archaeological horizons resulted from carnivore or from human activities. The two can be distinguished by noting the size of prey; type of anatomical elements; pattern of fragmentation; and presence or absence of gnawing (Haynes, 1980; Shipman, 1981), but such work has yet to be done on most European pleistocene assemblages. The presence of small carnivores might similarly indicate either that man was not the only creature to inhabit caves, or that he killed these for their meat or pelts. The best indication of fur-trapping is when an entire skeleton is found except for its paws, which are normally removed with the pelt when the animal is skinned. Although this practice is evidenced in the later Upper Palaeolithic (see next chapter), there is little evidence of it in earlier contexts.

Another quandary concerns the bear. In many high-altitude caves, this animal is very commonly represented, and one of the more popular myths about Neanderthal Man is that he practised an elaborate bear cult. However, in the Alps at least, most of these remains represent animals that died whilst hibernating (Jequier, 1975), and man probably used these caves during summer months whilst hunting other animals.

Mammoth and rhino provide further instances where the use of an animal resource as part of human diet is unclear. In eastern Europe where trees were scarce, their remains were often used for building, toolmaking, or as fuel. Thus it is often unclear whether these came from animals that man killed and ate, or from ones that died naturally and were dismembered for their skeletons.

VII. NORTHERN SPAIN

This area has lately regained its former importance to European palaeolithic studies, thanks to recent reappraisals of old evidence and the collection of new data.

In the early 1970s, Freeman reviewed the faunal evidence from cave deposits containing mousterian, chatelperronian, aurignacian and gravettian assemblages, and noted that the type and frequency of prey species from each were generally similar. He thus concluded that:

> "despite the . . . postulated great differences in technological efficiency between the Mousterian and Upper Palaeolithic . . . the Cantabrian case is one in which any differences before magdalenian times seem minor in comparison with the apparent continuities in subsistence-related behaviour".

This claim was subsequently upheld by Straus (1977), who also noted that the average number of species in assemblages from each period clustered around 5·5 from the Mousterian to the Magdalenian. This point thus conflicts with S. Binford's (1970) proposal that the advent of the Upper Palaeolithic may have been accompanied by a heavier reliance upon a smaller range of animals. Whether or not the relative importance of the major animal resources changed significantly through time is questionable. According to Straus, red deer increased gradually at the expense of large bovids, whilst the frequencies of horses remained stable from the Mousterian to the lower Magdalenian. However, as noted in the previous chapter, long-term trends of this kind may be illusory when very long periods are sampled in an intermittent manner, and when the samples may not be truly comparable. However, if one assumes that hunters generally took what was most readily available, this data may show that the biotopes favourable to red deer became more prevalent in Cantabria during the last glacial.

Freeman's (1973:38) second conclusion was that minor changes may have occurred in the early Upper Palaeolithic: "Whatever technological or organizational factors precluded the successful exploitation of suids, felids and alpine ungulates were overcome once and for all during the Aurignacian". However, these trends may be more apparent than real, and the impression that hunting strategies were more efficient in the Upper Palaeolithic may largely result in this instance from the scarcity of reliable mousterian data. Pig, for example, is rare throughout the entire palaeolithic sequence in the region, and did not become a major food resource until the Holocene (see Straus *et al.*, 1980). The evidence for the systematic trapping of small carnivores is also unconvincing. Whilst they are commoner in aurignacian and gravettian assemblages than in the few reliable mousterian ones, they are nevertheless rare, and there is no way of telling whether they died naturally in caves, were killed casually for their meat, or were trapped for their furs. Again, the absence of ibex and chamois from mousterian assemblages in this area need not mean that they were not hunted at this time. The apparent importance of these animals in aurignacian and gravettian assemblages is largely brought about by the inclusion of the samples from Lezetxiki and Bolinkoba which lie in mountainous terrain, unlike the mousterian sites which are located at lower altitudes, where these species would have been scarce. We can note also that mountain species *are* well represented in mousterian contexts elsewhere, where local habitats were more suitable for them—for example, at Gorham's Cave on Gibraltar (Davidson, 1976), and Shanidar in Iraq (Perkins, 1964).

It is equally hard to detect any marked changes in the location of sites from the Mousterian to the end of the Gravettian, as both are distributed over a large part of the coastal plain. Changes in the numbers of sites between each period are also inconclusive in showing whether or not population levels increased through time. According to Freeman's (1973) data, there are five sites with only mousterian assemblages, three with aurignacian but no mousterian, and four with both. If site densities and exploitation patterns had remained the same, we might expect a predominance of sites with only mousterian assemblages, since these were made over a far longer period than aurignacian ones. At the same time, the minute size of the archaeological sample available to palaeolithic archaeologists should be borne in mind when evaluating claims that pleistocene population levels changed through time. If, for example, northern Spain had been occupied by only one subsistence group over the 70 000 years during which mousterian assemblages were used, and if they had moved only once during each year to a new camp-site, they would nevertheless have created 70 000 sites. As palaeolithic archaeologists have often only one-thousandth of this number to study, their ability to discern population trends in the Pleistocene is clearly very limited (see Foley, 1981).

VIII. CENTRAL GERMANY

The faunal evidence from several caves in this area, and the methods used for studying it, are broadly similar to those we have just considered for northern Spain. After studying mousterian and upper palaeolithic faunal collections from various caves in the Swabian Alb, Gamble (1979:46) concluded that:

> "the majority of sites indicate a broad similarity between the communities preceding the Magdalenian. Large species size, high mobility and potential for aggregation are the main characteristics of the prey communities . . . between *c.* 60 000 and 20 000 b.p.".

The most detailed information comes from the cave of Stadel. In levels X-VIII, dating to the end of the last interglacial, *Bos*, red deer and horse are the ungulate species most commonly represented. Levels VII-V (early part of the last glaciation) contain more remains of horse, and reindeer was by far the commonest animal represented in levels IV and III, which also contained upper palaeolithic assemblages. Unfortunately, the remains of wolf and hyaena were very common in all levels, and these animals may have killed many of the herbivores represented in these assemblages. This potential source of confusion could be clarified in the manner suggested earlier. Secondly, the upper palaeolithic levels at Stadel were undifferentiated, and so it is unclear exactly when reindeer became important. However, the evidence from other sites in the region indicates that this animal was the main prey species around the glacial maximum at 20 000 b.p. (Gamble, 1978).

The evidence from other sites is very coarse but suggests that the range and type of prey taken during the Mousterian and Aurignacian were similar. The number of herbivore species per level varied from only 4·1 to 5·1, and by noting the percentage of levels in which a species occurred, Gamble (1978) suggested that mammoth, rhino, red and roe-deer were commoner in these periods than in the Magdalenian. What Gamble (1978) suggested in the way of a regional synthesis was that during the

Middle and early Upper Palaeolithic, subsistence groups utilized the
Swabian Alb during the summer months, and then followed herds of
horse and red deer perhaps 150 km to the Rhine Valley for the winter.
Present evidence does not suggest that this seasonal pattern of movement
was altered to any great extent over this long period.

Similar evidence for continuity in the type and frequency of prey
species between the Middle and Upper Palaeolithic can be found in other
areas. In western Russia (Klein, 1969a, 1973), the commonest medium-
sized herbivores in sites of both periods are *Bos*, red deer, horse/ass and
reindeer. Although there are no details of the age and sex of prey, there is
some hint of regional differentiation in species. In the Crimea, unlike the
Donets and Prut basin, roe-deer, ibex, wild sheep, saiga, elk and wild ass
were exploited; this is particularly true for ass, 60 000 bones and teeth of
which were found at the mousterian site of Starosl'ye. For reasons
already mentioned, the role of mammoth and carnivores as food
resources is uncertain until more evidence is available.

The faunal data from south-west France includes Bouchud's (1966)
important synthesis, as well as the valuable sequences from Combe
Grenal for the Mousterian (Bordes and Prat, 1965; Bordes *et al.*, 1966)
and for the early Upper Palaeolithic from the Abri Pataud (Movius,
1975; Spiess, 1979) and the Roc du Combe (Delpech, 1972). The
mousterian data permit few detailed observations beyond the somewhat
banal one that horse and reindeer replace red deer and *Bos* as the
commonest components of cave assemblages at the end of Würm I.
Whilst these changes may reflect more severe climatic conditions, an
abundance of reindeer need not indicate arctic-like conditions. As
Movius (1974:108) has reminded us, reindeer could tolerate the climate
of the Massif Central today, and their disappearance from this area since
the late Pleistocene could have resulted largely from vegetational changes
and competition from other herbivores, notably red deer. More detailed
observations can be drawn from the Abri Pataud, where very short units
of occupation, possibly as short as a single season, can be distinguished.
Spiess (1979) suggested that from 35 000 to 20 000 b.p., this site
functioned as an autumn to winter camp for the hunting of reindeer. His
attempts to calculate the numbers of man-days of meat represented in
each assemblage from the numbers of reindeer represented has brought
sharp criticism from Binford (1980b), whose own studies of modern
Eskimo hunting (Binford, 1978) suggest that only joints of meat rather
than entire carcasses would have been taken to a winter camp. (See also
Lyman (1979) for a similar criticism of the use of meat weights.) Leaving
this point aside, the French faunal data do not indicate any major differences
in prey species between the late Middle and early Upper Palaeolithic.

Other authors have commented upon the continuity in prey species over this time-range. Barker (1975a), for example, documented the composition of faunal assemblages from Italian caves with middle and upper palaeolithic assemblages, and highlighted the importance of red deer during the last glaciation. He further suggested that differences in the type of prey taken in the Middle and Upper Palaeolithic resulted mainly from climatic and vegetational changes than from alterations to the structure of hunting strategies. Looking further afield, it is of interest that similar claims for continuity in subsistence strategies have come from southern Africa. Klein (1977, 1978b) has shown that changes in the types and frequencies of animal resources during the last glaciation corresponded with changes in climate, and he was unable to detect any evidence for alterations in hunting strategies. The mortality patterns of different types of prey were also the same in both the Middle and Late Stone Age (broadly equivalent to the Middle and Upper Palaeolithic). In the case of large, solitary and dangerous species such as Cape buffalo, only the youngest and very old animals were killed, whereas with smaller, gregarious and more easily hunted species such as eland and reedbuck, prime adults were killed, possibly in communal drives.

IX. DISCUSSION

Much of the Mousterian and early Upper Palaeolithic is still uncharted territory, and the few landmarks that we have are soon left behind. The first step that can be made is to note that, apart from a possible colonization of Denmark in the last interglacial (Møhl and Hansen, 1964) and of the Ukraine during the Mousterian (Klein, 1969b), man remained confined to the Mediterranean and temperate regions of Europe. Secondly, although there are more early upper palaeolithic than mousterian sites, there is no evidence for any marked increase in population, since the loss of earlier sites cannot be assessed. Thirdly, the presence of both mousterian and upper palaeolithic assemblages in many cave sites indicates some continuity in usage, although possibly for different functions. Fourthly, the methods for killing prey seem to have relied upon stabbing at close range (and possibly stampedes) until the invention of snares, bows and arrows, and spear-throwers in the later Upper Palaeolithic (see next chapter). Finally, the choice of prey seems the same throughout and even beyond the Mousterian and early Upper Palaeolithic.

However, this last point does not mean that subsistence strategies remained unchanged. In the first place, the quality of the dietary data needs considerable improvement. In particular, more information is needed on the age and sex of prey; on the season(s) when sites were occupied; on the use of each resource; on the function of sites as parts of subsistence systems; and on the ways that animals were butchered, processed and cooked. These types of data will probably be obtained only be very precise analyses of well-defined and carefully-excavated occupational units rather than by the reworking of material retained from older excavations that were conducted under less exacting conditions. In addition, we need data from more open-air sites of the kind already known from a pitifully small number of localities (see Table 3).

Secondly, (as argued above), faunal evidence cannot be divorced from the strategies for obtaining and processing food that produced it. It is here that the lithic evidence is crucial, especially from south-west France. As is well known, the Mousterian of this area has been divided into five main variants: the typical, denticulate, Quina, Ferrassie and Mousterian of Acheulean Tradition (MAT) (see Bordes and Sonneville-Bordes, 1970). At this point, positions are taken behind barricades.

The first issue is the time-span involved. Most assemblages have been dated to after the end of the last interglacial, which was once thought to have ended around 70-60 000 b.p. Now that it has been recognized that the last interglacial was not followed *directly* by the last glaciation (see Fig. 7), it is apparent that some of these may date back to beyond 100 000 b.p. More serious than this doubling of the length of the Mousterian, however, is the question of its internal chronology. According to Laville (1973; Laville *et al.*, 1980) and Butzer (1981), all these variants were contemporaneous, and used throughout the last glaciation until replaced by the Upper Palaeolithic. This pattern contrasts completely with that seen in the Upper Palaeolithic of western Europe in two ways: first, mousterian cultures last 10, and possibly 20 times longer than upper palaeolithic ones; and secondly, upper palaeolithic lithic cultures are (by and large) sequential in that, for example, solutrean assemblages are earlier than magdalenian ones in the same areas. If this chronological patterning is accepted, the implication must be that mousterian tool assemblages — and possibly also the associated faunal remains — were produced by a very different type of behaviour from that in the Upper Palaeolithic.

However, this chronological scheme is opposed by Mellars (1969), who regards the Ferrassie variant as earlier than the Quina, and the MAT as immediately prior to the Upper Palaeolithic. In his favour is the point that the type of contemporaneity claimed by Laville and Butzer has not been found outside south-west France and northern Spain, even though other areas such as the Levant, southern Africa and central Europe are by now well researched. Secondly, the case for contemporaneity is based

Table 3: List of some European open-air mousterian sites.

Site	Type	Occupation	Main animal(s)	References
Salzgitter-Lebenstedt	Open-air	Mousterian: Early Würm	Reindeer	Grote, 1978; Tode *et al.*, 1953
Erd	Open-air	Mousterian: Mid Würm	Bear	Gabori-Csank, 1968
Molodova	Open-air	Mousterian: Early/Mid Würm	Horse, reindeer	Ivanova and Chernysh, 1965
Königssäue	Open-air	Mousterian: Early/Mid Würm	Reindeer	Mania and Töpfer, 1973; Mania, 1979c

upon highly technical analyses of sequences of cave sediments that have yet to be confirmed by absolute dating. Until that is done, it remains to be demonstrated that a highly elaborate edifice has not been built on sand.

Explanations of mousterian variability have been dominated by the well-known debate between Bordes (1973, 1978) and Binford (Binford and Binford, 1966; Binford, 1973) over whether these variants represent different cultures or tool-kits. Bordes' view that each represents a different people who inhabited the area year round is open to two major criticisms. The first is that the case for the round-the-year occupation of caves by hunters who used only a small annual territory rests heavily upon Bouchud's (1966) interpretations of the faunal evidence. These have been soundly criticized by several people (e.g. Binford, 1973; Spiess, 1979); instead, it is more likely that some form of herd following was practised over large areas (e.g. Bahn, 1977). Secondly, the notion of five "peoples" coexisting in an area as small as the Perigord for up to 2 or 3 thousand generations without any form of contact or exchange presupposes the existence of colossal and inexplicable cultural barriers. As Sackett (1981) has recently argued, this type of interpretation may reveal more about the history of French archaeology than about the last glaciation. On the other hand, the fact that none of the mousterian variants corresponds with particular climatic conditions (see Bordes, 1978; Butzer, 1981) suggests that whatever these might represent, they are probably not related to specific types of environment. One suggestion recently forwarded by Butzer (1981) is that these assemblages may be related more to the processing than procurement of food. However, the type of microwear and detailed faunal analyses needed to confirm or refute the identification of these tool-kits has not yet been done. The eventual interpretation of mousterian variability may well be complex (see e.g. Rolland, 1981), and involve a large degree of functional variability, some temporal change (e.g. Mellars, 1969) and perhaps the presence of more than one tradition.

At this juncture, we can make a temporary halt before leaving the mousterian miasma to seek a better vantage point from the Upper Palaeolithic. By now, it should be apparent that little further progress can be made in clarifying mousterian subsistence until three important, if mundane, chronological conundrums are resolved. First, the question of whether the Upper Palaeolithic and modern man entered Europe together requires better dating of the middle/upper Palaeolithic interface. Secondly, the evolutionary relationships of European Neanderthals to later populations will continue to be obscure until Neanderthal skeletal remains are firmly dated; and thirdly, explanations of mousterian variability will remain insecure until it can be demonstrated whether these variants are contemporaneous or sequential. Even then, considerably more data will be required on Neanderthal diet and on the function of mousterian artefacts.

What can be said with reasonable certainty is that the main meat resources—in most cases, red deer and reindeer—taken by Neanderthal hunters retained their importance in the Upper Palaeolithic. That is not to say, however, that the hunting strategies—the "rules" by which resources were obtained and processed—remained the same. In this context, the technological evidence is highly relevant, but needs to be seen in contrast with that of the Upper Palaeolithic. For this reason, it is worth moving on to events after 30 000 b.p.

5. The New Technology and the Advent of Modern Behaviour

Abstract

This chapter looks at some developments that occurred after 30 000 years ago, and concludes that substantial behavioural changes did occur. Motor and conceptual abilities were very different, as were the ways that subsistence activities were organized and implemented. These differences are masked if the types of stone tools or prey are studied in isolation from each other. Overall, behavioural systems after 30 000 years b.p. can be regarded as fully "modern", and radically different from that of Neanderthals. Whether these developed locally, or were intrusive, is a question best left open at present.

Given the confusion that envelopes the Mousterian, it is hard to determine whether early upper palaeolithic societies after 35 000–30 000 b.p. were substantially different from those of the Middle Palaeolithic, or basically similar but more artistic. Initially, the contrast between the two was considered to be well-nigh total: modern man replaced Neanderthals, introduced a technology based on blades rather than flakes, made widespread use of bone, ivory and antler as raw materials, and conceptualized his world through art. This landmark is by now seriously eroded, and indeed from some viewpoints is scarcely visible. It is uncertain that Neanderthals were replaced by incoming populations of modern man; the earliest upper palaeolithic assemblages of central and western Europe are regarded by some as local developments from a mousterian background; blade assemblages are known from middle palaeolithic contexts; and (as seen in the previous chapter) the faunal evidence has been widely interpreted as showing that subsistence strategies remained largely unchanged across the middle to upper palaeolithic transition. Only cave art and sculpting have remained as phenomena peculiar to the Upper Palaeolithic but not the Mousterian.

Because of such erosion, it has not proved easy to classify the behaviour of upper palaeolithic societies in ways that distinguish them from mousterian ones. Some (e.g. Clark and Piggott, 1965) have labelled these societies as "advanced hunters". However, the term "advanced" is vague, and implies only that some kind of change had occurred without explaining how earlier societies were "primitive". A minority of prehistorians (e.g. Bahn, 1978; Higgs and Jarman, 1972) have also maintained that the term "hunting" opens a Pandora's box of whether these communities relied solely upon wild resources. Others, noting the extreme dependence of some of these societies upon a single resource — notably reindeer — have suggested that these were "specialized" hunters, unlike earlier "generalized" ones (e.g. Gamble, 1978). However, as we saw in the previous chapter, changes in the type and relative frequency of prey between the Middle and Upper Palaeolithic were very slight in many areas; indeed, if one takes the faunal data alone, it is hard to see how the middle palaeolithic reindeer hunters at Combe Grenal at the height of the penultimate glaciation were any less "specialized" than those in the same area 100 000 years later. This view is also in apparent conflict with claims that late glacial communities actually broadened their subsistence base and exploited a "broad spectrum" of resources (e.g. Hole and Flannery, 1967). Some (e.g. Mellars, 1973) have tried to reconcile both views by proposing that these societies specialized upon one particular resource, but at the same time diversified their activities to include other prey, either to supplement an otherwise monotonous diet, or as failsafe alternatives if the main resource became scarce.

The main weakness of these views is that they place too much emphasis upon *what* was obtained and too little upon *how* food and other resources were procured and used. As way of reiteration, faunal evidence for pleistocene subsistence has to be seen in the wider context of the behavioural strategies that produced it. As these operate through the use of technologies — both abstract and physical — it is useful to start by examining the differences between mousterian and upper palaeolithic technologies in some detail.

I. TECHNOLOGICAL IMPROVEMENT AND INNOVATION AFTER 30 000 b.p.

Discussions of the technological changes between the Middle and Upper Palaeolithic have focussed largely upon differences in tool types, the way that these were made, and the choice of raw materials. These categories stem from descriptions of the most obvious features of tool assemblages, rather than from a framework that integrates all the stages of tool-making, beginning with the concept of an artefact through its production and ending with its usage and discard. A further weakness of the traditional approach has been the divide between "artefacts" and "art": the former comprising items made for physiological purposes, and the latter for aesthetic reasons. The two are treated—as in our own society, perhaps—as substantially different, in that art is commonly regarded as being somehow ethereally aloof from the banality of technology. Yet both often use the same techniques, and both are technologies in a general sense: painting, music and personal adornment are all ways of communicating feelings, beliefs, status and personal identity.

We can take first the number of *techniques* used for working raw materials. As Table 4 shows, mousterian—and for that matter, acheulean and oldowan—technology largely involved the use of no more than four basic techniques—percussion, whittling, scraping and cutting. These all used the same kind of hand motion: a repetitive and usually rapid motion of one hand in the same plane, the wrist flexible, with leverage from the elbow and shoulder, whilst the other hand held immobile the material being worked.

After 30 000 b.p., the range of techniques expanded enormously to include pressure flaking, drilling, twisting, grinding, and many others. Indeed, it is unlikely that the range of techniques for working raw materials increased again until the development of methods for making ceramics and annealing metal after 8000 b.p. Many of the techniques introduced after 30 000 b.p. required different motor abilities from those used in the Mousterian; for example, the use of both hands simultaneously but in opposite directions (as in drilling); repetitive and simultaneous movement of both fore-fingers against the thumbs (as in twisting); a very slow, firm, precise motion of one hand (as in engraving); or rotary movements (as in grinding and polishing).

Secondly, the range of *raw materials* increased. As many have commented, the three basic materials used since the Oldowan—stone, wood and skin—were supplemented by bone, ivory and antler, as well as shell and clay, although these last two were of minor importance. Leaving aside the highly controversial "osteodontokeratic" industry

Table 4: Techniques for working raw materials in the Middle and Upper Palaeolithic.

Middle Palaeolithic		Upper Palaeolithic	
Technique	Material	Technique	Material
Percussion	Bone, stone		→
Whittling	Wood		→
Scraping	Wood, skin		→
Cutting	Wood, skin, meat		→
		Pressure flaking	Stone
		Drilling	Bone, ivory, antler
		Splintering	Bone, ivory, antler
		Twisting	Fibres
		Lashing	Skins, wood
		Carving	Stone
		Engraving	Stone
		Kneading	Clay
		Grinding/polishing	Stone, bone
		?Matting	Animal hair
		Compression:	
		—straightening	Ivory
		—?bending	Wood
		?Tension:	
		—stretching	?Bow string

Table 5: Numbers of components in middle and upper palaeolithic artefacts.

	1	2	3	More than 3
Middle Palaeolithic	Wooden spears ? Clothing Scrapers, knives, etc. if unhafted	Stone-tipped spears Scrapers, knives, etc. if hafted		
Upper Palaeolithic	As above plus: needles ivory spears bone/antler polishers etc. if unhafted grinding stones	Bone/antler polishers etc. if hafted	Arrows (shaft/tip/flights)	Ladders Multi-piece clothing Necklaces Nets
		———— Bows (single or composite) ————		
		———— Traps ————		

claimed at some South African australopithecine sites, bone and ivory were hardly ever used before 30 000 b.p., and the few items made tended to be very simple modifications of a piece of bone, tusk or antler (see e.g. Mania, 1979b), quite unlike the bâtons de commandment, spear-throwers and barbed harpoons of the Upper Palaeolithic which required much more complicated methods of manufacture. Although several have drawn attention to this greatly increased use of bone, antler and ivory, no explanations have been offered as to *why* three readily available materials should have become so much more important only after 30 000 b.p.

Thirdly, the numbers of *components* in artefacts increased markedly in the Upper Palaeolithic (Table 5). Again, the use of composite tools of bone and stone has elicited much attention, although the concept of

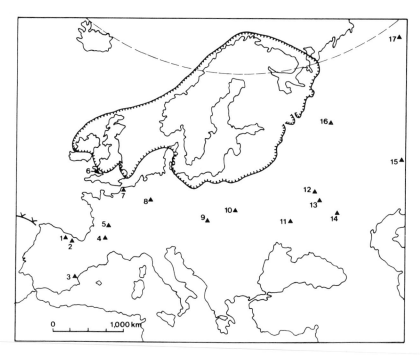

Fig. 10: Upper palaeolithic sites mentioned in text.

Key: ⊔⊔⊔⊔⊔⊔ maximum extent of British and Scandinavian ice-sheets.
           _ _ _ _ _ maximum extent of winter pack-ice.

Sites: 1 La Riera; 2 Altamira; 3 Parpallo; 4 Abri Pataud; 5 Lascaux; 6 Paviland; 7 Hallines; 8 Gönnersdorf; 9 Dolni Vestonice and Pavolov; 10 Spadzista; 11 Mezherich; 12 Elisavichi; 13 Mezin; 14 Kostienki; 15 Kopova; 16 Sungir; 17 Byzovaia.

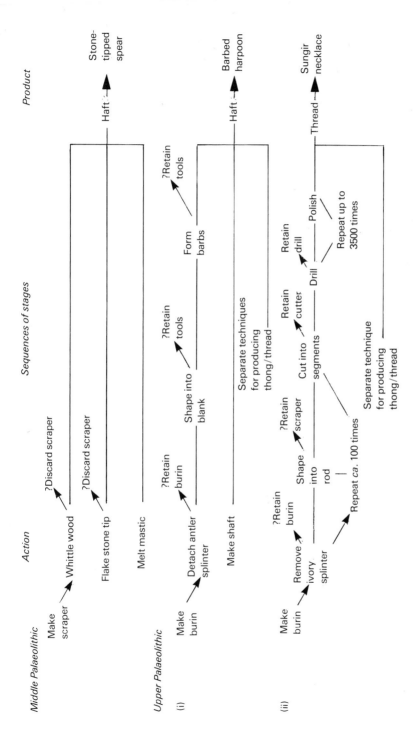

Fig. 11: Stages in tool-making in the Middle and Upper Palaeolithic.

composite tools was not in itself novel. For example, the mousterian stabbing spear was a composite tool, made of stone and wood. Where the upper palaeolithic composite tools were substantially different from their middle palaeolithic predecessors was in using more than two components, albeit of the same material in most cases. In terms simply of the number of separate items in one artefact, the palaeolithic record must be held by the necklace adorning one of the burials at Sungir (Fig. 10) (Shimkin, 1978) that was made of 3500 drilled ivory beads. However, more commonplace items using several components can also be cited from the Upper Palaeolithic; for example, the ladders at Lascaux probably had a dozen components, as may have some items of late glacial clothing.

Fourthly, the numbers of *stages* involved in making artefacts increased significantly; it is this feature that probably constitutes a crucial

Table 6: Differences in the ways that activities were performed in the Middle and Upper Palaeolithic.

Activity	Middle Palaeolithic	Upper Palaeolithic
Killing	Stampeding ?Sling Stabbing—broad-based stone point Spearing—wooden spear	Stabbing—narrow ivory/bone point Spearing—ivory/bone tip spear-thrower Shooting—bow and arrow Trapping—snares/nets
Cooking	Unlined hearths on surface	Cobble-lined hearths in ground
Storage	???	Pit-caches; ?drying/smoking
Keeping warm	Single-piece clothing	Multi-piece clothing: ?sewn mittens; head-gear; footwear
Moving	On foot	?Sleds, snow-shoes; ?riding, dog-traction
Communicating	Speech	Visual arts; personal adornment; music

difference between middle and upper palaeolithic technologies. This point can be made by comparing the stages of manufacture involved in making a mousterian stabbing spear—one of the most complex artefacts of the period—with those used in manufacturing an upper palaeolithic spear or the Sungir necklace. As Fig. 11 shows, the contrasts are striking.

These differences allow some observations to be made. Mousterian (and earlier) technology was essentially *immediate*, and involved only a short series of single-stage operations. By contrast, artefacts after 30 000 b.p. were often made by processes that involved several stages of manufacture between concept and product. The differences between the two technologies lie not so much in the *type* of material being worked, as in the *number* of processes and techniques involved, as well as the degree of conceptualization needed to follow the manufacture of an item from its initial design to the finished product.

These comments may help explain why bone, ivory and antler were used so little before the Upper Palaeolithic. There are very few items that can be made from these materials in one single operation; whilst one can "see" a spear in a branch and make one by only slightly altering its shape, one could not make a barbed point from a piece of antler except through a long series of separate operations. If these largely conceptual problems deterred Neanderthals, but not people after *ca.* 30 000 b.p., from using these materials for all but the simplest made types of tool, there may also be some interesting implications on the way that resources were perceived. First, however, we should look at how ways of doing things changed after 30 000 b.p. (see Table 6).

II. TECHNOLOGIES FOR DOING THINGS

A. Killing

Neanderthals probably killed most of their prey by stabbing, using short spears that were thrust rather than thrown and which had a large, broad stone point that caused death by massive haemorrhaging (see Geist, 1979). Wooden spears of the kind found at Clacton and Lehringen were probably used as well. Although these may have had greater penetrating power than stone-tipped stabbing spears, these too would have been thrust, and their tips would easily have been blunted by a thick hide.

Such methods of killing would have had four drawbacks. First, it is dangerous to the hunter, since the animal may take some time to die, and injure the hunter in the process. Secondly, because this method of killing is safer and more successful if undertaken by a group than by an individual, it requires cooperation and coordination of personnel that could be used for other activities. Thirdly, the join between the shaft and tip of this type of stone-tipped spear is weak and likely to break, especially if deflected laterally by, for example, a rib. Finally, if the join or stone tip of such a spear was damaged, repair would be difficult. Other methods of killing may have included stampeding animals over cliffs or into gullies, and possibly the sling, a poorly documented but lethal device.

Killing techniques improved markedly after 30 000 years ago. First, spears were tipped with a narrow bone or ivory point that was less liable to lateral displacement than the broad-tipped mousterian spears. They also had greater penetrating power than previous types of narrow-tipped spears made of wood. These new types of spears could reach those parts other spears could not reach, thus making a clean kill more likely and at less risk to its user. Since the points were replaceable, spears were also easier to rehaft and repair if damaged. Examples of these might be the bone points in several aurignacian assemblages, and the 37 cm long "darts" at Mezherich (Shimkin, 1978:245). Some spears were even made entirely from ivory; for example, two were found, 1·6 m and 2·4 m long in the grave of two children at Sungir, *ca.* 20 000 b.p. (Shimkin, 1978:233).

The innovations of which we can be reasonably certain were the spear-thrower, well represented in magdalenian contexts, and the bow and arrow, which were probably in use by 23 000 b.p. (Davidson, 1974), if the tanged stone points from Parpallo in Spain were arrow-heads. The advantage of these devices over the mousterian stabbing spear must have been comparable to that of the gun over the bow and arrow, for prey could have been killed over a greater distance—perhaps as great as 75-100 m—and in more safety. These items would also have made hunting more successful, since it was no longer necessary to get right up to an animal before attempting to kill it. Finally, and very importantly, the hunting of large animals could be successful if undertaken by only a few individuals rather than by several, and thus surplus manpower could be diverted to other activities.

Other techniques for catching prey after 30 000 b.p. are more difficult to establish. Evidence for snares, traps and nets is circumstantial but strongly hinted at by the presence (and often abundance) of small, elusive prey such as fish (Mellars, 1973), birds (e.g. Desbrosse and Mourer-Chauviré, 1973) and rabbit (e.g. Davidson, 1976), as well as by representations of fish on upper palaeolithic engravings. It is also worth noting the engraving of what looks very like a net on a piece of ivory from Elisavichi in the Ukraine, dated to the late glacial (see Clark, 1975:151). Several Russian upper palaeolithic sites also contain skeletons of hare lacking only their paws; this feature has been explained as the result of skinning animals for their pelts (Klein, 1973). If so, they would probably have been caught in winter, and most easily in some type of trap. Interestingly, Klein (1976) has also argued from the abundance of fish and birds (excluding the flightless penguin) that snares and nets were in use in southern Africa by the late Pleistocene.

To summarize: after 30 000 b.p., large animals could be killed at a greater range than before, by fewer people, and in greater safety. Because small game could also be taken by the use of snares and traps, a wider range of resources could be obtained.

B. Food processing

One of clearest indications that food was cooked in a more effective manner in the Upper Palaeolithic comes from the discovery of cobble-lined pit-hearths at cave sites such as the Abri Pataud (Movius, 1975) and La Riera (Straus *et al.*, 1980). Their advantage over the open hearths of the Mousterian were that heat was retained longer and at a more even temperature, and thus meat would have been better cooked and more palatable. Culinary innovations of this kind may have been at least partly responsible for the reduction in tooth size during the Upper Palaeolithic noted earlier (Brace, 1979).

Evidence that meat was dried or smoked and then cached after 30 000 b.p. is slight, but some of the pits and structures in East European upper palaeolithic open-air sites have been interpreted as storage facilities (Shimkin, 1978). Further evidence might be obtained by examination of the ways that animals were butchered. If meat was preserved and stored in the autumn for use in the winter, most of the faunal remains from winter occupation sites should represent joints of meat rather than entire carcasses (see e.g. Binford, 1978b; Lyman, 1979). Food storage also involves conceptual as well as technical developments to become effective. In particular, it would have necessitated *forward planning* so that the correct amount of food was cached in the right place, and also the concept of *delayed* consumption. So far as can be seen from present evidence, food consumption in the Lower and Middle Palaeolithic tended to be more or less *immediate*: some of a carcass might be eaten where the animal was killed, and the rest taken to a home base and eaten perhaps only a few hours later.

C. Keeping warm

The Upper Palaeolithic may have seen the invention of warm winter clothing, and of items such as hoods, gloves and foot-mittens that helped prevent the loss of body heat. Figures of well-clad individuals from East European sites show that, by the glacial maximum, man was able to provide himself with adequate protection against the elements. The painstaking reconstruction of the clothing worn by the man buried at Sungir 20 000 years ago (Shimkin, 1978) provides a further and vivid insight into the tailoring expertise of late glacial society. The invention of eyed needles, first seen in the Solutrean of France some 20 000 years ago (Stordeur-Yedid, 1979)—and by implication, a fine thread—are further indicators of developments in this field. We know also that fur-trapping may have been practised by this time. Further insulation may also have come from the down of some of the birds represented in late glacial European sites.

The architecture of open-air upper palaeolithic sites, particularly in eastern Europe (Klein, 1973; Shimkin, 1978) is often more substantial than that of the Mousterian, and also indicative of better insulation against the cold. In passing, it is worth noting that the largest of these were probably not as grandiose as suggested by the initial reconstructions of the structures at sites such as Kostienki I (horizon i), which were thought to be up to 40 m long. As the recent excavations at Spadzista in Poland have shown, the areal extent of some of these structures may have been exaggerated by solifluction (Kozlowski, 1974).

Two further points are worth mentioning. The first is that in eastern Europe, many structures were built largely of mammoth bones. If these were obtained from beasts that were either killed or scavenged very shortly after death, it is possible that the sides of these structures were made of mammoth hide, rather than from the skin of other animals such as reindeer. As mammoth had a hairy coat (Ryder, 1974), some kind of felt may have been made by a process of matting and pounding, and used as tent coverings or for clothing. Secondly, as both bows and drills were invented in the Upper Palaeolithic, it is possible that the fire-drill— combining the action of a drill with the motion of a bow—stems from this time as well. The lighting of fires may thus have become much easier than when using flints.

One implication of these details is that human calorific requirements need not have been much higher during the glacial maximum than in earlier milder episodes, since energy expenditure could have been reduced. Estimates that late glacial people needed 10 000 Cals per day (Wheat, 1973) seem far too high. Although it was once a FAO recommendation that for every drop of 1°C in mean annual temperature, an extra 100 Cals per day were needed, it now seems that food requirements in cold environments are no higher than those in temperate latitudes providing that insulation is adequate and people are able to schedule their activities to avoid excessive exposure to cold. In other words, by improving the quality of their clothing and dwellings, and by more efficient hunting, these societies may well have reduced significantly the amount of prey they needed in winter, and thus the time spent in obtaining it.

Perhaps the most eloquent testimony of man's ability to provide himself with adequate insulation at the height of the last glaciation is the site of Byzovaia in north-west Siberia, dated to *ca.* 20 000 b.p. (see Fig. 10). At latitude 65°N and only 100 km from the shores of the Arctic Ocean, this site is the most northerly one known from the Eurasian palaeolithic, and at present represents the earliest encounter between man and polar bear (*Thalarctos maritima*). Even allowing for the possibility that this area was warmer then in summer than today (see below, p.98), man could never have survived so far north except by using very sophisticated techniques for keeping warm.

D. Transport

The possibility that man had devised new means of transport by the final part of the last glaciation opens up a fascinating field of speculation. Bahn (1980) has championed the view that horses were ridden in the late glacial, but Littauer (1980) has bridled at these claims of palaeo-equestrianism. Nevertheless, the representation of a horse's head from St Michael d'Arudy in France appears to depict some kind of halter (Jarman and Wilkinson, 1972:84).

The case for arguing that such items as sledges, snow-shoes, skis and skates were used in the late glacial is tenuous but intriguing. First, confirmation of claims for dogs (Musil, 1970) in upper palaeolithic contexts in Central Europe would raise the possibility that they were used in harness. A second strand of evidence comes from items that were made or used in the late glacial. For example, the ladders used by the artists at Lascaux (Leroi-Gourhan and Allain, 1979) involved the same type of lashed frame as used in a sledge. Similarly, if the fibres made at this time were sufficiently strong for stringing a bow, they would also have sufficed for stringing a snow-shoe. We might also suppose that the grease used in making paints would have been suitable for lubricating the runners of a sledge or skate. As animals such as musk-ox (Wilkinson, 1975) and arctic fox and hare are likely to have been hunted only during the winter, some kind of method for moving easily over compacted snow must have been in use. Finally, indirect evidence for the use of sledges in the late glacial may come from some of the structures at sites such as Mezherich in Russia. As some of these incorporated up to 15 tons of mammoth bones (Soffer, 1981) and as a young mammoth skull weighs 100 kg (Klein, 1973:53), some method for transporting these quantities of materials around the landscape seems likely.

The most interesting aspect of these innovations is that they would have considerably facilitated mobility during the winter. Sledges and skis are mainly useful on hard snow once winter sets in, whilst snow-shoes are best used on soft snow during the fall. Movement during the spring thaw would still have remained difficult, however.

E. Communicating

An exhibition of middle and lower palaeolithic art would attract few visitors at present, for it could show only a few lumps of ochre, used for decorating bodies (dead or alive), some daubed pebbles, and perhaps the occasional hand-axe that seemed too carefully made for whatever utilitarian function it may have served. To this meagre total we might also add mention of a possible ochre mine from the last interglacial at Lovas in Hungary (Dobosi and Vörös, 1979), and the so-called "churinga" from Tata, also in Hungary, now dated to *ca.* 100 000 years ago, but incised by lines that appear to be natural rather than artificial (Schwarcz and Skoflek, 1982). By contrast, painting, sculpting and engraving were widely used after *ca.* 30 000 years ago, for both representational and abstract design as well as jewellery. The discovery of what appear to have been musical instruments at Mezin in Russia (Bibikov, 1978) indicates that this art form may have a similar antiquity to the visual arts. Although attention has focussed on the rich glories of south-west France and north Spain, art seems to have been a world-wide phenomenon after *ca.* 30 000 b.p. Engravings of animals at Apollo Cave in southern Africa have been dated to 26 000 b.p. (Wendt, 1976) and art in Australia probably has a similar antiquity (Mulvaney, 1975:275).

Explanations of why art should appear at this time have tended to be weak, and based largely on the tautology that upper palaeolithic man created art because he was more artistically creative than Neanderthals. It may again be worth considering art as one of the technologies in use at this time in terms of the degree of conceptualization involved. As noted already, a considerable degree of abstraction and design went into the production of such mundane items as bone needles, ivory beads, spear-throwers, ladders and bows; each required the ability to retain an image or concept through several stages of production. The ability to "see" a perforated bead in an elephant's tusk is no different from seeing an animal's head in a piece of stone, or realizing it three-dimensionally on a two-dimensional surface. Each also used similar techniques, such as engraving and carving, some of which also required motor facilities not evidenced to any great extent in mousterian technology.

The same point may be true of notation. Marshack (1972a, 1972b), has claimed that many of the apparently random or accidental notches, dots and scratches on late palaeolithic engravings may represent some form of calendrical or numerical notation. Discoverers of similar finds have tended to be cautious (e.g. Tratman, 1976), whilst reviewers have not always been sympathetic. Nevertheless, whilst Marshack's interpretations of specific items may be open to alternatives, the ability to conceptualize an abstract such as time in terms of spatial and numerical patterning is probably no greater than retaining the image of an animal, and reproducing that image in its correct proportions and at a reduced scale.

The art work forms part of the evidence that communication was better structured than before, over considerable areas of the late glacial world. On an inter-regional level, we can note the distribution of material items. Highly specific artefacts such as Kostienki points have been found from the Ukraine to Austria, 1500 km to the west (Klein, 1973), and the decoration of many Venus figurines and bone/ivory pieces show a number of remarkable similarities in detail over much of western and eastern Europe. The same can be said of the similarities uniting the art styles of Kapova in the Urals with those of south-west France, 7000 km to the west. We do not have to explain these distributions by supposing that these peoples were eternal and foot-sore wanderers who covered vast distances in their lifetimes; instead, these distributions are more likely to have resulted from social networks operating over large distances between groups whose annual territories were much smaller. A pertinent example might be the way that various shells were exchanged between aboriginal groups living on the north and south coasts of Australia (Mulvaney, 1975:113).

On a regional level, indications that contacts between subsistence groups may have been tightly structured comes from so-called "aggregation sites". Two types have so far been recognized. The first are sites that contain too much ceremonial evidence to represent the material needs of one autonomous subsistence group. Examples here are some of the structures at Mezin and Mezherich in the Ukraine (Shimkin, 1978). Three of the four structures at Mezherich were each made from more than 15 tons of mammoth bone, many of which were positioned in a highly patterned manner, involving herring-bone arrangements of skulls and mandibles and sections of walls built alternately of long bones and mandibles (Soffer, 1981). The second type concerns some of the painted cave sites. Conkey (1980) has argued from the range of motifs used in northern Spain that Altamira served as an aggregation site for several groups in the region, and la Peña may have functioned as another. If the same is true of other "art" sites—such as Parpallo in Spain, the south-west French caves, and Gönnersdorf in Germany—art may have played an important part in the way that periodic encounters between groups were structured (Gamble, 1980).

The significance of these innovations is shown in Fig. 12, which makes three points. The first is that many of these inventions and improvements would have been highly useful in enabling man to adapt to the conditions of a glacial maximum. Obvious examples are improvements in methods for killing large game, for trapping small animals, for coping with low temperatures and so on. That is not to say, of course, that these necessarily were invented because it was colder, or

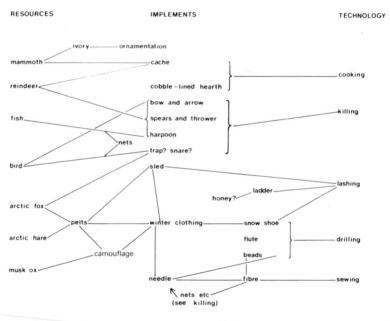

Fig. 12: Technological inter-dependence and resource procurement after 30 000 b.p.

becoming so; they are perhaps better viewed as "exaptations" (Tudge, 1981) in the sense that they later turned out to have an adaptive value that was not foreseen at the time.

Secondly, many of the innovations and improvements after 30 000 b.p. could have enabled communities to schedule their activities more effectively to cope with winter conditions. For example, more efficient ways of killing large animals could have enabled groups to kill more than they needed for immediate consumption during the summer or autumn, and the surplus could then have been stored for use in the winter. If it was no longer necessary to hunt in winter on a day-to-day basis, winter activities may have been largely those of fur-trapping and fuel-collecting (both of which would have been aided by the ability to move easily over snow), and in making and repairing clothing, or tool-kits for use in the spring and summer. As a consequence, energy expenditure and the risk of exposure in the winter months would have been minimized.

Thirdly, these technologies reinforce each other to a far greater extent than mousterian ones did. For example, bows and arrows may have facilitated the killing of reindeer, but the arrow flights would have come from the feathers of birds trapped by nets or snares; the same devices could also have been used for trapping arctic fox and hare; however, fur-trapping requires the ability to traverse snow if the pelts are to be in prime condition and white; in return, white pelts provide better camouflage when hunting reindeer in winter.

In short, each innovation of this period became an integrated part of what was overall, in modern parlance, a "new technology". Like its modern counterpart, its introduction would have profoundly affected both the ways that the environment was exploited, and how activities and roles were organized. Unlike middle palaeolithic tool-kits, these assemblages involved items with highly specific functions that were used in a tightly defined set of anticipated circumstances; to use a term from satellite jargon, these items were "dedicated" to specific tasks. Many of these would thus have been made in advance of the time when needed, and given the care and labour required for making at least some of the items (e.g. bows, harpoons, needles, spear-throwers), their use must have been prolonged as long as possible. In other words, many of these tools would have been curated, rather than used expediently as "one-offs". One archaeological corollary of this point is that the places where tools were discarded need have little relation to where they were made and used (an excellent and thought-provoking discussion of these points can be found in Binford, 1978b, 1979).

The social consequences of these innovations also deserves comment. Labour would probably have been used more effectively after *ca.* 30 000 b.p. than in Neanderthal societies using a mousterian technology. In the first place, it was no longer essential for all able-bodied members of a group to combine in obtaining meat (as in, for example, mobbing a horse with short stabbing-spears); instead, disparate activities such as fur-trapping or bird-snaring could have been undertaken simultaneously.

Moreover, those too old to hunt, or infirm and thus confined to base camps, could still have played essential roles in maintaining labour-intensive tool-kits, by making, for example, bone/ivory tools and the like, which required little expenditure of energy per hour, but much in the way of time and skill. Although leisure has been described as a product of affluence (see Sahlins, 1974), it may result less from any absolute increase in resources than from a more efficient use of man-power.

Secondly, some activities—such as winter trapping, tailoring and engraving—required considerable skill, and are unlikely to have been activities that all could do equally well. Roles may thus have become more clearly defined, and people thus less interchangeable in what they could do. One interesting and intriguing demographic consequence of this point is that random mortalities could have had far more severe consequences upon the viability of subsistence groups than when the roles of its members were less differentiated, as was probably the case in mousterian society. This point may have a bearing upon the rapidity with which traditions changed in south-west France during the Upper Palaeolithic, and complements David's (1973) suggestion that these resulted from periodic short-term collapses of the resource base.

Finally, the scope for personal differentiation could have been more easily expressed than before through the possession of items involving heavy expenditure of time and skill. Evidence that this may have occurred comes from some late palaeolithic burials from eastern Europe. Many were very elaborate, and may have involved some kind of roofed burial chamber in which the deceased was placed, lying down or sitting. The goods in these graves are often very spectacular. At Sungir, one grave contained an old man buried in a costume which contained the 3500-bead necklace alrady mentioned. The other contained two children, aged 12 and 9, who were buried in similar dress along with 16 ivory spears and knives, including one spear 2·4 m long. Similar, though less elaborate, burials of children are known from Mal'ta in Siberia and Kostienki (sites XV and XVIII) in the Ukraine (Shimkin, 1978). Why children merited such ceremony is an interesting question. One possibility is that they were offspring of a high-status person who was still alive when they died; another is that authority may have been hereditary. Either way, such elaborate burials of adults and children imply a considerable degree of social complexity, and should caution us against viewing all palaeolithic hunter-gatherers as necessarily egalitarian in authority, material possessions or, for that matter, diet.

As way of a summary, the differences argued here between societies before and after *ca.* 30 000 b.p. are shown in Table 6 and Figs 12 and 13.

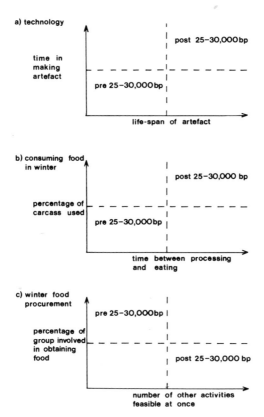

Fig. 13: Summary of differences between Middle and Upper Palaeolithic (post 30 000 b.p.) technology and subsistence.

III. CLIMATE, ENVIRONMENT AND SETTLEMENT, 30 000 TO 16 000 b.p.

Between 30 000 and 16 000 b.p. the climate was generally colder and drier than before, but often interspersed with short episodes of slightly milder conditions. The glacial maximum, usually placed around 18 000 b.p., is more accurately described as a period of extreme cold and aridity that lasted in Europe from *ca.* 20 000 to 16 000 b.p. than as the time when all ice sheets had reached their maximum extent. Although the European and Laurentide ice sheets were largest at this time, the Antarctic ice sheet may have attained its greatest area some 3000 years earlier, whilst the greatest expansion of ice over Greenland and the Arctic did not occur until *ca.* 10 000 b.p. (Hjört, 1979; Salinger, 1981).

Despite the vast amount of data on the European environment around the glacial maximum, reliable estimates of temperatures are still hard to come by. One recent review (Peterson *et al.*, 1979) lists only 11 palaeo-environmental sites in Europe that are reliably dated to 18 000 b.p., of which only two provide temperature estimates. One, based on insect assemblages (Coope *et al.*, 1971) suggests that mean summer temperatures in England were *ca.* 10°C, i.e. 7° less than those of today. On the assumption that seasonal contrasts were as great then as at present in areas like Siberia, where similar insect assemblages are found, average winter temperatures were probably 30°C colder. Florschütz *et al.*, (1971) estimated from the pollen profile at Padul in Spain that mean annual temperatures there were 6°C cooler than at present.

These estimates can fortunately be supplemented by those from CLIMAP's (1976) reconstruction of the world's oceans around 18 000 b.p. While the resulting picture is coarse-grained in that few of the ocean cores can be dated to within 4000 years, its overall view of global climate at this time cannot yet be matched by terrestrial data. One salient feature of ocean surface temperatures 18 000 years ago is that they were on average only 2·3°C cooler than today's; however, the greatest anomaly lay across the North Atlantic, which was then 8°C cooler, and which cooled western Europe to the extent that winter pack ice extended as far south as northern Spain (Ruddiman and McIntyre, 1981). Simulation studies of prevailing atmospheric conditions over land suggest that summer temperatures were 8–10°C less than today's over much of Europe (Gates, 1976). One interesting detail here is that western Siberia may have been one of the few places in the world where summer temperatures 18 000 years ago were actually higher than today's by 4–6°C. The most striking feature of the Mediterranean was the pronounced temperature gradient from east to west; off the Levant, surface temperatures were only 1°C cooler than today's, whereas they were 9°C colder off the south coast of Spain. (The anomalously low temperatures in the Aegean will be discussed in the next chapter.)

Although it is difficult to estimate the level of precipitation during the glacial maximum, Europe (and the Near East) would have been drier than today, and too dry, as well as too cold, to sustain extensive tree cover except perhaps along river valleys and the lower parts of mountains.

The most striking feature of the European landscape 18 000 years ago were the ice sheets over the British Isles, Scandinavia and western Siberia. Their ultimate extent is still controversial. Hughes' (1977) proposal that a continuous sheet linked the European, Greenland and American ice-caps has been criticized as an unjustified extrapolation of Antarctic conditions to the northern hemisphere (Boulton, 1979).

Grosswald (1980) has suggested that there was a continuous ice sheet from Ireland to western Siberia that was 6000 km wide, up to 3km thick and covering 8 million sq. km (an area only slightly smaller than the United States). At the edge of these sheets, vast amounts of dust produced by the flow of ice over rock were picked up by wind and deposited as loess, forming a mantle often several metres thick over the "polar desert" of northern and eastern Europe as well as areas further south.

Estimates of how far sea levels fell due to the transfer of ocean water to ice-caps vary from 85 to 140 m; the most widely quoted (and easily remembered!) estimate is of 100 m. A drop of this magnitude would have exposed much of the English Channel, the Bay of Biscay, and the Adriatic and Aegean seas, and would have prevented salt water from entering the Black Sea. A significant area of coastal plain would thus have been available which has since been drowned, along with any evidence for how it was used.

The European flora extant during the glacial maximum has been intensively investigated, especially in northern and eastern Europe. One point that did not emerge until fairly recently is that tree cover was extremely slight in southern as well as northern Europe at this time; a more appropriate image than that of forests retreating southwards as it got colder is that they evaporated, leaving only residual patches. The uniqueness of the late glacial flora of northern Europe unfortunately impedes attempts to estimate its productivity. Although many of its individual constituents are found today in the arctic tundra, late glacial France or Poland was never the land of the midnight sun, and they provided favourable conditions for many plants that cannot tolerate the extremes of day and night of the far north, as well as entirely different growing conditions for those that can. Its productivity must have been far higher than that of present-day tundra, since it was able to maintain viable populations of mammoth (see Stanley, 1980), whose feeding requirements probably exceeded 100 kg per day. However, despite the diversity of this flora, it is not one that could have provided much in the way of plant foods suitable for man, and his diet must have consisted almost entirely of meat at this time.

These conditions would have affected human populations in three main ways compared to earlier periods, besides the loss of plant resources. First, the diversity of medium-sized prey would have decreased. Reduction in tree cover and browse as well as the increased cold itself would have adversely affected elk, roe deer, aurochs and pig over most of Europe; in northern Europe, red deer would also have been disadvantaged by the lack of suitable grazing. It is thus hardly surprising that faunal assemblages from sites dated to around the glacial maximum show, with monotonous regularity, that reindeer and/or horse were the commonest prey from south-west France to the Ukraine, or red deer from northern Spain (Straus *et al.*, 1980) through Italy to Greece (Jarman, M., 1972).

These changes do not, however, in themselves indicate that hunting strategies were substantially different from when a wider range of prey was available (as in the early Upper Palaeolithic), nor that they were similar to middle palaeolithic subsistence patterns at the height of the previous glaciation, when reindeer were also abundant. If we take the faunal evidence in isolation, we could conclude that hunting strategies had changed to some degree in response to these environmental changes: thus one animal resource would have been eaten more often than before, and others less frequently; and slightly different techniques could have been used in hunting one animal rather than another. However, these changes would be no greater than when wolf-packs adjust their behaviour to hunting solitary elk instead of part of a reindeer herd. These responses to changes in the structure of the environment are very different from — and minor when compared with — the changes already mentioned that altered the technology and organization of subsistence activities after *ca.* 30 000 b.p.

Secondly, reindeer and horse in northern, and perhaps red deer in southern, Europe would have been subject to considerable short-term fluctuations, both temporally and spatially. Several analogies are known from the Arctic in recent times. That weather conditions can change markedly is dramatically shown by the pronounced fluctuations in snow cover over the northern hemisphere between 1960 and 1970; in one spectacular instance, 3 million sq km of Siberia was covered by snow within a week (Matson and Wiesnet, 1981). Clearly, whilst such short-term changes are undetectable in the archaeological record, they would have spelt disaster for human groups caught in the wrong place at the wrong time. Even without such obvious climatic fluctuations, resources would have varied in their availability from super-abundance to disappearance. The cyclical fluctuations of arctic hare provide one clear historical example, as does the periodic collapse of reindeer herds (see Burch, 1972; Wilkinson, 1975).

The third consequence is that some areas of Europe probably became uninhabitable around the glacial maximum. There is, for example, no clear evidence of year-round settlement in Britain (Jacobi, 1980), northern France (Hemingway, 1980), Switzerland (Sonneville-Bordes, 1963) or Moravia (Valoch, 1980), although some of these areas may have been visited occasionally on ivory-collecting expeditions (see p.132). The same point may be true of the Ukraine. As this area contains most of the excavated late glacial open-air sites, it should provide crucial evidence on the extent to which human groups coped with the full severity of a glacial maximum. Unfortunately, many of them are dated only vaguely from their geological context, and some of the ^{14}C dates are suspect. However, the dates do provide at least a hint of a hiatus, or at least some contraction, in settlement between 20 000 and 16 000 b.p. (see Fig. 14). At Molodova V, the best-dated Ukrainian palaeolithic site, horizons 7 to 9 are dated to between 23 000 and 28 000 b.p., and levels 4 to 6 to around 16 000 b.p. Between

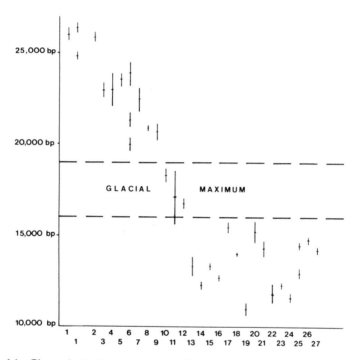

Fig. 14: Chronological patterning of East European sites dated to between 15-30 000 b.p.

List of sites: 1 Pavlov; 2 Dolni Vestonice; 3 Nitra-Cerman; 4 Molodova V layer 7; 5 Kostienki XII; 6 Kostienki XVIII; 7 Sungir; 8 Afontova Gora II; 9 Berdyzh; 10 Byzovaia; 11 Molodova V layer 4; 12 Molodova V layer 6; 13 Molodova V layer 3; 14 Molodova V layer 2; 15 Kokorevo II; 16 Kokorevo III; 17 Kokorevo IV; 18 Kostienki I; 19 Kostienki II; 20 Kostienki XI; 21 Kostienki XIV; 22 Kostienki XIX; 23 Borshevo II; 24 Kursk I; 25 Kokorevo I; 26 Mal'ta; 27 Volchiya Griva; Based on Shimkin, 1978; Vogel and Waterbolk, 1964; Vogel and Zagwijn, 1967.

horizons 5 and 7 is a metre of loess, in which there is no evidence for occupation. Most of the Ukrainian sites probably date to the final part of the last glaciation, and may indicate that some areas which had become uninhabitable were recolonized at a later date. This argument is not in conflict with the evidence for human activities near the Arctic Circle in north-west Siberia during the glacial maximum. As noted already, this area may be exceptional in having been one of the few areas of the late glacial world that was actually warmer than today.

V. CONCLUSIONS

In my opinion, human behaviour after 30 000 b.p. can be regarded as fully "modern", and substantially different from that of Neanderthals. The primary differences between the two types of behaviour are *conceptual* and *organizational*. Particularly important here were the developments of highly specific technologies that required much greater investment of time, labour and skill than before, together with more specialized expertise in their deployment. Inter-group relations were also much more highly structured than previously, and operated through elaborate exchange networks and aggregation sites that served as regional foci. Since none of these changes is evident by looking at simply the range and type of prey that were taken, these points emphasize the need to study palaeolithic subsistence within a wider perspective than that provided by the study of dietary evidence alone.

When, and at what rate, these changes occurred are uncertain. In terms of formal tool types, the earliest upper palaeolithic assemblages of central and western Europe may well have been derived from a local mousterian background and—if the evidence from St Césaire is confirmed—made by Neanderthals. If so, major changes in the ways societies organized themselves, their subsistence and technology might not have occurred until sometime after 30 000 b.p., rather than at the middle-upper palaeolithic interface some 2000 to 4000 years earlier. Whether these changes occurred through the immigration of new populations from outside Europe is also an open question. Whilst the differences in hunting techniques and strategies, social organization and technology before, for example, 40 000 b.p. and after 30 000 b.p. are profound, they need not have been introduced from outside, since there are plausible ways of explaining rapid and major cultural transformations in purely local terms (e.g. Renfrew, 1978).

6. The Last Deglaciation and Its Consequences in Southern Europe

Abstract

This and the following chapter are concerned with the last deglaciation in Europe, which began around 16 000 years ago, and was largely completed by 6000 b.p. The climatic and environmental changes that occurred are first discussed, and then the archaeological evidence from southern Europe. Here, it is argued that the techniques for procuring large animals remained much the same as before, but that foraging became much more important. Southern Greece, the Iron Gates region of the Danube, and northern Spain are taken as examples of these developments.

The end of the last ice age is usually defined by the end of the Younger Dryas period some 10 millennia ago, since which time an interglacial climate has prevailed. This boundary also marks the transition from the Palaeolithic to the Mesolithic. The reasons why the Palaeolithic and Pleistocene ended at the same time seem clear enough at first sight; the onset of interglacial conditions led to fundamental changes in the life-styles of European communities. Perhaps the most notable of these was that man no longer depended upon the reindeer, horse and mammoth, occupying a more or less treeless environment, but upon red and roe-deer, elk, pig and aurochs: animals that lived in a largely forested environment. In addition, as the ice sheets melted, the European landscape changed radically to assume its present form, and new land areas in north and north-west Europe were opened up for colonization.

Two points can be made about this view. The first is that it rests upon a sharp, sudden transition from a glacial to an interglacial climate and environment, even if one allows for a minor preamble to the Holocene in the Allerød "interstadial" between 12 000 and 11 000 b.p. As is now apparent from research over the last decade, the last deglaciation was a very protracted affair that lasted some 10 000 years, a period as long as that normally ascribed to the present length of the Post-Glacial. During this long period, the input of solar energy, the extent and volume of ice sheets, air temperatures and circulation, as well as the soils, vegetation and fauna, were rarely, if ever, in equilibrium with each other. Thus the fact that late palaeolithic communities in northern Europe lived in a predominantly "glacial" environment stems largely from the slow rate at which the vegetation and fauna could respond to a rapid rise in temperature, whilst the speed with which these changed following a comparable rise in temperature after 10 000 b.p. owes much to the subtle but real consequences of the late glacial warming. Similarly, the swift disintegration of the ice sheets after 10 000 years ago largely results from the fact that their volume had already been halved during the late glacial.

The second point is that the contrast between the late Palaeolithic and the Mesolithic has been greatly exaggerated by historical factors, for whereas the former has been best documented from south-west France, northern Germany and the Ukraine, the latter has always been dominated by evidence from Britian and Scandinavia. Only scant attention has been paid to the southern half of Europe, where continuity rather than change in the way of life of human communities is apparent between 14 000 and 8000 b.p. Even in northern Europe, however, the features that are supposedly distinctive of the Mesolithic—a microlithic technology, the use of shellfish, the domestication of the dog, or the colonization of previously uninhabitable areas—have firm roots in the late Palaeolithic.

In order to study how human societies were affected by and responded to the climatic and environmental changes of the last deglaciation, the late Palaeolithic and the Mesolithic should be treated as a single unit. The beginning of the last deglaciation can be set at *ca.* 16 000 b.p. and its end when the world's oceans attained their present condition some 6000 years ago. First, the climatic and environmental changes that occurred during these 10 millennia can be briefly outlined; a summary is provided in Table 7.

Table 7: Chronology of the last deglaciation (based on Coope and Pennington, 1977; Duplessy et al., 1981; Ruddiman and McIntyre, 1981).

Date (b.p.)	Temperature fluctuations	Vegetation	Insect fauna
18 000	Maximum extent of ice sheets		
17 000	Summer solar input rises to above present level	Tolerant of very cold, dry conditions	
16–13 000	Volume of ice sheets halved by calving of icebergs into North Atlantic → North Atlantic cold, area of sheets reduced by only 20%; cold, dry conditions dominated southern margins of ice sheets		
13 500	Ice sheets stabilize; few bergs shed into Atlantic → Sea temperatures rise, warmer moister air moves from south		Changes from arctic to temperate
	WINDERMERE INTERSTADIAL		
12 000		Trees reach northern Europe (Allerød)	
11 500	Temperatures begin to fall		
11 000	Sharp fall in temperatures; Younger Dryas — readvance of polar water	Reversion to cold, dry-tolerant vegetation	Arctic
10 000	Rapid rise in temperature		
9–8 000	Remaining half of ice sheets melted; sea levels rise to present level	Gradual invasion of trees	Temperate
6 000	Oceans assume present form	Deciduous vegetation in northern Europe	

I. THE LAST DEGLACIATION, 16 000 TO 6000 b.p.

As a result of eccentricities in the earth's orbit, the amount of solar energy received during the summer 17 000 years ago, shortly after the glacial maximum, was higher than today, and it continued to rise until 11 000 years ago (Berger, 1978). Consequently, the southern edges of the northern hemisphere ice sheets became unstable, and vulnerable to melting. As a result, and probably also because of internally-generated stresses on their marine edges (Andrews and Barry, 1978), their volume was halved between 16 000 and 13 000 b.p. through the calving of icebergs into the North Atlantic (Ruddiman and McIntyre, 1981). Most of this reduction was achieved by thinning, since the area of the ice sheets at 13 000 b.p. was still *ca*. 80% of that during the glacial maximum. Such a vast influx of ice into the North Atlantic meant that the increase in summer insolation was fully absorbed in melting this ice. Because the North Atlantic remained cold, and the areal extent of the Eurasian ice sheets was little changed, warmer, moister air from lower latitudes was prevented from moving northwards, and much of Europe remained cold and dry "polar desert". It was only after 13 000 b.p. that the influx of ice slackened to the point where temperatures in the North Atlantic and western Europe could rise (Ruddiman and McIntyre, 1981).

Evidence for this late glacial warming comes from two sources. Analyses of cores taken from the North Atlantic floor show that between 13 500 and 11 500 b.p., summer surface temperatures rose rapidly from 6·6°C to 14·0°C, and winter ones from 0·9°C to 9·0°C; during this period the front of the cold polar waters retreated some 1700 km from west of the Bay of Biscay to a position south-west of Greenland (Ruddiman *et al.*, 1977). Independent confirmation for this marked late glacial warming comes from studies of insect assemblages. Between 13 500 and 13 000 b.p., mean summer temperatures in Britain rose from *ca*. 10°C (7°C cooler than today's) to near modern values, and temperate insect faunas replaced arctic ones as far north as Scotland (Coope and Pennington, 1977). Similarly, a recent oxygen-isotope study of late glacial sediments from south-east France indicates a rise of 7°C in mean annual temperatures between 13 000 and 12 000 b.p. (Eicher *et al.*, 1981).

These warm conditions in western Europe—best termed the Windermere Interstadial (Coope and Pennington, 1977)—were abruptly halted by a short cold episode known generally as the Younger Dryas. Within only 700 years after 11 500 b.p., summer and winter surface temperatures off the coast of western Europe fell from 14·3°C to 7·4°C and from 8·2°C to 1·8°C respectively, and polar waters readvanced some 800 km south. In Scotland, summer temperatures fell by at least 3°C around 12 000 b.p., and then by a further 4°C after 11 000 b.p. However, there is little indication that the area of ice sheets increased to any great extent.

After 10 000 b.p. temperatures rose again and as rapidly as in the thousand years after 13 500 b.p. In the North Atlantic, summer surface temperatures rose from 7·4°C to 15·4°C, and winter ones from 1·8°C to 10·1°C at a mean rate of 12°C/1000 years. Additionally, within only 500 years, polar water retreated to where it had been before the previous cold episode. The final warming of the Norwegian Sea continued until 6000 b.p. when the oceans' present interglacial character was attained (Ruddiman and McIntyre, 1981). In Britain, insect assemblages indicate that summer temperatures had reached present levels by 9500 b.p.— a rise of 7°C in only 500 years (Osborne, 1974). Since then, mean annual temperature have fluctuated from this level by only 1-2°C.

It is, however, after 10 000 b.p. that the remainder of the ice sheets disappeared. Their final demise had far-reaching consequences upon Europe. The first, and most striking, was that most of Scandinavia and Britain became available for colonization between 9500 and 8000 b.p.; this area of "new" land consisted of some 1·4 million sq km. Other smaller areas were also opened up by the retreat of glaciers from the Alps and Pyrenees. This increase in the size of habitable Europe must, of course, be partially offset by some loss of land caused by a rise in sea level of 70-100 m. Although in no way as dramatic as the drowning of Beringia or much of the Australian margins, the amount of land so lost was still considerable, particularly in the Adriatic, Aegean, Gulf of Lyons, Bay of Biscay, the Celtic and North Seas and the English Channel. Most of this was drowned fairly rapidly: Ireland was severed from Britain by 9500 years ago, and the low-lying land in the southern part of the North Sea by 8300 b.p., thus marking the beginnings of British insularity.

The melting of the ice sheets also resulted in major hydrological changes to Europe's two inland seas, the Baltic and Black Sea.

A. The Baltic

As has been well-known for several decades, the rate at which the Baltic region uplifted following the removal of the Scandinavian ice sheet has not always matched the rate at which sea levels have risen since the ice sheets melted. Consequently—and as indicated in Fig. 15—its western exit has twice been blocked, turning it into an inland lake rather than a saline inlet of the North Sea. These changes have probably affected the inhabitants of the Baltic region in two ways. The first is that winters may

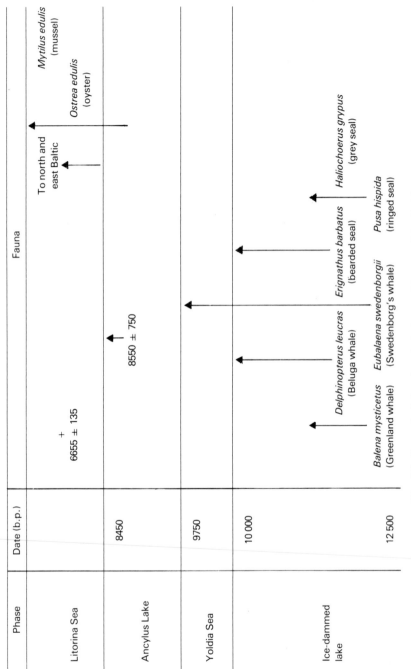

Fig. 15: Late glacial and early holocene history of the Baltic.

have been more severe when the Baltic was separated from the North Sea, since fresh water freezes more readily than salt water and would thus have had a greater cooling effect upon the region. The second is that the present salinity of the western Baltic lies only slightly above the tolerance of many marine organisms, and so even minor changes in the influx of fresh water from the east or saline water from the west would have had marked consequences upon its marine life and thus the resources available to man.

B. The Black Sea

Like the Baltic, the Black Sea receives a substantial influx of fresh water from rivers, is only slightly saline, and is connected to adjacent ocean systems by a single narrow channel. In this instance, the Bosphorous channel at Istanbul is only 35 m deep and 2 km wide, and greatly impedes the exchange of water between the Aegean and the Black Sea.

The history of the Black Sea over the past 20 000 years is a complex one, and is summarized in Fig. 16. Events before 12 000 b.p. are still unclear. According to Thiede (1978) and Thunell (1979b), the Aegean 18 000 years ago used to receive a large influx of cold fresh water from the Black Sea that was ultimately derived from western Siberia. On the other hand, Stanley and Blanpied (1980) have argued that the Aegean, the Sea of Marmara and the Black Sea formed three separate systems before 12 000 b.p. However, none of the cores in their study extended back beyond 12 000 b.p. or came from the Aegean, and their data may show only that no saline water entered the Black Sea at this time — thus the outflow of fresh water into the Aegean is not excluded.

Between 12 000 and 9500 b.p., some saline water from the Aegean managed to penetrate the Sea of Marmara but not the Black Sea itself. after 9500 b.p., sea levels rose, the flow of meltwater into the Black Sea slackened, and so salt water from the Aegean was able to enter the Black Sea. By 7000 b.p. its present features had established themselves; incoming saline water from the Aegean sank below the less dense fresh water entering the Black Sea from rivers and impeded circulation so that the water 200 m below the surface to its floor at 2200 m became increasingly anaerobic and uninhabitable to fish and plankton.

These developments must have considerably affected the marine life of the Aegean, as well as the environment and human societies of surrounding regions. One consequence of a large influx of cold fresh water from the Black Sea before 9500 b.p. may have been to render the Aegean unsuitable for fish such as tunny, which later became an important resource. Another is that the surface temperatures, evaporation

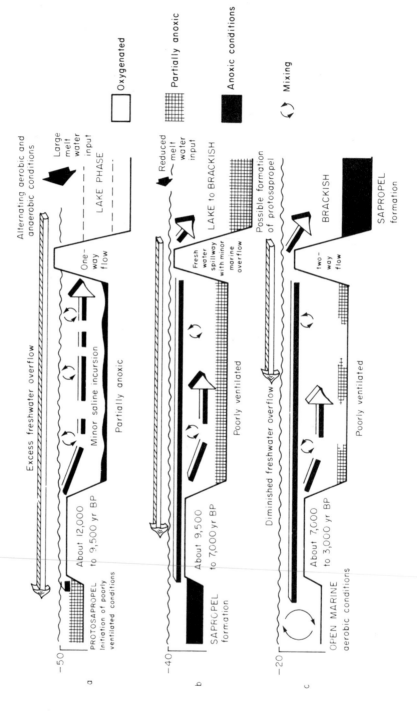

Fig. 16: Post-glacial history of the Black Sea (Stanley and Blanpied, 1980, p.540).

rates and rainfall of the Aegean would have remained low until Mediterranean water managed to enter the Black Sea after 9500 b.p. This in turn may have delayed the spread of tree growth in the Aegean area until well after 10 000 b.p. (see below).

C. Vegetational changes

The vegetational history of the last deglaciation is now known in immense detail for the northern half of Europe, but only scantily that for the southern part. Interpreting this record is difficult, for it results from several factors, including climatic change, the rates at which different plants could migrate, interspecific competition, ecological preferences, and the location of late pleistocene plant refugia. What is now evident is the extremely slow rate at which trees could respond to rapid rises in temperature. This is especially true of the late glacial warming. In the Lake District of northern England, for example, the local vegetation was largely composed of grasses and sedges when temperatures began to rise after 13 500 b.p., and it took 500 years for woodlands, at first of birch and later of birch and juniper, to become established (Coope and Pennington, 1977). By the time that woodlands had become established over many parts of northern Europe, temperatures had already begun to fall. Thus one of the oddities of our present understanding of late pleistocene climate is that the Allerød (*ca.* 12 000–11 000 b.p.), traditionally regarded as an interstadial on account of its high percentage of tree pollen, was in fact a period when temperatures were already falling (Eicher *et al.*, 1981). This point is made clearer if we consider the rates at which trees can migrate. As Goudie (1977:57) has pointed out, birch—a fast mover by arboreal standards—migrates at a mean rate of only 200–260 m year. Even at that heady pace, it would extend its distribution by only 260 km in 1000 years.

The same point seems to hold for the early Holocene. As indicated above, temperatures rose very rapidly between 10 000 and 9500 b.p. to modern values; yet, as the pollen record indicates, it was not for another 3 millennia that deciduous woodland was established over Britain and Scandinavia.

Although the vegetational record from southern Europe is still sparse, it is sufficient to refute any notion that deciduous forest retreated southwards from northern Europe during the glacial maximum. In southern and central Italy (Bottema, 1978; Grüger, 1977) as well as Greece (Bottema, 1974), the pollen record shows scarcely any woodland until after 10 000 b.p. This picture is essentially the same as that for south-west Turkey (van Zeist *et al.*, 1975) and Syria (Niklewski and van

Zeist, 1970), and emphasizes the point that the climate was cold and arid during much of the last deglaciation. As indicated above, the Aegean may have remained especially cool until the influx of meltwater through the Black Sea had slackened, and this may have deterred potential tree colonizers. Even during the late glacial warming, tree growth in southern Europe may have been discouraged because increased temperatures led to higher rates of evaporation rather than more precipitation (Bottema, 1974).

D. Faunal changes

The last deglaciation saw for certain the extinction of three large mammals in Europe—the mammoth, musk-ox and Giant Irish Elk—and possibly also the woolly rhino, steppe bison, hyaena and lion. At present, the mammoth is the animal whose extinction is best detailed. It appears to have lasted in western Europe almost as long as in Siberia. The most recent find from Switzerland is dated to 12 270 ± 210 b.p., and from France to 13 390 ± 300 b.p.; in north-east Siberia, a mammoth from the Taimyr River is dated to 11 450 ± 250 b.p. (The date of 9780 ± 260 b.p. for one from Estonia may be suspect; see Berglund *et al.*, 1976:189.) Eurasian musk-ox finds are very rare, but the most recent one is probably from Diuktai in Siberia and dated to *ca.* 12 000 b.p. (Wilkinson, 1975:44). *Megaceros*, the beast that was neither Giant nor Irish nor an Elk (Gould, 1980), is last known from the Younger Dryas, *ca.* 11–10 000 b.p.

The causes of these animals' extinction are unclear. Although mammoth, woolly rhino and musk-ox are most unlikely to have survived the sudden rise in temperatures in late glacial times, due to changes in vegetation and competing animal species, the role of man cannot be excluded. A few years ago, Mosimann and Martin (1975) showed in a simulation model how an initial population of 100 people entering North America could have exterminated over 3·3 million mammoth in only 500 years; a more recent study by Campbell (1978) has suggested how only sporadic and small-scale hunting could result in the extinction of populations of animals such as wild sheep. Yet the roles of man in causing the extinction of the late pleistocene megafauna in many parts of the world is still equivocal (see e.g. Gillespie *et al.*, 1978; Grayson, 1977), and after a careful review of this problem, van Valen (1969) felt unable to reach any definite conclusions.

E. Changes in animal distribution

During the last deglaciation, some animals extended their distribution, whilst others became more restricted; some became locally extinct but also colonized new areas. These changes partly reflect climatic and vegetational changes, but also the social, migratory and reproductive behaviour of each species as well as its ability to compete with others.

The most noteworthy change in the European fauna after 10 000 b.p. was the northward expansion of red and roe-deer, elk, pig and aurochs into areas previously occupied by reindeer and horse. The rate at which these particular replacements occurred probably owes more to vegetational than climatic changes, given that reindeer can tolerate the climate but not the vegetation of the Massif Central in France today (see Movius, 1974:108). As seen already, temperatures changed more rapidly than could the vegetation during the late glacial warming. Consequently, the lichens, mosses and sedges preferred by reindeer persisted over much of northern Europe throughout most of the late glacial, and it was not until after 10 000 b.p. that these were replaced by the grasses and forbs that reindeer dislike but which are preferred by red deer. This degree of disequilibrium between the rates of climatic and vegetational change must have led to a curious situation, in which cold-adapted animals died out, but others such as red deer and pig that were better adapted to warmer conditions could not replace them because their plant foods and concomitant shelter had not migrated sufficiently far.

Similar relationships between vegetational change and herbivore movements can be seen with other species. For example, the rate at which elk dispersed was strongly constrained by the availability of birch, one of its main foods. As noted above, this tree migrates fairly quickly, and so elk was able to reach northern England by *ca.* 12 000 b.p. (Hallam *et al.*, 1973). However, elk (and roe-deer) never reached Ireland, although it was then still joined to Britain; presumably, by the time that the vegetation in Ireland had changed to the elk's liking, the sea had risen and barred it from further colonization (Stuart, 1977:310). A similar fate befell the beech marten, which never reached Britain because the sea beat the beech to the area that is now the English Channel.

The responses of other species to the climatic and vegetational changes during the last deglaciation are less well detailed. So far as birds are concerned, their likely responses can sometimes be inferred from their present migratory behaviour. The wheatear (*Oenanthe oenanthe*) is a clear example. Today, this has four sub-species: two are African residents, one spends the summer in Greenland, Iceland and the Faroes, and the other in north-eastern Siberia. In late glacial times, these migrations were clearly impossible, and these latter two sub-species are likely to have developed only after the ice sheets had retreated (Baker, 1978:705). Given the variety of birds represented in magdalenian (Desbrosse and Mourer-Chauvire, 1973) and maglemosian (Clark, 1975:245–247) sites, it would be interesting to know more about the readjustments each had to make to a deglaciated Europe. The same point applies to shellfish, a food resource that has elicited an immense amount of attention in discussions of post-glacial subsistence. Its dispersal into northern Europe will be outlined in the next chapter.

As the main consequence of the rises in temperatures between 13 500 and 11 000 b.p. and after 10 000 b.p. was to warm Europe from south to north, it is appropriate to follow this process northwards by looking first at how the last deglaciation affected southern Europe.

II. SUBSISTENCE STRATEGIES DURING THE LAST DEGLACIATION IN SOUTHERN EUROPE

Perhaps the most noteworthy feature of the archaeological record from southern Europe during the last deglaciation is its continuity. This is especially evident in two ways. The first is the repeated use of many sites —although not necessarily for the same function—and the second, the importance of red deer as a major source of meat. Nevertheless, significant developments did occur, and chiefly concern the greater usage of small resources—fish, shellfish, seeds, nuts, rabbit and other small game—which may in turn imply notable changes in the way that subsistence strategies were organized. All these features are shown by the data from three widely separated areas—southern Greece, the Iron Gates gorge of the Danube and northern Spain, as well as by less detailed evidence from southern France.

A. Southern Greece: Franchthi

The importance of Franchthi cave lies in its long sequence of occupation across the pleistocene/holocene boundary (Jacobsen, 1976), the meticulous nature of its excavation (see Diamant, 1979), its plethora of over fifty ^{14}C dates, the quality of its dietary evidence (Hansen and Renfrew, 1978; Payne, 1975; Shackleton and Andel, 1980), and supporting geomorphic data (Andel *et al.*, 1980). The main trends are summarized in Fig. 17. When first occupied around the time of the glacial maximum, *ca.* 20 000 b.p., the cave lay 5-6 km inland. The importance of onager during this phase is consistent with pollen data from northern Greece (Bottema, 1974) that indicate open grassland steppe vegetation and a cold, arid climate. After a long hiatus, the cave was reoccupied around 12 500 years ago, by which time the sea had risen some 40 m so that the cave was only 3-4 km from the coast. In these phases (B and C), some aurochs, pig and goat are represented in a sample

Phase	Sea level	% of no. of bones of large mammals					Shellfish	Fish	Botanical remains	Date (b.p.)
A	− 90m	Cervus	Equus				—	—	—	ca. 22 000
				HIATUS						
B	− 50m	Cervus	Equus	Bos	Capra		Patella	small; rare	*Hordeum spontaneum;* *Vicia* sp; | *Lens* sp.	ca. 12 500
C		Cervus	Equus	Capra	Sus		Patella	small; rare	→	ca. 10 500
D₁		Cervus		Sus			Cyclope	small; rare	→	
D₂	− 25m						Cerithium	tunny-size; common	→	ca. 8 500

Fig. 17: Summary of evidence from Franchthi cave, southern Greece (based on Jacobsen, 1976; Payne, 1975; Shackleton and Andel, 1980).

otherwise dominated by red deer and onager. At this time, the vegetation is still likely to have been predominantly treeless. A few small fish bones in these layers also indicate some fishing—unless they are derived from bird gullets—that may have been done in the nearby river, or on the coast. Small numbers of *Patella* shells may also indicate small-scale usage of coastal resources.

Phase D begins some time after 10 500 b.p., a date that roughly coincides with the inception of tree growth in the Aegean (Bottema, 1974). The wooded environment of this phase is clearly shown by the dominance of pig and red deer, and the absence of onager and goat. In the latter part of this phase, *ca.* 8500 b.p., there were three important and related changes that concerned the sea. The first is that 20-40% of the total weight of bone consists of fish remains, many of which are large vertebrae, 2-4 cm in diameter, and comparable to those from a 20-25 kg tunny. A radiocarbon date of 8740 ± 114 b.p. from this phase agrees well with the evidence that cold, fresh water was no longer entering the Aegean from the Black Sea (see above), since a rise in the salinity and temperature of the Aegean after 9000 b.p. would have made it more attractive to fish like tunny. Alternatively, the appearance of marine species at the cave may simply reflect that the rise in sea level had brought the coast to within only 1 km of the cave (Andel *et al.*, 1980). Important local changes also affected the type of shellfish gathered by the cave's users. After 9000 b.p., *Patella* was largely replaced by *Cyclope*, a small shellfish that lives on muddy shores and in brackish water. This in turn was supplanted after 8000 b.p. by *Cerithium*, a rock-dwelling mollusc. This latter change is probably a local consequence of the rise in sea level that inundated the mudflats on which *Cyclope* populations lived, and simultaneously resulted in a rocky shoreline favourable to *Cerithium* (Shackleton and Andel, 1980). The third important development after 8500 b.p. is that 10% of the lithics are made from obsidian brought from the island of Melos, 130 km away by sea. If we exclude claims of palaeolithic flints from Cyprus (Vita-Finzi, 1973), the presence of Melian obsidian at Franchthi is currently the earliest evidence for seafaring in the Mediterranean.

The botanical evidence from Franchthi provides one of our rare glimpses of early holocene plant husbandry. As Hansen and Renfrew (1978) show, wild barley, oats, three types of legumes and two types of nuts were used between 8000 and 12 000 b.p. The bearing of these finds on later cereal and legume-based economies in south-east Europe will be explored later (see Chapter 8).

B. The Iron Gates

One hundred km downstream of Belgrade, the Danube flows through the gorges of the Iron Gates, some 130 km long. For 7 km of this stretch it is forced through a narrow canyon less than 100 m in places, between the 300 m high limestone massifs of the Cazanele Mari and Mici, with resulting flows of up to 18 km/h. As a result of excavations during the 1960s, Roumanian and Yugoslav archaeologists established an impressive sequence of sites in this area that date from 12 000 to 7000 years ago. Although the evidence is drawn from several sites, their local environments are probably sufficiently similar to have had only minor effects upon the main chronological trends. In all cases, sites are adjacent to two resource zones: the fish of the Danube and the mammals and fowl in the surrounding hills. Most are also near small enclosed basins along the Danube that provide good grazing or potential arable land. Access inland is usually easy along river valleys running into the main river.

Collectively these sites show a stable cultural tradition lasting over 4 millennia, and practised by the same ethnic population (Zivanovic, 1975). During this time, deer, pig and fish provided the main sources of meat; as at Franchthi, there are also a few tantalizing hints for early (pre-neolithic) use of cereals. The only changes in the resource base of the region were that elk, chamois and ibex became rarer or, in some cases, extinct.

Four sites can be examined briefly. The earlier pair are Roumanian, and the latter Yugoslav. A slight problem arises in integrating the faunal evidence from these sites, since it was analyzed by different investigators whose methods were not always directly comparable.

Cuina Turcului (Bolomey, 1973a, 1973b):
The occupation in this rock shelter, at the foot of the Cazanele Mici, is one of the earliest in the area. The lowest layer is dated to 12 600 ± 120 b.p. and 12 050 ± 120 b.p., and the upper to 10 125 ± 200 b.p. The associated artefactual material is described rather unsatisfactorily. Boroneant (1970) regarded both assemblages as Romanello-Azilian, whilst Srejovic (1969a) called layer I late palaeolithic and layer II epi-palaeolithic. The distinctions between these terms are very vague, and the absence of marked or sudden change is probably more important than minor points of dissimilarity.

Pollen analysis shows that by the time layer II was accumulating, elm, lime and oak had expanded at the expense of pine. As noted above, these changes were probably only partly a result of rises in temperature.

The faunal assemblages are summarized in Table 8. One problematic feature is that wolf remains were common in both layers. As man may have used the shelter only seasonally (Bolomey, 1973a,b), wolf may have frequented it at other times and eaten some of its kills there. This possibility could be clarified by examining the bone debris for evidence of gnawing. Similarly, the other carnivores in these assemblages may have been trapped for their meat or pelts, or have inhabited the cave when man was absent.

As is readily apparent, the remains of ibex and chamois are common in both layers; those of elk and pig are rarer in the later horizon, whilst *Bos/Bison* is more frequently represented. The samples are not large enough to show details of the age at which animals were killed. Bolomey (1973a, 1973b) suggested that ibex and chamois descended to the Iron Gates region in the winter, and that man then followed these and other herbivores into upland areas during the summer. On the other hand, chamois and ibex could probably have lived year-round in the rocky environment of the Iron Gates, and fishing is likely to have been an important summer activity. An alternative interpretation is that Cuina Turcului was only one of several sites used locally during the year, and that its users exploited both aquatic and terrestrial resources in the summer and hunted during the winter. Toothring analysis could provide one way of showing if chamois and ibex were killed in winter, as suggested by Bolomey.

Icoana:
This open-air site lies in much the same type of setting as Cuina Turcului. The main faunal assemblage has been dated to 8070 ± 130 b.p. and 8010 ± 120 b.p., and is associated with an artefactual assemblage which Srejovic (1969a) classed as part of the Lepenski Vir culture, a tradition of local origin that lasted until the eighth millennium b.p. As Table 8 shows, pig, red and roe-deer are the commonest animals represented, followed by *Bos* and, less commonly, chamois; ibex is absent. As at Cuina Turcului, several other animals may have been killed for their pelts or meat, or have occupied the cave when man was absent. Very large quantities of fish bones were found, and suggest that fishing was important at least in terms of time spent procuring them, if not in absolute quantities of food. Data on the age at which pig and red deer were killed show that around two-thirds of pigs were killed when less than 2 years old, and most of the remainder when senile. This culling pattern seems reasonable: piglets and very old pigs are much easier to kill than prime adult ones. This point is succinctly expressed in a Balkan proverb that runs to the effect that if you hunt bear, you should take a doctor, but if you hunt boar, you should bring a priest (Freeman, 1973:12). Pig also have very high reproductive rates, so that large

Table 8: Composition of faunal assemblages from Cuina Turcului and Icoana (based on Bolomey, 1973a).

	CUINA TURCULUI				ICOANA IV	
	I		II			
	N. spec.	MNI	N. spec.	MNI	N. spec.	MNI
Large herbivores						
Sus sp.	118	7	6	1	2038	40
Capra ibex	74	5	111	8	—	—
Rupicapra rupicapra	62	3	49	5	22	4
Bos/Bison	5	1	68	6	21	2
Alces alces	14	3	5	1	—	—
Capreolus capreolus	16	3	1	1	237	14
Cervus elaphus	?	—	21	1	1474	26
Equus caballus	2	1	3	1	—	—
Total		23		24		86
Fur-bearing animals						
Castor fiber	72	7	52	4	34	9
Canis lupus	35	3	49	5	9	2
Vulpes vulpes	14	1	15	2	—	—
Ursus arctos	23	2	2	1	16	2
Martes sp.	29	3	10	2	44	8
Felis silvestris	1	1	1	1	7	3
Putorius putorius	—	—	1	1	—	—
Lepus europeus	1	1	27	2	11	1
Meles meles	—	—	—	—	13	3
Lutra lutra	—	—	—	—	2	1
Lynx lynx	—	—	—	—	2	1
Total		18		18		31

numbers of young can be culled without endangering the viability of the herd; whether this factor would deter people from hunting adult boar more than concern for their own personal safety is perhaps a moot point. Of the 22 red deer that could be aged, only 7 were less than 14 months old. In Bolomey's opinion, this might indicate deliberate conservation of stock; alternatively, sub-adults—especially male—are usually easier to kill than young or mature animals because they are more curious and less wary.

An intriguing part of the evidence from Icoana is the cereal-type pollen found in some coprolites. The identification of cereal pollen is rarely certain, and is normally made on the basis of size. Pollen grains of cultivated cereals are usually 35–50 microns in diameter, whereas most — but not all — grass pollens are smaller (see Godwin, 1975:405). Cârciumaru (1973a, 1973b) has been suitably cautious on this point. The cereal-type grains are larger than those attributed to grasses, and up to 52·5 microns in diameter. As she states, these large pollen grains are largely "des formes primitives des graminees du type Cerealia et seulement de facon sporadique des Gramineae Cerealia proprement dites". Even if rare, their presence in a Balkan context at *ca.* 8000 b.p. is difficult to explain. No carbonized plant remains were found in the excavations of these sites, and the artefactual evidence is ambiguous. Cereal pollen — except for cultivated rye — does not usually travel long distances (see Edwards, 1979:257), so these pollen grains were probably derived locally. The most parsimonious explanations appear to be either that the grains are not of cereals, but from a grass with large pollen grains, or that cereals were present in this part of south-east Europe at least a millennium before the Neolithic. The latter possibility would do little to help the prevalent view that cereals had to be introduced to this part of Europe during the Neolithic.

Vlasač (Bökönyi, 1975; Srejovic and Letica, 1969):
This open-air site has three layers which Srejovic (1969a) considers span some 2 millennia, from *ca.* 10 200 to 8000 b.p. — roughly equivalent to Cuina Turcului II and Icoana. However, Bökönyi (1975) regards the site as dated to *ca.* 8000 b.p. The faunal samples are unfortunately treated as one assemblage. As with the other sites (see Table 9), red and roe-deer and pig are the commonest animals, although several types of other mammals (mainly small carnivores) and birds are also present. One interesting feature of the assemblage is the large numbers of canid bones, which Bökönyi (1975) considered to be from domestic dog. This suggestion seems reasonable in view of the widespread evidence of domestic dog from the late Pleistocene onwards (e.g. Davis and Valla, 1978).

An enormous number of fish bones were found, and strongly suggest the importance of fishing. However, one cannot infer, as did Bökönyi (1975), that two-thirds of the meat eaten by the inhabitants came from fish simply because two-thirds of the bones were from fish. A "head count" of the minimum number of individuals of each type of mammal

Table 9: Composition of faunal assemblages from Vlasač and Lepenski Vir (based on Bökönyi, 1970, 1975).

| | Vlasač | Lepenski Vir | | |
		I	II	III
Large herbivores				
Bos primigenius	54	14	7	549[a]
Rupicapra rupicapra	22	—	—	2
Cervus elaphus	6732	115	111	862
Capreolus capreolus	510	4	1	36
Sus sp.	1185	10	6	219[b]
Asinus hydrantinus	—	—	—	7
Ovis/Capra	—	—	—	81
Total	8503	143	125	1748
Canis familaris	1914	21	23	149
Other mammals	778	11	4	63
Birds	146	6	1	10
Fish				
Cyprinus carpio	1552	—	—	—
Cyprinidae	5230	86	1	14
Esox lucius (pike)	11	—	—	—
Silurus glanis	2283	3	5	22
Unidentified fish	8372	154	47	364
Total	17 448	243	53	400

[a] Included here are 375 bones attributed to *Bos tauros*.
[b] Included here are 9 bones attributed to *Sus scrofa* dom.

and fish might be more useful in this context, so long as each animal has been butchered in the same manner (and none of the fish-heads had been thrown into the Danube!). At present, the most promising way of establishing the dietary importance of fish relative to other sources of meat might come from ^{13}C analyses of human skeletons (see Box 2).

Most of the fish represented at Vlasač were carp. These prefer warm temperatures and still water, and feed at the bottom of shallow pools (Wheeler, 1969). In this part of the Danube, their main habitat was

---

Box 2: Prehistoric diet and human skeletons

One of the most difficult problems for the economic prehistorian is to estimate the relative importance of plant to animal foods in prehistoric diet. One way in which this might be done is by analysing the chemistry of human skeletons. Providing that their composition has not been altered by prolonged burial, the % of some elements—such as strontium, zinc and calcium—can indicate whether or not the intake of meat within a community varied according to age, sex or rank. Unfortunately, this type of study does not show the actual proportion of the diet that was formed of meat. Another line of approach is to see how the incidence of diet-related diseases varied through time, or within communities. Shifts towards a diet containing a higher proportion of cereal starch and a lower one of meat protein may, for example, be indicated by higher frequencies of dental diseases and infectious lesions.

One new technique that may prove extremely useful is to monitor the ratio of ^{12}C to ^{13}C in bone tissue. This is because some plants, such as maize, contain significantly higher ratios than others. Use of this technique has enabled researchers to identify the point at which maize became an important component of the diet in parts of North America; recently, the technique has been developed further to show the proportion of fish in the diet of mesolithic groups in Denmark.

References: Lallo and Rose, 1979; Lambert *et al.*, 1979; Tauber, 1981; Vogel and van der Merwe, 1977.

---

probably the shallow water close to the banks where they could have been taken in summer, and perhaps preserved for consumption during the winter. Unfortunately, too little is known about the late pleistocene history of the Danube to establish the time when it became sufficiently warm for carp to colonize.

As at Icoana, cereal-type pollen was found in coprolites, and raises the same intriguing question as before.

Lepenski Vir (Srejovic, 1969b):
This, the most famous site in the whole region, lies in a small and inaccessible cove immediately by the Danube, and is best known for its substantial buildings and its graves and unusual sculptures. The site has three phases of occupation. The first two ("epi-palaeolithic") have trapezoid houses containing hearths; the first phase contained 95 structures distributed through five sub-phases, and the second, 45. It was clearly a substantial settlement, very likely occupied throughout the year, whose inhabitants depended upon harvesting the resources of both the Danube and neighbouring forests. The faunal list (Table 9) presents

few surprises in the light of the evidence from other sites in the area except for the appearance of sheep and goat in the final period of settlement, a feature which will be mentioned later (Chapter 9).

Finally, skeletal remains from Vlasač and the slightly later site of Padina provide some indirect, if sometimes ambiguous and contradictory, information on dietary trends in this region in the early Holocene. Zivanovič (1975) attributed increasing wear on anterior teeth to their use for cracking nuts; however, Y'Edynak (1978) suggested that it may have been caused by using teeth instead of the local quartzite tools for cutting. The frequency of enamel hypoplasia — an alteration of the tooth surface caused by seasonal deficiencies in diet — also decreased, possibly because better techniques for storing food helped overcome seasonal food shortages. One odd feature of the Padina skeletons is that many had suffered from rickets. This vitamin D deficiency disease is unlikely to have been caused by insufficient sunlight and may therefore be due to dietary inadequacies.

C. Northern Spain

This area shares many of the features seen in southern Greece and the Iron Gates region, but has the added advantage of also showing late pleistocene subsistence in considerable detail. The main trends are conveniently summarized by the cave of La Riera (Straus *et al.*, 1980), now 1·5 km from the coast, in the province of Asturias.

Layers 4 to 20 contain solutrean and lower magdalenian assemblages that date from *ca.* 21 000 to 16 000 b.p. and show the main sources of food during the severest part of the last glaciation when winter pack ice extended as far south as this area. In this period, almost all food seems to have been obtained from hunting medium-sized mammals, especially red deer and ibex. However, a few salmon and sea-trout that spawn in fresh water are also represented, as are some limpets. At this time, shell-gathering from La Riera would have involved a round trip of 20 km between cave and coast. As the energy costs of obtaining small amounts of food over this distance would have been very high, shellfish may have been obtained as only an adjunct to other activities.

After a 2000-year hiatus, the cave was reoccupied *ca.* 13 000 b.p., by which time sea levels had risen by perhaps 40 m and polar water had retreated from the Bay of Biscay. Red deer were still the most commonly hunted animal, followed by ibex. However, coastal resources had grown in importance. Top-shells, periwinkles and sea-urchins were collected as well as limpets, and by *ca.* 10 750 b.p. the weight of shell was up to 70%

of that of bone. During the Younger Dryas, when polar water again approached the North Spanish coast and reindeer made a brief appearance in the area, shellfish diminished in importance, but were supplemented by birds and ocean fish such as sea-bream.

These trends continued after 10 000 b.p., when present interglacial conditions were established. Red deer retained their importance, but ibex and horse were replaced by forest animals such as roe-deer and pig. Shellfish continued to form an increasingly larger proportion of the volume of archaeological layers; by 8500 b.p., the weight of shells in layers averaged 4·6 times that of bone (see Fig. 18). Interestingly, limpets may have been over-exploited, since their size decreased markedly once they were collected on a large scale. However, the apparent importance of shellfish has to be offset against the point that by 8000 b.p., the cave was probably six times nearer the coast than it had been 8 millennia previously; late glacial shell-gathering may be under-represented as most shells were probably eaten on the (now drowned) coast, and only a small proportion taken inland where they can be discovered today.

D. Southern France

This area deserves a brief mention, for although the evidence is less precise than that from northern Spain, the overall trends are much the same. During the late glacial, red deer, aurochs and horse provided most of the food. In the early Holocene, horse became rarer and pig and roe-deer commoner. Small animals—notably rabbit, hare, snails, birds and tortoise—were also taken, and their importance appears to have increased through time (see Courtin, 1978). The origin and role of sheep in this area will be discussed later (see Chapter 9).

III. DISCUSSION

Throughout the last deglaciation, there was considerable continuity from northern Spain to southern Greece in the importance of red deer as the main animal resource, in the stability of lithic traditions, and in the repreated usage of many caves. Consequently, it has proved very difficult to draw a clear-cut line between the Palaeolithic and Mesolithic in southern Europe. Changes in the availability of other food resources were also very similar over this area, but tended to span several millennia. Vegetation and temperature changes after 10 000 b.p. resulted in woodland habitats favourable to pig, roe-deer and aurochs at the expense of other animals such as horse, ibex and chamois. Static resources also became more important. These included shellfish from the

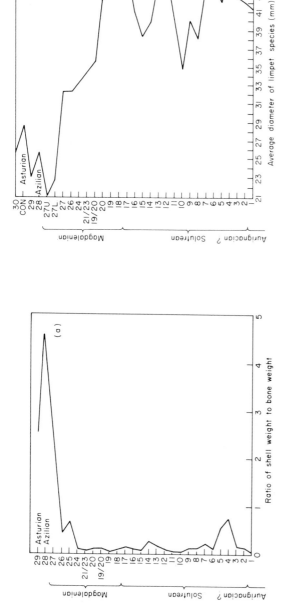

Fig. 18: Changes in exploitation of shell-fish in northern Spain during the last deglaciation. Source: Straus *et al.*, 1980. (a) IMPORTANCE OF SEAFOOD in the diet of the sojourners at La Riera is traced in this graph in terms of the ratio between the gross weight of mammalian bone and the gross weight of mollusk shell. Such a ratio does not, of course, reflect the actual yield in vertebrate protein and invertebrate protein. The numeral 1 on the ordinate indicates a one-to-one weight ratio. This was much exceeded at La Riera during the Azilian phase. Both in the early Solutrean and in the later Magdalenian, however, the weight of shells occasionally reached 70 percent of bone weight. (b) INTENSIVE USE OF THE MOLLUSK FISHERY at La Riera is reflected in this graph, which shows an average of the maximum diameter of the two limpet species whose shells are found in the cave. Whereas some of the decrease in size reflects the exploitation of the smaller limpet species starting in Magdalenian times, part of it is probably also due to overfishing.

late glacial onwards, plants, and fish, which although mobile, could be taken by net or line from static locations such as river banks and coasts. One other static resource that almost certainly became more important during the last deglaciation was honey, the main sweetener before the use of cane and sugar-beet in recent times. Although this has left no direct evidence, paintings from this period in southern Spain clearly show people collecting honey (e.g. Dams and Dams, 1977). One other important change would have been the increased availability of wood after 10 000 b.p. This would have meant first that fuel was more easily available (although perhaps required in lesser amounts for keeping warm) and secondly, that wood could be used more commonly for making artefacts.

It could be argued from continuities in the importance of red deer, in lithic traditions and site usage, that changes in subsistence strategies in southern Europe between the late Pleistocene and early Holocene were only minor. This is perhaps an over-simplification, however, and may underestimate the role of static resources after 13 000–10 000 b.p. As argued in the previous chapter, one consequence of the technological innovations after 30 000 years ago was that only part of a subsistence group needed to hunt, and thus manpower could be diverted to other activities such as fur-trapping, maintaining tool-kits at base, and preserving food. When — as during the glacial maximum — most food was derived from one or two animal resources, most of a group need not have been directly involved in food-procurement. However, once shellfish, plant foods, fish and honey became available, not only was the range of food resources widened, but those not needed for hunting could also have contributed to the food supply by foraging. If we can return to a point made already (p.55 ff.), static resources tend to be dependable and easily located, and also help to lower the energy costs of obtaining other foods such as small mammals, crustacea, insects and reptiles. We might thus expect that a larger proportion of subsistence groups at this time were engaged directly in obtaining food than when most was derived from the hunting of large mammals. In this context, it is perhaps significant that Spanish rock art seems to show males hunting deer, but women gathering honey.

The most vexing question here is how to estimate the dietary importance of fish, shellfish and plant foods in different areas between 16 000 and 8000 b.p. Although their importance is likely to have risen almost universally in this period, it is currently impossible to tell by how much. As noted already, the numbers of fish and mammal bones in an assemblage cannot be directly compared. Nor, unfortunately, can the numbers of shells and mammal remains, since the latter may represent

joints of meat and not entire carcasses. However, as Bailey's (1975, 1978)
work has shown, shellfish were much less important than the numbers of
their shells in middens would imply; on his estimates, one red deer
carcass represents the calorific equivalent of over 50 000 oysters, and
shellfish may have provided no more than 10% of the total annual diet of
coastal groups along the Atlantic coast in the early Holocene. Certainly
in northern Spain, shellfish do not seem to have been sufficiently

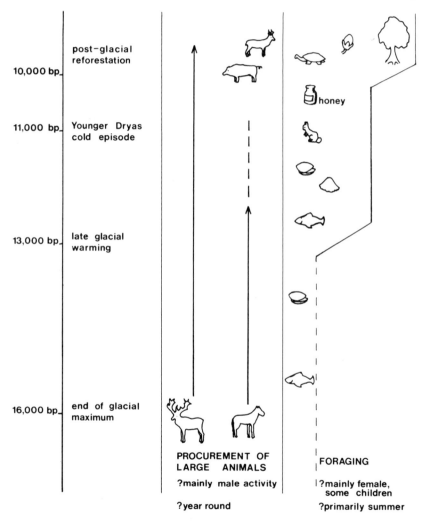

Fig. 19: Summary of subsistence trends in southern Europe during the last
deglaciation.

important to have warranted the abandonment of inland settlements in favour of coastal locations. So far as plant foods are concerned, our knowledge of pre-neolithic plant husbandry in Europe is so derisory that we have only the vaguest notion of what types were eaten, and even less idea of their importance. The issue will perhaps be resolved only by trace element and isotopic analyses of human skeletons (see Box 2). Meanwhile, it would seem a reasonable supposition that although red deer increased its proportional representation in faunal assemblages from southern European sites between 13 000 and 8000 b.p., mammals as a group became less important as a source of food.

The increase in the availability of fish and shellfish from the late glacial onwards, and the rise in plant and mammal biomass after 10 000 b.p. may also have had social consequences that extended beyond the individual subsistence group. One is that groups may have become larger, or have required smaller annual territories than before; either possibility could have locally increased population densities. Another is that where static resources were important, the location of groups throughout the year could have been more predictable, and thus mating networks easier to maintain. The demise of cave art, once seen as irrefutable proof of post-glacial degeneration and impoverishment, may have been more a case of shelving a redundant technology if, as Gamble (1980) suggests, its main function was as a means of communication between widely scattered and highly mobile groups in the same mating network. (An alternative explanation is that the rise of foraging removed much of the mystique associated with hunting, since almost anyone could feed him/herself in favourable circumstances.)

In conclusion, the transition from glacial to interglacial conditions in southern Europe may have been accompanied by changes in the way food procuring was organized. In particular, the harvesting of static resources, perhaps by women and children, may have provided a substantial part of the diet during the summer, and thus have complemented the hunting strategies developed after 30 000 b.p. (see Fig. 19), and discussed in the previous chapter. Although the importance of foraging must remain unclear until the dietary significance of fish, shellfish and plants is clarified, it could easily have been overlooked by focussing attention upon the hunting of one of two large animal resources that are easily visible in the archaeological record.

7. The Last Deglaciation and Its Consequences in Northern Europe

Abstract

This chapter first divides the archaeological evidence of northern Europe into two phases. The first began in the late glacial, and resulted in the recolonization of the North European Plain, Denmark, southern England, the Alps and the Pyrenees; the second was largely post-glacial, and witnessed the colonization of Ireland, northern England, Scotland and most of Scandinavia. The second part of the chapter looks at the main types of subsistence economies, and how these can be studied. It ends by noting our woeful ignorance over the role of plant foods, and whether or not these societies were food extractors or food producers.

As long as man has inhabited Europe, he has probably moved north at the end of each glaciation into areas previously near or under ice sheets. Unfortunately, with the exception of the 200 000 year old occupation of Pontnewydd in Wales (Chapter 3) and some fallow deer bones from the last interglacial that were dredged out of Copenhagen harbour (Chapter 4), there is little trace of these earlier movements. Thus, whilst the Mesolithic of north-west Europe is probably only the most recent colonization of these parts, it is unique in being the only one recorded in detail. Its uniqueness is further enhanced in that it also represents the only time that *Homo sapiens sapiens* has had to adjust to the onset of interglacial conditions in northern Europe.

Attitudes to the Mesolithic have altered enormously over the years. At one time, it was seen as little short of a human catastrophe: late glacial societies, living in a world where large herds of reindeer amply satisfied their food requirements, and visibility was uninterrupted across a largely treeless landscape, suddenly found themselves engulfed in thick forests in which the occasional red deer could sometimes be glimpsed; or were hemmed in on the shoreline, ekeing out a wretched existence on limpets. So overcome were they supposed to have been by post-glacial depression that their artists could do little more than daub a few pebbles. Decline, depopulation, degeneration and impoverishment were all terms applied to these hunters who had fallen on hard times, and who supposedly felt only unbounded relief when the sound of bleating sheep and rustling wheat heralded the arrival of the Neolithic. These days, we are less inclined to regard the Mesolithic as a Dark Age, interposed between the rugged artistic splendour of the late Palaeolithic and the secure domesticity of the Neolithic. Perhaps the greatest triumph of mesolithic studies over the last 40 years has been to demonstrate how successfully these societies adapted to the environmental changes at the end of the last glaciation. The notion of the affluent hunter-gatherer society, with its low labour requirements and an adequate diet, has further led us (perhaps more than is warranted) to seeing these communities as secure, satiated with venison, pork, oysters and a profusion of plant foods, and with no incentive to abandon their way of life for agriculture.

Although still widely used, the term "mesolithic" has lost most of its former chronological, typological and economic definitions, and now has little value, apart from its convenience as a label. Its previous distinctiveness from the late Palaeolithic has become blurred since the discoveries that microliths, shell middens and dogs are common to both, and that—as noted before (Chapter 6)—both took place during the most recent deglaciation. As the "mesolithic" way of life continued in many parts of northern Europe long after the inception of the Neolithic (see e.g. Zvelebil, 1978), contrasts between the two in terms of hunting versus farming are of dubious value.

A more useful local definition of what the Mesolithic represents is that it is part of the process of the recolonization of northern Europe by communities reliant upon traditional resources (as defined earlier, p.20). This process began in the late glacial, continued well into the Holocene, and in some areas was not significantly interrupted until the appearance of novel resources in the last millennium. It can be broadly divided into two phases, one late glacial and the other early holocene.

I. PHASE I: LATE GLACIAL EXPANSION

This phase began in the late glacial warming, and resulted in the colonization of much of northern France, the North European Plain, Denmark and northern England, as well as the higher parts of the Alps, the Pyrenees and Moravia. The colonization of these areas was closely tied to changes in the distribution of both terrestrial and marine resources. On land, the northward dispersal of animals such as reindeer, elk, horse and perhaps mammoth was probably the major incentive for the expansion of settlement into northern Europe during the late glacial. In coastal areas, such as western Norway and the shores of the Baltic, however, it was probably the marine resources—such as various whales and seals—that provided the main subsistence base. First, the terrestrial evidence.

When temperatures began to rise in western Europe some 13 000 years ago, there is little indication of human activity north of a line running from the Paris basin to the southern edge of the North European Plain as far east as Poland (Fig. 20). North of the Massif Central, there are no dated lower magdalenian sites, and very little material that can be assigned to this period on typological grounds (Hemingway, 1980).

However, there are two sites that are problematic, in that they lie well to the north of what appears to have been the main area of settlement, and have been dated to the cold interval between the glacial maximum and the late glacial warming. The first is Paviland in South Wales, where Dean Buckland exhumed a skeleton in 1823, and pronounced it to be the remains of a Roman scarlet lady, since the skeleton was covered by red ochre and the site lay near a Roman camp. However, a radiocarbon date of 18 460 ± 340 b.p. (Oakley, 1980:22) on the femur and tibia shows it to be one of the most elaborate upper palaeolithic burials yet discovered; the skeleton is, in fact, that of a 25-year old male. The second site is Hallines, near the Pas de Calais, where a mammoth skeleton was found, dated to 16 000 ± 300 b.p., and associated with large numbers of burins (Agache, 1971).

Both sites could be dismissed by special pleading. For example, the radiocarbon date from Paviland could be too young; alternatively, the man may have been buried at Paviland 18 000 years ago, but have died elsewhere. It is, however, stretching credulity to its limits to suggest that he was buried some 600 km north of where he died. So far as Hallines is concerned, the mammoth found there could have died 16 000 years ago, but have been re-exposed later and quarried for its ivory during the late glacial warning, as suggested by Jacobi (1980). However, unless the mammoth was buried very shortly after death, its ivory would have

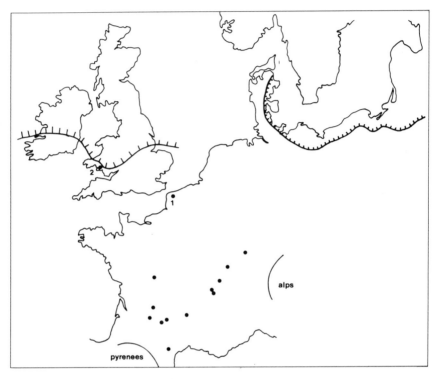

Fig. 20: Distribution of European sites between 18-14 000 b.p. (based on Jacobi, 1980). Note the rarity of archaeological sites north of the Paris Basin. Key: 1 Hallines; 2 Paviland; ⌐⌐⌐⌐ ice-front at c. 18 000 b.p.

exfoliated and been unsuitable for working at a later date (see e.g. Behrensmeyer, 1978).

Both sites might be explained more satisfactorily in terms of ivory-collecting. As is evident from the large numbers of carefully worked beads, bracelets, points and other items, ivory was a highly valued commodity in the Upper Palaeolithic. As commented before (p.54), mammoths were probably rare because of their high feeding requirements. In western Europe, they also seem to have lived in areas unoccupied by man, and close to the margins of ice sheets; hence the concentration of their remains in Denmark, the Alps and north-west Siberia (Berglund *et al.*, 1976). Consequently, ivory may have been collected in western Europe on trips beyond the area of habitual settlement. At Hallines, the large numbers of burins (46%) and the absence of butchering tools imply that the carcass was not used for its meat but for its

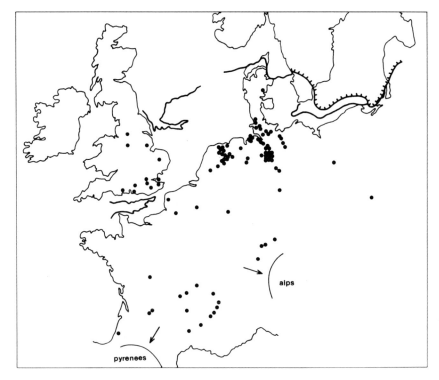

Fig. 21: Distribution of archaeological sites between 14-12 000 b.p. (based on Jacobi, 1980).
Arrows indicate recolonization of the Alps and Pyrenees.

ivory. The same may also be true of Paviland. First, the corpse was buried with a bracelet, pendant and 40-50 polished rods of ivory; secondly, at the time of burial, the cave was used as an ivory workshop as the pendant could be fitted back onto part of a mammoth skull found in the cave (Jacobi, 1980:31). As Paviland was then only 6 km from the edge of the ice sheet, it was also in the type of area where mammoth would have lived. In view of the hardships involved, ivory procurement by a 25-year old male is also entirely reasonable. The Paviland male may thus represent an individual who lived far to the south, but who died whilst on an ivory-collecting expedition near the ice margins during the summer. Other ivory procurement sites may be those of Diuktai in northern Siberia (Wilkinson, 1975:44), and Praz Roudet, La Croze and La Columbière in the Alps (Berglund *et al.*, 1976), all of which contain large numbers of ivory fragments and lay near the edges of ice sheets. If so, it may be necessary to distinguish between areas of late palaeolithic *habitual* settlement and those visited *occasionally* for specific purposes. One intriguing implication of this argument is that areas such as northern France and southern Britain would have been known about before the late glacial warming, even if they were unoccupied. Thus, when these regions were colonized in the late glacial warming, expansion was not necessarily into a *terra incognita*.

The expansion of human settlement that had occurred by the time the late glacial warming was drawing to a close some 12 000 years ago can be seen from the distribution of archaeological sites shown in Fig. 21; the chronological patterning is shown in Table 10. In northern France, late magdalenian sites are common from Brittany to the Belgian frontier, and eastwards into northern Germany. The well known sites of Meiendorf and Stellmoor show that man was in the Hamburg area by 12 300 years ago. He had probably also reached Denmark by this time, although the evidence is tenuous; one of his favourite prey species, reindeer, had already moved in (evidenced by a skeleton at Villestofte, indirectly dated to *ca.* 12 400 b.p.), and a projectile point of the same age has been found at Hvejsel (Clark, 1975:93). As is shown by Bromme and other sites (Becker, 1971), man was definitely present in Denmark between 11 800 and 11 000 b.p. (i.e. in Allerød times), and was thus almost certainly in the Hamburg region as well, despite the present lack of sites from this period in that area. Further east in Poland, the sites of Calowanie III and Widry Welikie I, both dated to the Allerød, show that man had also colonized this area by the time that birch had migrated into this part of the North European Plain (Schild, 1976).

The British evidence is less satisfactory as it is not always clear whether the artefacts in cave deposits are contemporaneous with or later than the bones of animals in the same layer and dated by ^{14}C. For this reason, Jacobi (1980) was inclined to doubt whether man was in Britain until the late glacial warming was well advanced. However, conclusive evidence that man was in northern Britain by 11 500 b.p. comes from an elk skeleton found near Blackpool in which several barbed projectile points were embedded, and which is dated to midway through the Allerød; presumably man was in southern England at an earlier date.

It is not known when reindeer and man first entered northern Norway, nor is it clear from what direction(s) they came. As will be seen shortly, reindeer are unlikely to have migrated from the south, and may instead have arrived from the White Sea region to the east. Since arctic ice reached its maximum extent around 10 000 b.p. (Boulton, 1979), this route might not have been feasible until holocene times. As is known from Odner's (1966) work in the Varangerfjord around the North Cape, both man and reindeer were present by 5500 b.p., Komsa sites in the area

Table 10: The late glacial colonization of the Alps, Pyrenees and Moravia.

Region	Site	Date (b.p.)	Assemblage	Fauna
Alpes du Nord/Jura	La Croze	14 440 ± 260 14 850 ± 350	Magdalenian	Reindeer, mammoth, horse, bison, *Megaceros*
	La Columbière DI	13 390 ± 300	Magdalenian	Mammoth, woolly rhino
	Abri du Calvaire	13 450 ± 300 12 970 ± 300	Magdalenian IV Magdalenian III	Arctic fox and hares, horses, reindeer, birds
	Pierre-Châtel III	12 980 ± 240	Magdalenian	Mammoth, reindeer, ibex, birds
	Freydières	11 380 ± 180	?Azilian	Marmot, ibex, red deer; no reindeer
Switzerland	Moosbühl I	10 300 ± 180	Magdalenian	
Pyrenees	Fontanet	13 810 ± 740	Middle Magdalenian	Reindeer, bovids
	Le Portel	12 760 ± 170	Middle Magdalenian	Ibex, reindeer
	La Vache 4	12 850 ± 60	Upper Magdalenian	Ibex, reindeer
	Les Églises	11 800 ± 500	Upper Magdalenian	
Moravia	Brno	14 450 ± 90	Late Gravettian	Mammoth, horse, reindeer
	Kulna 6		Magdalenian	Reindeer dominant
	Kulna 5		Magdalenian	Horse dominant; *Bos* and red deer
	Kulna 4	11 470 ± 105	Magdalenian	Roe deer, elk, pig; no reindeer
	Kulna 3	10 070 ± 85	Epi-Magdalenian	Roe deer, elk, pig; no reindeer

Sources: Desbrosse, 1976; Phillips, 1980; Clottes, 1976; Valoch, 1980.

have not been dated absolutely, but some may be up to 8000 years old. One interesting feature of the late glacial expansion of man and reindeer impinges on the notion that man followed reindeer northwards as the ice sheets retreated. To some extent, this is only partly true, for reindeer colonized three areas that remained uninhabited by man. The first was Norway. At Blomvag, near Bergen, reindeer bones that do not seem to have been derived from earlier deposits have been found in contexts dated to *ca.* 12 400 b.p. As Norway would then have been separated from Denmark by at least 100 km of open sea, and previously entirely covered by ice, this find raises the question of how reindeer managed to make the crossing. Although Indrelid (1975) has suggested that reindeer migrated across sea-ice in winter, an unforced migration of this distance over ice seems improbable. An alternative is that some were carried by drifting ice during the summer, or entered Norway via southern Sweden, having earlier made a short crossing over sea-ice from Denmark. The other two areas occupied in the late glacial by reindeer but not man were Scotland and Ireland (Lacaille, 1954; Stuart, 1977); the latter was probably reached by a land bridge across the northern Irish Sea. This evidence would seem to suggest that man was reluctant to colonize areas where conditions were unduly severe, even though food resources were potentially available; although often omitted from discussions of late glacial economies, fuel was probably at least as important to man as food.

II. OCEANIC EVIDENCE

The northward expansion of reindeer and other cold-tolerant animals in the late glacial was paralleled by equally major changes in the distribution of seals and whales. Although their range at the height of the glacial maximum is unknown, they were able to migrate southwards into the North Sea between 13 000 and 10 000 b.p. (Fredén, 1975), presumably after the British and Scandinavian ice sheets had separated. Several other finds of late glacial seals have also been made around the coast of Jutland (Møhl, 1970). Although undated, innumerable engravings of seal and whale along the Norwegian coast, as well as the presence of their bones in coastal middens, show the importance of these sea mammals as food resources since conditions in the Norwegian Sea reached their present state, some 6000 years ago.

III. PHASE II: EARLY HOLOCENE EXPANSION

This phase was marked by the expansion of red and roe-deer, aurochs and pig across land, and of fish, shellfish and seal into and sometimes beyond areas of coastal waters colonized in the previous phase. Man also extended his range: into Ireland, Scotland, highland Wales and England, coastal Norway, northern Sweden and Finland.

In the southern part of the area covered in this chapter, this expansion began as the first phase was drawing to a close in northern Europe. Its first stages are difficult to monitor. This is partly because there are few early holocene open-air sites that contain bone and artefacts that are clearly associated with each other and dated. A second problem is how to interpret cave sequences where the two are associated. In south-west France, changes in the frequencies of large animal species represented in cave deposits containing palaeolithic artefacts have been used primarily for palaeoclimatic reconstructions (see e.g. Laville *et al.*, 1980). This type of faunal sequence can provide a detailed climatic account only if caves were always used for the same purpose and in the same season by groups that practised a "catch-as-catch-can" existence, and killed whatever they happened to encounter within a uniform radius of their cave. For reasons discussed in Chapter 5, it is unlikely that this type of subsistence was prevalent in south-west France in the late Palaeolithic. At times, it is obvious that the function of a cave has changed; for example, the extremely large numbers of marmot skeletons at the cave of Freydières (Bouchud and Desbrosse, 1973) probably means that the cave was used at that time as a fur-trapping base, but not that the area was for a time overrun by marmots. For any cave assemblage one has to take account of the probability that the season and type of use of a cave changed through time, especially if the climate was also changing.

In any case, the rate at which red deer replaced reindeer as the main food resource in northern Europe depended only partly upon climatic factors; as noted already (pp.112–114) the social behaviour of the animals themselves, as well as vegetational changes, were also important. In this instance, the replacement of "arctic" by "temperate" resources during the last deglaciation would have been a complex process as the animals involved can tolerate a very wide range of conditions. This is particularly true of red deer, whose present distribution overlaps with that of reindeer in Norway and gazelle in Iran. Thus it is not surprising that red deer was represented at Remouchamps, dated to the Younger Dryas, in an assemblage dominated by reindeer (Bouchud, 1974); conversely, reindeer probably persisted in parts of France for some time after red deer had colonized more northerly areas.

Table 11 gives some idea of the complexity of this changeover in south-west France. At Pont D'Ambon, red deer formed over 80% of the faunal assemblage between 12 000 and 13 000 b.p., whilst reindeer formed a similarly high proportion at the nearby site of La Madeleine. Later sites show reindeer, horse, red deer and pig in the same area during the

Table 11: Faunal changes in south-west France during the last deglaciation (based on data in Laville *et al.*, 1980; Delpech 1968, 1970).

Date (b.p.)	Flageolet II	Madeleine	Pont D'Ambon	Gare du Couze	Faurelie	Duruthy
9 000			82% red deer; roe +, horse +, pig +			
10 000			9 830 ± 130 level 3a	10 900 ± 310 level C, reindeer +, red deer +, pig +		
11 000						11 150 ± 220 level 3, 3a reindeer 13% red deer 60%, 3b reindeer 26% red deer 47%
12 000		12 640 ± 260 level F reindeer +++, 12 750 ± 240 level G reindeer +++, 12 970 ± 190 level I horse = reindeer	12 130 ± 160 level 3b red deer 89%, roe deer +, pig +, 12 840 ± 920 level 4	12 430 ± 320 level H reindeer +++	11 780 ± 180 reindeer +, horse +	
13 000		13 890 ± 300 level J				13 510 ± 120, 13 840 ± 120 level 4 reindeer ++, horse ++, *Bos/Bison* ++, red deer +
14 000	14 110 ± 690 reindeer +++, Level IX red deer +, ibex +, saiga +, chamois +					
15 000	15 250 ± 300					

+ present   ++ common   +++ abundant

following millennium. It was probably not until after the Younger Dryas that reindeer died out in this region.

After 10 000 years ago, the rate at which temperate animals colonized new areas was rapid. By 9500 years ago, red and roe-deer, aurochs and pig were as far north as Star Carr in northern England, and probably Denmark; shortly after the same time, red deer and pig had reached Ireland. We can safely assume that territories further south were filled at an earlier date.

This expansion was accompanied by the isolation and often local extinction of some of the species that had been involved in the first phase of expansion. Reindeer that had colonized upland areas in the late glacial were isolated on islands of high ground such as the Alps, Pyrenees and Massif Central, and probably died out shortly after the end of the Younger Dryas. In southern Norway, reindeer probably retreated to the high plateau of the Hardangervidda, where flint scatters more than 8000 years old have been found. Although no bones are present, the most plausible explanation for man in this area is that he went there to hunt reindeer once lowland areas became forested (Indrelid, 1975). Reindeer probably left Ireland soon after the end of the Younger Dryas, and may have died out at around that time in Scotland; claims that reindeer persisted there until 1200 A.D. seem to have arisen through the misidentification of some red deer bones (Leavy, 1979:27).

A similar fate befell other animals. Horse is thought to have persisted into the early Holocene in Denmark and Britain, as it is present in some Danish maglemosian assemblages (Brinch-Peterson, 1973), and at Thatcham, *ca.* 9500 b.p. (Stuart, 1977). In the latter instance, however, the horse remains may be intrusive (Carter, 1975), and thus horse may already have died out in the late glacial. In France, horse lasted well into the Holocene; for example, it is recorded at Gramari in south France until 7700 b.p. (Poulain, 1971). In Britain, elk declined with the expansion of deciduous forest at the onset of the Atlantic period, but survived for some time thereafter. Its last, if somewhat undignified, record in this country is via one of its droppings in a Fenland peat deposit dated to *ca.* 3300 b.p. (Godwin, 1978:165). In Zealand, it had disappeared by 7000 b.p. along with aurochs (Aaris-Sørensen, 1980). Similarly, the Giant Irish Elk is not recorded after the Allerød in France (Bouchud, 1965) or the British Isles (Gould, 1980); however, it was present at Remouchamps in Belgium at *ca.* 10 250 b.p. (Bouchud, 1974). Finally, the ringed seal (*Pusa hispida*), which probably colonized the Baltic soon after it was opened to the North Sea, later became trapped, and is now confined to the northern and eastern parts only.

Two areas whose post-glacial development stand out as unusual are worth noting. The first is Sweden and the eastern Baltic, where elk, rather than red deer, became the dominant ungulate, presumably because of its ability to overwinter in boreal forest and in deep snow by feeding on twigs and bark (Welinder, 1975). It thus increased in this area, whilst declining in Britain, Denmark and the North European Plain. The other exception is Ireland, where the only large mammals to have colonized it in the early Holocene were pig and red deer (Woodman, 1978).

The extension of man's distribution into north-west Europe during this second phase of colonization can be only cautiously recorded, and is summarized in Fig. 22. In Ireland, the earliest settlement now dates from

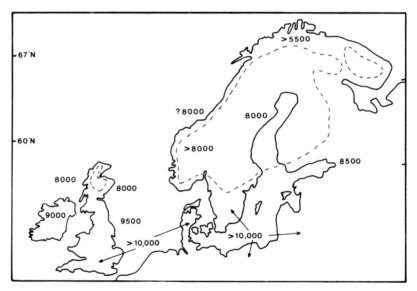

Fig. 22: The recolonization of northern Europe, 11-8000 b.p. The dotted line indicates extent of ice-sheet at c. 10 000 b.p.

9000 b.p. (Ryan, 1980: Woodman, 1978), and in northern Britain, to *ca.* 9500 b.p. or slightly earlier (Jacobi, 1978). At present, the earliest date from mainland Scotland is one of 8000 b.p. from area 46 at Morton, where most of the occupation has been dated to *ca.* 6000 b.p. (Coles, 1971). A date of 6200 b.p. from the island of Jura is currently the earliest indication of man's presence in the Western Isles (Mercer, 1974). Coastal Norway remains enigmatic, as no ^{14}C dates are available for its earliest occupation, but may have been settled by 8000 b.p. by people exploiting whales, seals and fish. Similar dates have now been obtained from northern Sweden (Broadbent, 1978). The land which was emerging from beneath the Baltic and eventually became Finland was occupied by 8300 b.p., probably by people moving in from Russia (Clark, 1975:221).

IV. OCEANIC EVIDENCE

The expansion of marine and freshwater resources during this second phase is at present difficult to document. The easiest method is to record their earliest occurrences in archaeological contexts. However, the date at which they were first eaten need not, of course, coincide with their first appearance in an area. The record is additionally incomplete as many coastal areas have been submerged or eroded over the last 8000 years. Species of shellfish harvested in northern Spain 13 000 years ago (see previous chapter) were in the English Channel by 7000 b.p. (Palmer, 1976), and eaten at Oronsay in the Hebrides by 6000 years ago (Mellars and Wilkinson, 1980). The earliest middens around the Baltic also date from roughly this period. There, subtle changes in the salinity and surface temperatures of the water must have considerably affected the distribution of shellfish. As the presence of shell middens in Zealand 6000 years ago show, the Litorina Sea was at times sufficiently saline for mussels and oysters, which are nowadays confined to the Limfjord in northern Jutland. The harp and grey seal seem, however, to have found the Baltic inhabitable throughout most of the Holocene, and probably colonized it soon after it became an inlet of the North Sea.

Regrettably little is known of the rate at which fish colonized the lakes and rivers of a newly deglaciated Europe. One interesting insight into this otherwise murky pool is that fish had probably not reached the northern parts of England when the first occupants of Star Carr camped by the lake (Wheeler, 1978).

V. SUBSISTENCE AND DEMOGRAPHY

In recent years, the literature on late glacial and early holocene societies has grown phenomenally, and no attempt will be made here to evaluate more than a small fraction of it. Instead, some of the main issues and problems of this material will be discussed, as well as some of the approaches that have been developed to overcome them.

In general, the simplest prehistoric subsistence strategies are those in which almost all food was derived from one or two animal species. For this reason, the subsistence of the late glacial and the far north of Europe is usually more easily modelled than that of the Holocene and more southerly areas. We can thus begin with some relatively straightforward examples which attempt to integrate excavated faunal data, using the season of death of a species identified in an archaeological context, and comparing it to modern data for its behaviour and favoured habitats. The exploitation of reindeer in the late glacial of northern Europe provides a good example of this approach.

As is clear from numerous excavations, reindeer was by far the commonest resource represented in late glacial sites on the North European Plain. This animal is migratory, and can cover up to 800 km between its winter and summer pasture. In winter, reindeer seek areas where snow cover is thin and easily scraped by their hooves so that they can graze; in summer, they try to seek relief from insects by migrating (Spiess, 1979; Sturdy, 1975). Fortunately for the prehistorian, reindeer can be sexed from their antlers, and the time of year they were killed reckoned from whether these were shed or unshed.

According to Sturdy (1975), the vast majority of reindeer at Ahrensburg were adult males; most were killed in the autumn, and a few in the spring. This pattern differed from that in southern Germany, where the faunal data—although often of poor quality—showed little evidence for winter occupation amongst late magdalenian groups. Sturdy thus argued that human groups migrated with the reindeer between these two areas, and used an ahrensburgian assemblage for their winter activities, but a magdalenian one for different activities during the summer. A few groups may have moved north in the summer into Jutland to hunt seal. Each autumn they would kill a large number of reindeer in northern Germany and store the meat for winter consumption, and then a few more in spring just before the herds began their southwards migration. Sturdy further suggested that during the summer, reindeer were not killed *en masse*, but as and when required. From studying the location of sites in southern Germany, he suggested that those animals eaten in the summer were isolated in small valley basins and killed when needed; those that were to be slaughtered in northern Germany later in the year were contained in larger adjacent basins where they could be kept under observation but otherwise undisturbed, in what he termed an extended territory, i.e. an area containing resources associated with a human group but rarely visited.

The useful features on his model are first, that it provides a plausible explanation of the ahrensburgian sites in northern Germany, and secondly, the notion of the extended territory is consistent with the way reindeer are managed in present-day Greenland (Sturdy, 1972). Whether the ahrensburgian sites of northern Germany and the magdalenian ones further south were part of the same economic system seems debatable. The two are not always contemporaneous, and the evidence that southern Germany was occupied only in the summer is open to alternative interpretations. The paucity of late glacial sites in Central Germany could be the result of inadequate survey, or high rates of erosion. Also, a site such as Gönnersdorf, one of the richest late glacial art sites, and only a little south of Cologne, seems an unlikely candidate for the type of ephemeral transit site that this area should, on his model contain (see Hahn, 1978). Finally, Burch (1972) voiced serious doubts as to whether human groups could follow reindeer on long-distance migrations. An alternative model might therefore be that the makers of ahrensburgian assemblages remained in north Germany year-round, and subsisted on preserved meat obtained during spring and autumn.

The types of subsistence strategies that may have characterized this area in the late glacial are shown diagrammatically in Fig. 23, which also shows the types of archaeological sites which should be found. So far, it

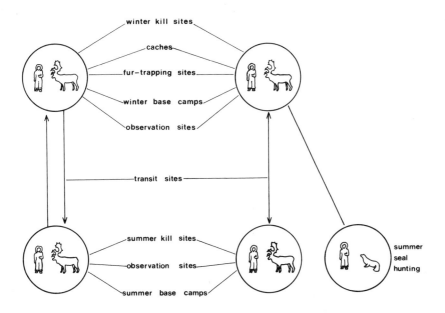

Fig. 23: Two models of late glacial reindeer economies in northern Europe.

would seem that only autumn and spring kill sites have been safely identified.

Similarly structured economies have been claimed from later contexts. One example is northern England during the eighth millennium b.p. (Clark, 1972; Jacobi, 1978). During the summer, red deer—commonly represented at Star Carr—probably grazed in the Pennines and Cleveland Hills where there would be little irritation from insects, and in winter moved into lower areas. Human groups may have spent the summer hunting red deer in the hills, and winter at low-lying sites such as Star Carr, living off red deer and other animals that were resident in the area throughout the year. On this model, Star Carr was occupied only during the winter, and the numerous small sites in the Pennines during the summer months. Alternatively, only part of a group (perhaps young males?) followed deer into the uplands during the summer, whilst the remainder stayed in the lowlands to hunt pig, elk and roe-deer (which have only small annual movements), and perhaps to exploit plant foods (see Fig. 24).

These examples highlight three problems that are not easily resolved. The first is the evidence for seasonal occupation. If a site (such as Star

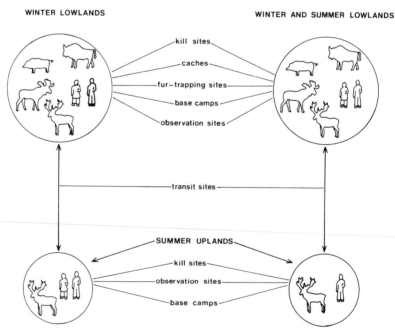

Fig. 24: Two models of early holocene subsistence in northern England.

Carr) is known to have been occupied at one time of the year, it does not necessarily follow that it was unoccupied at other times, but simply that specific evidence for these times of the year is not available. Secondly, even when there is convincing evidence for summer habitation in one area, and winter occupation in an adjacent region, it need not follow that all members of a subsistence group moved from one to the other. Thirdly, the function of sites within the annual subsistence round is difficult to establish from on-site information. For example, the well known site of Star Carr has been variously interpreted as a winter base camp (Clark, 1972), a winter industrial site (Jacobi, 1978), a winter ambush site (Andresen *et al.*, 1981), or a summer tanning site (Pitts, 1979). For these reasons, the data may be equally well explained by a variety of models.

Identifying systems of resource procurement becomes considerably more complicated when there is no clear contrast between areas of winter and summer occupation, and where there is a wide variety of potential resources besides mammals, such as shellfish, fish, birds and plants. At first sight, the main reason for these difficulties is simply that the dietary evidence is very heavily biased towards mammals or shellfish. For example, it was only through a meticulous sieving programme that the Oronsay middens in northern Scotland were found to be largely composed of fish bone and not limpets, although the latter were far more conspicuous (Mellars and Wilkinson, 1980). One sorry implication of this discovery is that in some areas the notion of shell middens rather than "fish middens" may be an artefact of inadequate excavation techniques. A second point about middens is that they can easily give a false impression of the importance of shellfish relative to mammals. For example, a few bones of red deer dispersed through a midden could well be considered unimportant, but the meat of one individual may have represented the equivalent of 70 000 limpets (Bailey, 1978). As dogs were present in many mesolithic settlements, mammal bones may also have been preferentially destroyed through scavenging. Bird bones too are small and fragile, and often leave little trace archaeologically, or are missed by lack of sieving.

However, it is plant foods that present the greatest problems of differential preservation. In most cases, the only plant resources that are likely to be preserved archaeologically are those which require parching or roasting. For this reason, it is not surprising that the commonest plant food evidenced in mesolithic northern Europe is the hazel nut, the shells of which have been found in sites from Ireland to Finland. Evidence for the consumption of roots, tubers, rhizomes, leaves, fruit and fungi are always unlikely to be preserved except in the most exceptional circumstances.

However, even under ideal conditions of preservation, and even by using the best sieving and flotation techniques available, the major problem of investigating prehistoric diet is one of sample comparability; in other words, how does one estimate from the numbers or weight of plant and animal remains the relative importance of plant to animal resources? Because the two types of evidence are not comparable, it is impossible to tell from excavated data whether plant foods constituted 1% or 99% of the total diet consumed by the inhabitants of a prehistoric site.

For this reason, ecological models have been developed to estimate the productivity of the resources represented in a site, or potentially available to its inhabitants. On a continental scale, Clarke (1976) showed how plant resources could have provided a much greater biomass than herbivores. In one of the most stimulating of recent works on prehistoric subsistence, Jochim (1976) tried to estimate the importance of each type of resource potentially accessible to the inhabitants of mesolithic sites in Germany by ranking each in terms of its calorific value, abundance and predictability. This ingenious approach was perhaps the first serious attempt to assess the role of plant relative to animal resources in mesolithic European diets. It is, however, uncertain whether all the sites whose catchment areas he studied were base camps from which all potentially accessible resources were tapped. Others have tried smaller-scale models. Welinder (1978), for example, showed how types of finds and the location and number of sites in Scania changed through time, and compared these with known environmental changes. The resulting associations led him to suggest that the preferred areas for settlement changed from inland forest areas to shallow lakes, and finally to the coast.

However, when it comes to translating estimates of potential productivity into ones of actual yield, serious difficulties are encountered. First, there is a regrettable shortage of relevant data on the rates at which people can extract and process different types of resources. Ethnographic data, mainly from arid regions, have been stimulating in showing how plant gathering can supply more food per man/woman-hour than hunting, but these areas are usually poor in animal resources. As Hawkes and O'Connell (1981) point out, the role of plant foods in modern gatherer-hunter diets seems to fall where animal resources are more abundant, because the *total* expenditure of energy in obtaining and then processing plant foods is often greater than that in hunting and butchering animals. Thus it does not necessarily follow that plant foods would have been important in mesolithic Europe simply because they may have been abundant. A second problem is that many estimates of the productivity of plant and animal resources in early holocene Europe are based on the assumption that these communities lived in a "natural" environment, unaltered by man. Since hunter-gatherers can significantly raise the productivity of their surroundings, these views may be simplistic, and will be mentioned again shortly in the context of population pressure in late mesolithic northern Europe.

A third difficulty is that resources should not be considered individually, but collectively. This point may be shown by the role of shellfish. Although these seem to have contributed only a minor part to the overall annual diet (Bailey, 1975), their importance may have been enhanced by two factors. The first is that they could have had a "spin-off" effect, in that shellfish might not have formed much of the diet, but could have led to the harvesting of other resources nearby—such as coastal plants (including seaweed) and crustacea—which, when taken together, formed a significant part of the diet. Secondly, they may have been eaten by people who went to the coast in order to obtain enough fish to last several months, but required an easily obtainable food whilst fishing was in progress, or the catch was being processed.

Because of these various problems, early holocene economies in northern Europe can be modelled in several ways, and in most instances it is not yet possible to vindicate one by eliminating all others. Some of the main types that were probably practised are shown diagrammatically in Fig. 25. The first is the classic foraging model, whereby a group occupies several sites throughout the year, and obtains resources within a uniform distance of the site until they are depleted and less abundant than elsewhere. The next example shows a variation on this theme, in which a group is entirely sedentary and obtains all its resources locally from one location. The preconditions for this type of subsistence would clearly be that food was either available locally throughout the year, or of the type that could be stored, and that it was in higher concentrations than elsewhere so as to deter movement. Although rare, sedentary hunter-gatherers have been recorded ethnographically (as on the British Columbian coast); Rowley-Conwy (1981) has recently suggested that some groups in late mesolithic Denmark may have been largely sedentary and able to live year-round off fish, shellfish, plants and game. The other two examples involve a degree of aggregation in one season and dispersal in another. Finally, there is the type of logistic pattern mentioned in an earlier context (see Fig. 2).

The next few years are likely to see considerable progress in using archaeological data to test hypotheses on mesolithic subsistence that are based on ecological and ethnographic sources. Improvements in the recovery and analysis of dietary data from mesolithic sites, especially middens, have already been rapid. In addition to obtaining the necessary quantitative data on the precise composition of middens, the use of growth rings in otoliths and shells, and oxygen isotope analyses are likely to yield invaluable information on the time of year they were used. An alternative approach, developed by Bailey (1975) has been to estimate from the rate at which middens accumulated, the proportion of the total

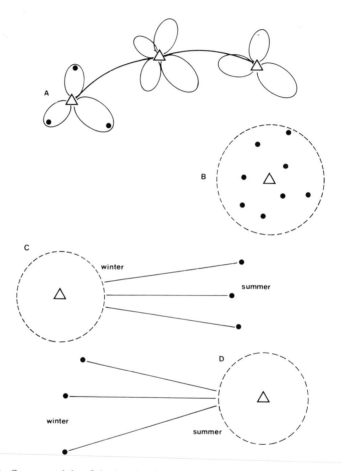

Fig. 25: Some models of the kinds of subsistence economies that may have been practised in early Holocene northern Europe.
Key: (a) "catch-as-catch can", using a series of base camps and associated ancillary sites; (b) year-round occupation of one site, and use of nearby ancillary sites; (c) winter aggregation at one site, and dispersal during the summer to several locations; (d) summer aggregation at one site, and dispersal during the winter to several locations.

annual diet that was provided by shellfish. His estimates that perhaps only 5–10% of the total diet came from this source may at last dispose of the notion of mesolithic strand-loopers whose lives were an interminable round of limpet-bashing.

A second and equally valuable source of data will come from studies of the size of sites, as well as of the size, type and spatial patterning of material contained in them. At present, the function of most mesolithic sites within the overall annual round of activities is obscure, especially when faunal material is not preserved. Analyses of the kind pioneered at Pincevent (Leroi-Gourhan and Brézillon, 1972) and since developed at Meer (Cahen and Keeley, 1980) have shown the detail that can be extracted from sites that would previously have been studied only in terms of their cultural affiliations.

One source of evidence that might become crucial in the next few years is human skeleton material. If ^{13}C and trace element analysis of this type of material can indicate what type of resources were eaten, it may at last be possible to evaluate the role of plant foods in the total annual diet. There may even be possibilities of investigating whether the type and quality of diet varied between different age and sex groups, as has been shown in North America (Lambert *et al.*, 1979). One preliminary study of the skeletons from the Danish site of Vedbaek (Tauber, 1981) suggests that fish constituted the largest proportion of the diet; the dietary remains from this site include fish, shellfish and large mammals.

VI. HUNTING AND GATHERING, AND FOOD PRODUCTION

One of the more unfortunate legacies of eighteenth and nineteenth century European observations of hunter-gatherers was that they practised a "catch-as-catch can" (Braidwood and Howe, 1960:1) or "parasitic" (Childe, 1958:34) existence that was wholly characterized by the extraction from the environment of whatever resources were required. In contrast, agriculturalists were food-producers, who invested labour and materials in raising the productivity of their environment. Food production and agriculture thus became synonyms, and very different from the food extraction of hunter-gatherers. This dichotomy between hunter-gatherers and farmers became applied to the European Mesolithic and Neolithic at a very early stage of enquiry.

It is highly unlikely that this distinction is valid today. In the first place, food production is a feature of many hunter-gatherer societies. Australian examples of fish-channels and fire-stick farming have already been noted (p.16), as have instances where plants were protected and transplanted. Another example, this time from New Guinea, is the capturing of young cassowaries and pigs, and rearing them in captivity until required for slaughter. Secondly, a large body of evidence from the British Mesolithic indicates that areas of woodland were cleared by burning (Mellars, 1976; Simmons and Innes, 1981). As these episodes are associated with human activity, the firing seems to have been deliberate, and done in order to increase the forage available to red deer (Simmons, 1979) or the plant foods eaten by man (Clarke, 1976). On much the same lines, Simmons and Dimbleby (1974) suggested that the high frequency of ivy pollen at Oakhanger resulted from the collection of this plant as winter fodder for deer.

This evidence can be interpreted in two ways. One is that it indicates attempts by mesolithic populations to increase the *productivity* of their environment, perhaps in response to population pressure. This argument is one that fits neatly with Cohen's (1977) hypothesis that agriculture was adopted in many parts of the world, as a common response to population pressure, by hunter-gatherers who were forced into more labour-intensive techniques to obtain the necessary amount of food. The second interpretation is that forest-clearance represents ways of improving the *predictability* of the environment. In winter, deer and pig would be attracted to localities where food was abundant, and so less time would be wasted in searching for them. In latitudes where days in winter are less than 8 hours long, the advantages of minimizing the time spent in locating game are obvious. The elusiveness of prey such as roe-deer is succinctly shown by the results of a roe-deer census some years ago in Denmark (Andersen, 1953). After 3 years of careful observation, the number of roe-deer was estimated at 70. When the forest was cleared by shooting, the actual number was 213.

Whatever the reasons for mesolithic forest clearance may have been, its practice has two implications for prehistorians. The first is that estimates of mesolithic population levels based on the productivity of a "natural" environment may be too low. The second is that the Neolithic is unlikely to mark the inception of food production in prehistoric Europe. This point is especially pertinent to the question of when cattle were first domesticated. As we shall see in the final chapter, neolithic cattle are often smaller than mesolithic ones, and classed as the domestic *Bos tauros* rather than the wild *Bos primigenius*. However, it is dangerous to assume that the size of these animals provides an automatic indication of how they were exploited. Mesolithic cattle could, for example, have been provided with fodder, or even tethered and maintained in areas of cleared woodland. A preference for smaller animals in the Neolithic may have arisen more from the ways human groups were organized than from the methods used to manage cattle. For example, small cattle may have been selected for if groups were divided into household units of production; small cattle present smaller problems when it comes to consuming a carcass. If, on the other hand, food was obtainable and consumed on a communal basis, large animals are desirable, since there is more meat to go round. In both cases, however, animals could have been maintained in artificial environments, been provided with fodder, and kept under human control.

8. The Expansion of Novel Resources: the Development of Food Production in South-East Europe

Abstract

The expansion of cereals and sheep over Europe after 8000 years ago is the main theme of this and the final chapter. This one considers the origin of agricultural settlements in south-east Europe. It is argued that these are unlikely to have been founded by Near Eastern colonists. Instead, they probably resulted from local developments involving the use of einkorn, barley, legumes and sheep, and from the immigration of emmer and bread-wheat. These, it is suggested, could have dispersed into western Turkey and south-east Europe either naturally or through exchange networks, and without involving the movements of peoples.

Clark's (1978:1) comment that "there is a certain disadvantage in living in the same continent that invented prehistory . . . one has to put up with the aftermath of crude and often uncouth beginnings" is particularly applicable to the mesolithic–neolithic interface. This boundary, originally drawn on artefactual grounds, has been the most rigidly demarcated frontier in the whole of European prehistory, marking as it has for several decades the end of hunting and gathering societies in Europe and the beginnings of agriculture. Despite the realization over the past 20 years that the subsistence of prehistoric societies cannot be inferred from its technology alone, all too often the first appearance of pottery and polished stone in a region is still taken as automatic evidence that hunting and gathering had been replaced by farming.

This state of affairs can be traced back to the nineteenth century, when the difference between the Palaeolithic and Neolithic seemed so colossal that the former could never have given rise to the latter. When the Mesolithic was recognized in the 1890s, it was treated as little more than the scrag-end of the Palaeolithic; whilst it may have preceded the Neolithic, it no more contributed to the development of food production than did the aborigines towards the founding of Sydney. This outlook found its most influential expression in the writings of Childe. To him, the Mesolithic seemed a dark and gloomy cul-de-sac from which the inhabitants of Europe could not escape, and the Neolithic the point at which European civilization could begin. His explanation of how this great leap forward was accomplished rested on the assumption that agriculture developed in the Near East, but not in Europe. Supposedly, the village farming communities of the Near East grew rapidly, and produced a surplus population. Rather than absorb this by intensifying their food production, they initiated the agricultural colonization of the virgin lands of the Balkans. Agricultural settlers thus pushed ever deeper into the European hinterland, founded new settlements, appropriated the lands of the aboriginal (mesolithic) populations, and developed as they did so their own cultural traditions. Within only a few millennia, the frontier of farming advanced from the Aegean to the North Sea, and terminated the hunting-gathering way of life that had prevailed since Europe was first occupied.

Once the idea of colonization had colonized explanations of the European Neolithic, it successfully obstructed the immigration of other models. With hindsight, its pervasiveness is hardly surprising. In the first place, it was a chronological necessity, since the only way that the early neolithic cultures of Europe could be drilled into respectable order was by postulating that they were all agricultural and ultimately of Near Eastern origin. Secondly, this model mirrored very faithful nineteenth century experiences of both agricultural colonization and the hunting-gathering way of life. To most prehistorians of the last century, hunting and gathering seemed a crude, barbaric, precarious and parasitic way of living; in contrast, agriculture represented security, prosperity, and the opportunities for investment and leisure that ultimately led to civilization. The hunter-gatherers of nineteenth century Australia or southern Africa seemed completely incapable of making that jump themselves; whilst they might eventually benefit from European contact (assuming, of course, that they survived it), they seemed utterly incapable of raising themselves above their brute status. So too in prehistoric Europe; because local mesolithic populations were assumed to have been hunter-gatherers, they could never have developed agriculture of their own accord, and therefore it must have been introduced from the Near East by a similar process of colonization.

These views are no longer tenable in this post-colonial era. As has been apparent since the *Man the Hunter* symposium (Lee and DeVore, 1968), the hunting and gathering way of life is not always the brutish nightmare it seemed to many nineteenth century observers, but is often secure and easy. In contrast, it is agriculture that is frequently hazardous, time-consuming and hard work. Investigations of the prehistory of extant hunter-gatherers have also shown that these peoples are not "living fossils", but have often changed their mode of subsistence, and sometimes even developed their own kinds of food production. We can also appreciate more readily than could prehistorians of Childe's generation that the colonization of much of the world by European powers in the eighteenth and nineteenth centuries occurred under vastly different demographic, economic and technological conditions from those prevailing eight millennia previously.

Nevertheless, the colonization model proved so appealing (long after it was made redundant by ^{14}C dating) that it somehow managed to survive, despite the fact that it lacked any obvious means of support. Even by the late 1950s, there was not the slightest trace of any neolithic settlement in Turkey, from which these colonists supposedly came, apart from the site of Mersin on the south coast. Childe (1958:46) himself was forced into making what was probably his most ingenuous statement, that "The migrants who came hither (to the Balkans) have left no trace in the archaeological record". What these invisible immigrants brought with them was also unclear. Forty years after Childe first suggested that the early Neolithic of south-east Europe was the product of agricultural colonization, there was scarcely any evidence that early neolithic settlements in this region were agricultural. As recently as 1975, Barker (1975b:102) pointed out that "the vast majority of sites with early neolithic pottery in the Balkans are entirely without economic data of any kind, so that . . . it is impossible to equate 'neolithic' with 'early farming' or anything else at the moment". Evidence that mesolithic sites in the Balkans were entirely those of hunters and gatherers has been equally unimpressive, for "there is virtually no evidence of the mesolithic 'economy' outside of the Danube gorges and the mountains" (Tringham, 1973:555). We can now, of course, add Franchthi, which is located at the southernmost tip of Greece, several hundred kilometres from early farming sites such as Argissa and Achilleon in the plains of northern

Thessaly. In large areas of central Europe, few mesolithic sites have any faunal or botanical evidence at all, and it remains an important yet untested assumption that their inhabitants lived entirely by hunting and gathering. It is also a major assumption that these sites are entirely pre-neolithic; as Milisauskas (1978:90) points out, most are undated and many could be contemporaneous with the early Neolithic.

The colonization model, despite its lack of supporting data, still tends to exercise a powerful influence on explanations of the mesolithic-neolithic interface. Mesolithic societies are still assumed to have played no part in the expansion of food production over their own continent, and the possibility that they developed indigenously into food-producing neolithic societies is rarely considered. In many parts of Europe, neolithic prehistorians still look to the Near East for explanations of where food production originated rather than to a local, pre-neolithic background. Although the ghosts of land-hungry Asiatic farmers sweeping northwards into Europe in some kind of "wave of advance" (Ammerman and Cavalli-Sforza, 1971) are less frequently sighted in the literature than before, they have yet to be fully exorcized. These days, many prehistorians prefer instead to talk of "the spread of farming economy", rather than of farming peoples, to explain the origin of the European early Neolithic, but rarely specify how this spread was accomplished, or what it involved. Consequently, it is often hard to avoid the impression from much recent literature that early farming was like some kind of margarine or rising damp that eventually, and somewhat mysteriously, managed to cover most of Europe.

A useful starting point in the search for alternative explanations for the early development of agriculture in Europe is to consider how we can explain the appearance in south-east Europe after 6000 b.c. of permanent settlements whose inhabitants relied upon sheep and morphologically domestic cereals and legumes, as well as on cattle and pig.

I. THE ORIGIN OF SEDENTARY FOOD PRODUCTION IN SOUTH-EAST EUROPE

The prevailing explanation—that these communities resulted from Near Eastern colonization—is largely the result of three views. The first is the assumption that Europe and the Near East are separate entities, divided from each other by the Dardenelles as surely as the continent is cut off from Britain by the English Channel. Consequently, all early agricultural societies from Scotland to Greece are "European", and thus resulted from colonization; those from the Hellespont to Baluchistan are "Near Eastern", and thus developed locally. This view can be discarded at once;

as Clark and Piggott (1965) pointed out many years ago, the divide between the two is arbitrary, and largely irrelevant to discussions of prehistoric agriculture.

The second view that has permeated most discussion on the subject is that cereals, legumes and sheep/goat had a centre of origin in the Near East, and then dispersed outwards. Thirdly, it is assumed that this dispersal could have occurred only through human agencies, most notably migration resulting from population pressure.

The resulting colonization model has one notable strength, in that the ^{14}C evidence indicates that the age at which early farming settlements were first established becomes increasingly more recent from west Turkey to southern Yugoslavia, as might be expected if agriculture originated in the Near East and was then carried northwards by colonists.

It has, however, several serious weaknesses. The first is that the Near East cannot be regarded as a demographic cistern that was spilling its surplus population over south-east Europe by the seventh millennium b.c. Early neolithic sites in western Turkey are very rare, and although there are doubtless many awaiting discovery, it is hard to accept that the whole of that vast and fertile region was so densely populated by 6000 b.c. that it could absorb no further increase in population. In the Cumra basin of south-west Turkey, for example, Can Hasan III is the only site known to have been occupied around 7000 b.c., two millennia later, there were only three (French, 1970). In Iranian Kurdistan, settlements such as Asiab and Sarab had been founded in the Kermanshah area by the seventh millennium b.c.; yet in the adjoining Kangovar valley, no agricultural settlements existed for another 2000 years (Levine and McDonald, 1976; McDonald, 1979).

In Europe, the density of early neolithic settlements also seems to have been very low. In south Bulgaria, for example, there are only 12 early neolithic sites in the Nova Zagora region; in the Valley of Roses, Kazanluk is the only Karanovo I settlement; and there are only three in the Celopeč area (Dennell, 1978). So, too, in the islands of the east Mediterranean. At the beginning of the seventh millennium b.c. only four of the 80-odd islands were occupied; two millennia later, the number had scarcely doubled (Cherry, 1981). Large areas of southern Greece and Crete remained unoccupied by farming communities until the fourth or even third millennium b.c. (Halstead, 1981). This evidence would suggest both very low numbers of people in the initial phases of agricultural settlement, and very low growth rates for a long time thereafter.

Secondly, the colonization model does not explain why the early neolithic cultures of south-east Europe are regionally distinctive from the outset. This feature can be explained only by special pleading, by postulating either an as yet undiscovered donor culture in north-west Turkey or Thrace, or a diffusion of people with cereals and sheep who settled down before they began making pottery. The former is an open question until these areas are surveyed, and the latter possibility seems unlikely in view of the low rates at which settlements in the Near East budded off to found daughter communities. The hypothesis that people changed their material culture whilst migrating is ingenious but untestable, and reminiscent of Gosse's assertion in the last century that the Almighty created fossils to give palaeontologists the illusion that Genesis was untrue.

Thirdly, the prevailing model has one glaring inconsistency in its explanation of the Turkish and south-east European early farming settlements. In both areas, the only evidence for early holocene occupation comes from caves on the southern coast (Franchthi in Greece, Beldibi and Belbasi in Turkey); these are far from areas of early farming settlements, and both regions contain the same kind of neolithic tell settlements, with the same kind of resources. Yet those in Turkey are explained as the result of local developments, whilst the European ones are regarded as the result of immigration.

Finally, the early farming settlements in south-east Europe seem improbably successful to have resulted from colonization. We should consider this point in the light of historically documented colonial ventures. A conspicuous feature of these is the high rate of initial failure by the incoming pioneer populations. For example, American, Boer and Australian folklore is filled with instances of the failures and struggles of the early colonists — those who tried to till land that proved too infertile, stony or waterlogged; or built their settlements in areas that experienced periodic drought or flooding. In the early decades of the European colonization of North America, most of the early settlements on the east coast failed, and all experienced enormous challenges in their early years.

This does not seem characteristic of early farming settlements in south-east Europe. In many cases — particularly in Bulgaria and Macedonia — early farming settlements were placed in extremely advantageous locations, and were frequently occupied for several generations, if not centuries. Their success is perhaps best evidenced by a Bulgarian example. In the Nova Zagora region, the largest and longest occupied tells are virtually adjacent to modern communes established in the last 30 years in locations chosen by conscious economic planning. The only exceptions are those sites that have experienced post-neolithic alluviation in their local vicinity. In these cases, the new communes are located nearby, but on slightly higher ground (Dennell and Webley, 1975).

Unless one grants these early farmers a phenomenal amount of good luck and even better judgement, it is hard to see how pioneering immigrants had such detailed knowledge of the area they were colonizing.

In view of these weaknesses, it would seem worthwhile searching for alternative explanations. One is that most of the cereals, legumes and sheep used in south-east Europe after 6000 b.c. were derived from a local background.

II. INDIGENOUS FOOD PRODUCTION IN SOUTH-EAST EUROPE?

As Harlan (1971:468) stated "The idea of a center—an area in which things originate and out of which things are dispersed—is reasonable, logical, and intellectually satisfying, but does not always agree with the evidence". So far as the origins of food production in the Old World are concerned, the assumption that the Near East was a centre rests heavily upon the supposition that the "natural" distribution of wild cereals, legumes and sheep has remained largely unchanged and confined to that area since first used over 12 000 years ago. This notion is highly questionable, for the present-day distribution of these species is almost certainly a residual one, curtailed by millennia of climatic change and land use. It would be surprising if this were not so; the distribution of most plants and animals has altered substantially in recent, historic and geologic times (see Elton, 1972), and "a statement that a particular species is, or is not, a 'native' is rather an idle one, and of little scientific value" (Salisbury, 1964:29). As seen in the previous chapter, the last deglaciation saw enormous change in the distribution of plants and animals in northern Europe, from mammoths to moles, and from edelweiss to elm trees. Southern Europe and the Near East were not exempt from these changes. For example, woodlands did not colonize Greece until after 10 000 years ago, and in western Iran, oak did not colonize the Zagros mountains until after 14 000 b.p., nor reach its maximum extent until 6000 years ago (Bottema, 1978). As H. Jarman (1972:23) pointed out, if we are to take seriously the suggestion that most of the European forest was cleared in less than 5000 years, we should at least consider the possibility that more than 10 000 years of agriculture has greatly reduced the distribution of wild cereals in the Near East. What we need to consider is not where the species are now, but where they were likely to have been by the beginning of the last deglaciation.

A. Wild cereals

Today, these are confined largely—but not entirely—to the Near East. Wild barley (*Hordeum spontaneum*) is concentrated in an arc from the Zagros across southern Turkey and into the Levant, but is also found scattered across northern Africa, Crete, Cyprus and as far east as Baluchistan. Wild einkorn (*Triticum boeoticum*) is found over north-west Iran and most of Turkey, but also in eastern and northern Greece, southern Bulgaria and south Yugoslavia. The most restricted of the wild cereals is wild emmer, *T. dicoccoides*, which is confined to Palestine and south Syria, and parts of south-east Turkey and north-west Iran (Zohary, 1969).

Like many grasses, wild einkorn and barley are colonizing species that can occupy disturbed habitats before being displaced by arboreal species. During the extremely cold and arid conditions of the glacial maximum, these are likely to have been distributed in isolated refugia, and may have been absent from most of the Tauros and Zagros mountains (see Fig. 26). They may, however, have survived in western Syria, Lebanon and adjacent areas; wild einkorn may also have grown in eastern Turkey (van Zeist, 1969). There may also have been other isolated populations around

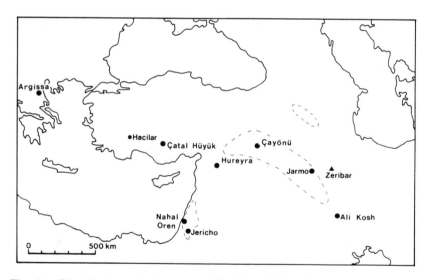

Fig. 26: Distribution of wild emmer (*T. dicoccoides*) and early food-producing sites mentioned in text.
Key: circles: archaeological sites; triangles: pollen core; dotted line: present distribution of *T. dicoccoides* (based on Zohary, 1969).

the Mediterranean perimeter (H. Jarman, 1972), and perhaps also in the southern Nile Valley, where grains of wild barley have been reported from contexts 18 000 years old (Wendorf *et al.*, 1979). This find would imply that the distribution of wild barley in the last glaciation may at times have extended far beyond its present range.

In the late glacial warming after 14 000 b.p., wild barley and einkorn would have been able to expand from their refuge areas. One area where this is likely to have happened is the Aegean basin; the presence of wild barley grains at Franchthi, and cereal pollen at Icoana (Chapter 6) and in late glacial/early holocene pollen profiles in northern Greece (Fig. 26; see Bottema, 1974: Figs 27, 31), indicate that barley and perhaps other cereals were present in south-east Europe before the appearance of "village-farming" communities around 6000 b.c. One intriguing hint that other European populations of cereals existed at the close of the Pleistocene comes from the Paris basin, where Planchais (1970) reported cereal pollen in a late glacial/early holocene horizon, along with high levels of Graminae. Although inconclusive, this find might indicate that cereals were among the grasses that moved into northern Europe at the end of the Younger Dryas ahead of woodlands.

It is, however, unlikely that wild emmer existed outside the Near East in the early Holocene. As noted already, its present distribution is the most restricted of all the wild cereals, even though it can tolerate a wide range of climatic conditions. Zohary (1969) explained this feature as the result first of its dislike of disturbed ground, and secondly of its strong preference for soils on basalts and limestone. Its archaeological record also suggests a very restricted distribution in the early Holocene. To date, it has been reported from only three sites. The first two—Jarmo in northern Iraq (Helbaek, 1960) and Çayönü in south-east Turkey (van Zeist, 1972)—are in the same general region of the northern Zagros, and date from the late seventh and eighth millennia respectively. The third is Abu Hureyra in Syria, where a few grains that were probably, but not certainly, of *T. dicoccoides* (Hillman, 1975) were found in the "neolithic" but not "mesolithic" levels.

What is strange about wild emmer is that it is absent from several Near Eastern early holocene sites where the domestic type, *T. dicoccum*, has been found, such as aceramic Hacilar (Helbaek, 1970), Can Hasan III (Hillman, 1972), Nahal Oren (Dennell, 1973), Ali Kosh (Helbaek, 1969) and the earliest levels at Jericho (Hopf, 1969). It was for this reason that I once suggested (Dennell, 1973) that wild emmer may be of recent origin, and that the ancestor of domestic emmer may have had the same type of grain as *T. dicoccum* but a brittle rachis. Unfortunately, the crucial spikelet fragments are rarely preserved archaeologically, and so the question is at present unresolved.

What does seem probable on present evidence is that *T. dicoccum*, rather than *T. dicoccoides*, extended its distribution after the eighth millennium b.c. At Ali Kosh (Bus Mordeh phase, *ca.* 7250 b.c.) it appeared in a fully developed form, and is assumed to have been introduced to that part of south-west Iran from elsewhere. At Abu Hureyra, its first appearance was in the neolithic levels (Hillman, 1975). To that extent, its presence in south-west Turkey at *ca.* 7000 b.c., northern Greece by 6000 b.c. and Bulgaria by 5300 b.c. may signify the further extension of this cereal's range from its point of origin.

The origin of bread-wheat (*T. aestivum*) is currently obscure, but is likely to have occurred outside Europe (van Zeist, 1976). At present, its earliest record is from Can Hasan III in south-west Turkey, where it was found in a context dating to *ca.* 7000 b.c. (Hillman, 1972). Its presence on Crete at 6000 b.c. (Evans, 1964) and sporadically in sixth millennium contexts in south-east Europe (Dennell, 1979) show that it featured in the earliest cereal crops evidenced in these regions. As it is a free-threshing wheat, it is less likely to be carbonized than einkorn and emmer, and may be under-represented in the archaeological record.

B. Legumes

As with cereals, the distribution of legumes during the last deglaciation is largely a matter for conjecture. Although prevailing opinion favours an Asiatic origin for most of the peas used in neolithic Europe, they may have descended from *Pisum elatius*, which has a circum-Mediterranean distribution, rather than *P. humile*, the Asiatic type, particularly as the seeds of these two species are hard to distinguish from each other. The same can be said of lentil, since the wild forms (*Lens elatius*, *L. nigricans*, *L. orientale*) are found in both south-west Asia and around the Mediterranean, are difficult to distinguish from each other by their seeds, and also seem to resemble early claimed domestic types.

It is easy to see how these difficulties over identification can lead to a circular argument. Since agriculture in south-east Europe is assumed to have originated from the Near East, neolithic finds of *Pisum* and *Lens* are assigned to a Near Eastern type; this can then be taken a evidence that agriculture developed in the Near East and spread outwards. As legumes have been found in early holocene contexts at Franchthi (Chapter 6), and also in southern France (Courtin and Erroux, 1974), it is at least as likely that the pulses used in neolithic Europe had a local origin.

C. Sheep

There are two reasons why these need not have first set hoof in Europe during the early Neolithic. The first is that these could almost certainly have tolerated the conditions that prevailed in late glacial Europe. For example, wild sheep in Kurdistan live in an area where the present pollen rain is composed largely of *Artemisia* and *Chenopods*, not unlike that in many late glacial pollen assemblages. Wild sheep also live in Mongolia, which Frenzel (1973) considered to be a good analogue for the cold, dry conditions of late glacial Europe. Additionally, of course, sheep (and other animals) would have been free to move across the Dardenelles during periods of low sea level.

Secondly, the fossil record indicates that sheep inhabited Europe both before and during the last glaciation (see Table 12). Their rare representation in palaeolithic contexts need not be surprising. Wild sheep live in

Table 12: Occurrences of Upper Pleistocene and Early Holocene sheep in Europe.

Site	Identification	Reference
Upper Pleistocene		
Pech de l'Aze, France	*Ovis fossilis* cf. *aries*	A
Lunel-Viel, France	*O. tragelaphus*	A
Balme de Glos, France	*Ovis* sp.	A
Petershöhle, Austria	*Ovis* sp.	A
La Bocca del Tasso, Italy	*Ovis* sp.	A
Certova-Dira, Czechoslakia	*O. argaloides*	A
Grotta Bella, Hungary	*Ovis* sp.	A
Tata, Hungary	*Ovis* sp.	A
Crvena Stijena, Yugoslavia	*Ovis* sp.	B
Adzhi Koba III, Crimea	*O. cf ammon*	C
Mezin, Russia	*O. cf orientalis*	C
Early Holocene		
L'Abri Pages, France	*Ovis* sp.	A
Gramari 7, France	*Ovis* sp.	D
La Adam, Roumania	*O. ammon orientalis*	E

References: A. Bouchud, 1956; B. Benač and Brodar, 1958; C. Korobitsyna *et al.*, 1974; D. Poulain, 1971; E. Radalescu and Samson, 1962. References kindly supplied by N. Ralph.

small, scattered groups; because of their low density, and their agility over broken and hilly ground, they are not likely to have been hunted by man to any great extent when other types of prey were more readily available.

It is likely that the spread of woodlands after 10 000 b.p. broke up European sheep populations into separate groups, and some of these may have died out. One population in southern France is known to have survived, for it is commonly represented in cave deposits from the early Holocene onwards. Whether they were "domesticated" in the sense of ownership and/or controlled breeding is unknown, and cannot be established from present evidence. What their presence does indicate, however, is that the sheep used in southern France since pottery was introduced need not have had an exotic origin.

This brief review would suggest that the development of morphologically domestic barley, einkorn, legumes and sheep could have occurred in a "non-centre" that extended from parts of the Mediterranean basin to south-east Europe and the Near East (and possibly eastwards into central Asia and China). If that were the case, the earliest village farming settlements in south-east Europe could have developed most of their features without any Near Eastern influences. Whilst this explanation avoids most of the weaknesses of the traditional colonial model, it does not explain why the earliest farming settlements in south Bulgaria are younger than those in northern Greece, or why these in turn are more recent than those in south-west Turkey. In addition to this failing, it is difficult on present evidence to argue that the ancestral forms of domestic emmer and bread-wheat were present in south-east Europe before 6000 b.c.

It is thus worth exploring the possibility that domestic species may have originated in a "centre" but then have dispersed outwards without ever having been part of the baggage of migrating colonists.

III. THE DISPERSAL OF PLANTS AND ANIMALS

The ways that the plants and animals used by or associated with human communities extended their distribution can be likened to different types of travellers. On a pleistocene time-scale, most were fellow-travellers, and made their own way into new habitats; the extension of reindeer and red deer into northern Europe during the last deglaciation is a good example of this type of movement independent of man. In more recent times, some species may have expanded their area of distribution as stowaways. The most successful of these is probably the rat, which has managed to accompany man to remote islands such as Tristan da Cunha. Others may have been hitch-hikers, granted a place on the human bandwaggon for their company or usefulness: cat and dog are perhaps suitable examples, as both are liable to hop off and become feral if conditions become unfavourable. One group of species that is assumed to have extended its distribution by being baggage rather than fellow-travellers, stowaways or hitch-hikers are the domestic cereals, since these are assumed to be unable to fend for themselves.

The extent to which this supposition is true of cereals has perhaps been overestimated. Under truly "natural" conditions, it is true that domestic cereals stand little chance of survival. This is clearly shown by a nineteenth century experiment at Rothamsted in England, where a field of wheat was abandoned: "In the following season, a fair wheat plant came up and gave about half a crop, but after it seeded the weeds increased their hold upon the ground until in the fourth season only two or three stunted wheat plants could be found" (Hall, 1917:41). However, they are more successful at surviving in disturbed habitats where competition from other plants is reduced. In southern France in the last century, for example, domestic einkorn was a troublesome weed of corn fields (H. Jarman, 1972:18), and in Britain, the testing of new cereal strains has to be carried out on land that has been free of cereals for at least two years to avoid the possibility of contamination with previous crop types (H. Jarman, 1972:23).

If, as suggested earlier, domestic emmer originated in a restricted part of the Near East, it could have dispersed in one of two ways, without involving human movements.

As noted in the introductory chapter, man is not the only animal that utilizes his resources; in the case of cereals, competition comes from rodents, birds and ungulates. Grain eaten by these would often have passed through the gut undamaged, and could have been defecated elsewhere, standing a chance of germinating far from its parent plant. Its chances of survival would have been increased if it was dispersed to habitats where other cereals were already growing. Providing that those cereals were already being exploited by man, an incoming cereal that had a large grain and a tough rachis which did not shatter when being reaped would have a fair chance of being selected for and taken under cultivation.

An alternative way that domestic cereals could have dispersed over large distances but without involving large-scale human movements is through exchange. To return to the analogy made earlier, domestic cereals may have dispersed as passengers, but in a series of short journeys. In the early Holocene, obsidian found its way from Çatal Hüyük to the Dead Sea Valley; that from near Lake Van has been found as far south as south-west Iran. In both cases, these distribution patterns can be explained as the result of networks of exchange (Renfrew *et al.*, 1968). What was exchanged for obsidian is unclear, but as these networks crossed areas in which domestic emmer and bread-wheat were used at an early date, these may have been some of the commodities that passed in the opposite direction into south-west Turkey.

In my opinion, the appearance of permanent village communities using cereals and sheep in south-east Europe after 6000 b.c. can be explained by a combination of local and intrusive developments, but without having to postulate the movement of invisible colonists. These developments could have taken place in three phases, and are summarized in Fig. 27.

The first stage would have occurred in the early Holocene, when conditions became more favourable to plant growth. Grasses, including wild einkorn and barley, would have become more abundant, and formed locally dense stands. As Harlan (1967) demonstrated in a now famous experiment, a prehistoric family could easily have obtained enough grain to suffice it for most of the year by only 2 or 3 weeks of harvesting. However, the amount of time needed to process large amounts of wild grain must have been considerable (Hawkes and O'Connell, 1981), and it is thus likely that groups processed perhaps a few weeks' supply of grain, and then dispersed to exploit other resources such as equids and deer that were more easily obtained. In addition, because the time of year when wild cereals can be harvested tends to be short and unpredictable (Zohary, 1969), people would probably have relied upon several stands, only a few of which might be harvested in any one year.

During the second phase, trees colonized areas previously occupied by grasses. Although the expansion of tree cover would have represented an increase in the total amount of edible plant biomass, it would have decreased the amount worth extracting by human groups because it was either too scattered, or involved too much effort in collecting and processing to be worthwhile. Wild cereals would thus have been worth maintaining as a seasonally important food resource. In undisturbed woodlands, yields from wild cereals are likely to have been too low to make their harvesting worthwhile, even though trees would probably have been sufficiently widely spaced for cereals to grow between them (Zohary, 1969). However, it would have been easy to maintain open areas of woodland by burning, coppicing or ring-barking. Once cereals in these disturbed habitats had been harvested, these clearings would have gradually reverted to woodland and, for a few years at least, provided young foliage for animals such as deer, sheep and cattle. A very simple kind of interdependence between plant harvesting and animal exploitation might therefore have developed in the early Holocene in

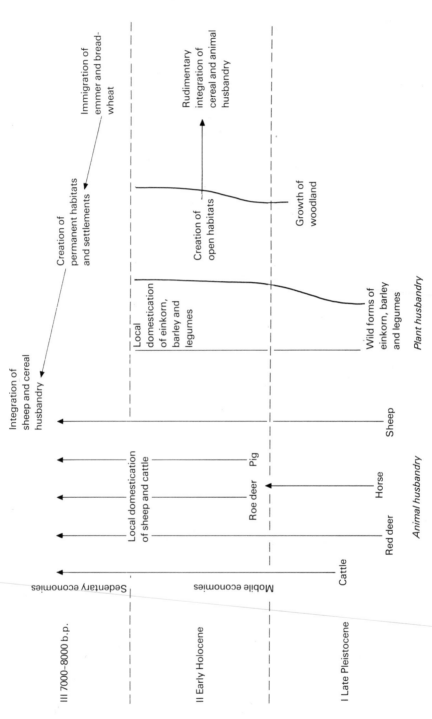

Fig. 27: Suggested developments leading to food-production in south-east Europe.

those areas where woodlands were expanding at the expense of cereals and other grasses.

The archaeological consequences of these two phases in early holocene south-east Europe should be broadly similar, and consistent with what I suggested characterized subsistence patterns in southern Europe in the last deglaciation (see Chapter 5). Settlement sites (when found!) should be small, and have been occupied briefly; those used at harvesting time should contain evidence of reaping and milling equipment and the remains of wild cereals (and other plants such as legumes), together with bones of ungulates, possibly including sheep. They should also have been organized along communal rather than household lines, for reasons that will be seen shortly.

It is during the third phase that permanent agricultural settlements became established. This transformation could have been initiated by the immigration (through natural means or exchange networks) of large-grained, tough rachis cereals, notably emmer, into areas where both the inhabitants and environment were already pre-adapted to their cultivation. Their arrival would have had profound social and economic consequences. This is because domestic emmer and bread-wheat are more productive and reliable than wild cereals, and more productive than domestic einkorn, but are also more labour-intensive. If yields are to be economic, they need sowing on ground that has been prepared, and then require weeding and protection against other competitors and predators. The choice of soil becomes more important, for it has to be sufficiently light to till yet with enough organic content to provide crops with the nutrients they need. Under these conditions, it would have been worthwhile establishing long-term habitats in the form of fields, and cultivating them from a permanent location. As domestic emmer and bread-wheat extract large amounts of nutrients from the soil, this needs replenishment from nitrogen-fixing legumes and animal manure. Animal husbandry and crop cultivation thus needed to be integrated, but a rudimentary form of integration would already have been in existence. Because these novel crops would have been more labour-intensive, there would also have been the incentive to organize food production along household lines, whereby individual families would be guaranteed the results of the labour they invested.

This model avoids many of the weaknesses of the prevailing colonial model. First, it avoids the need to postulate a surplus Near Eastern population, for which there is no evidence, and secondly, it explains the appearance of farming communities in south-west Turkey and south-east Europe as the result of one process rather than two. Thirdly, it explains the cultural diversity and idiosyncrasy of the Balkan early neolithic cultures as the result of predominantly local developments. Fourthly, it explains why the earliest of these tell settlements were located in areas extremely suitable for crop agriculture, since their inhabitants would already have had prior knowledge of the region. Finally, this model also explains the chronological patterning of early tell settlements in south-east Europe, in that it is consistent with a gradual drift northwards from western Turkey to southern Yugoslavia of cultigens rather than of peoples.

The Expansion of Novel Resources Over Europe: Neolithic Colonization and Mesolithic Assimilation

9.

Abstract

This final chapter looks at how cereals, legumes and sheep were adopted as food resources in temperate Europe. Two basic mechanisms are proposed. The first is that they spread through the movements of small numbers of colonists, as, perhaps in central Europe. The second is that they were acquired by local mesolithic populations who adapted them to prevailing circumstances. Britain—despite its position as an island—is cited as one instance where this explanation may be more applicable than those invoking neolithic colonization by agricultural immigrants.

Between 7000 and 5000 years ago, cereals, legumes and sheep spread to many parts of Europe. What this chapter will discuss are the two basic mechanisms by which this might have occurred. The first was through the movements of small numbers of colonists into areas already occupied by communities using traditional resources. The second, and probably more important, was that local mesolithic groups gradually acquired those new techniques and resources that they found useful, and assimilated them into existing practices.

I. THE EXPANSION OF NOVEL RESOURCES THROUGH AGRICULTURAL COLONIZATION

One region where cereals, legumes and sheep were probably introduced as part of the baggage of incoming colonists is central Europe, where these resources first appear in the *Bandkeramik* complex between 6500 and 6300 b.p. This complex is assumed to represent an intrusive phenomenon because it appeared suddenly; its material culture is very different from that of the local Mesolithic, but can be derived from that of neolithic sites in south-east Europe; and sheep, cereals and legumes as well as pottery are not thought to have been in central Europe before the appearance of *Bandkeramik* settlements. It is worth pointing out, however, that very little indeed is known about the late mesolithic communities in those areas where *Bandkeramik* settlements are found, and it has yet to be firmly demonstrated that the *Bandkeramik* complex owed nothing to local developments. It is possible, for example, that cattle, the staple animal resources of *Bandkeramik* settlements, were no less important in late mesolithic times, and may even have been managed in much the same way. This point aside, there are probably two reasons why this area was colonized by incoming agriculturalists from south-east Europe. The first is that the areas they moved into seem to have been only sparsely occupied by local mesolithic groups, and thus competition for resources was minimized. Secondly, the largely loessic soils of central Europe were easily tilled, fertile and probably only lightly wooded, and thus highly suitable for crop agriculture and a hoe technology.

As the main features of *Bandkeramik* settlements have been well described elsewhere (e.g. Tringham, 1971), only a few points need to be noted here. The first is that the initial phase of colonization was essentially small-scale. The distribution and chronological patterning of early *Bandkeramik* sites suggest that small groups of people migrated along the river valleys of central Europe, avoiding areas where mesolithic settlement was densest, and founded their first settlements in what have been termed *Siedlungskämmern*, or settlement cells, which remained the main foci for subsequent occupation. Bogucki (1979) has suggested that the earliest of these were sited in a variety of different locations because their occupants had yet to become familiar with their surroundings. Once these were better known, settlements were located so that the inhabitants could best exploit the landscape. If confirmed, this patterning would present an interesting contrast with areas such as Bulgaria, where farming settlements were well-positioned from the outset, implying that their occupants were already familiar with the area.

The density of *Bandkeramik* groups appears to have been low. In the Middle Neckar valley of central Germany, for example, there appears to have been only one *Bandkeramik* settlement per 1000 sq km in the earliest phase of occupation (Milisauskas, 1977:312). The areas they used were also small. Bakels (1978:141) suggested that the site territory of Hienheim in Germany covered only 200 ha, of which between one-third and one-tenth would have been needed for crop cultivation. An even smaller area was suggested by Milisauskas (1977:308), who considerd that only 12·5 to 30 ha of arable land would have been needed. Finally, the settlements themselves appear to have been small. Although *Bandkeramik* sites often extend over several hectares and contain many structures, only a few of these were used at any one time. Hammond (1981), for example, points out that these settlements are better described as "hamlets comprising farmsteads separated by distances in the order of 100 m" than as large nucleated villages. As an example, 95 long-houses were discovered at Elsloo in the Netherlands, a site covering 10 ha, of which one-third was excavated. Of the 300 structures that may have existed in the entire site, only 11 to 17 would have been used at any one time, assuming that each lasted for some 25 years. So too with other sites; at Bylany in Czechoslovakia there were only seven to ten houses for each of the seven phases of occupation, and around eight at Olszanica in Poland (Milisauskas, 1977). Estimates of the number of inhabitants of these settlements range from *ca.* 40 to *ca.* 150, depending upon the assumptions made about the ways long-houses were used. If each was occupied by one nuclear family, an estimate of *ca.* 40–60 people in total seems reasonable (e.g. Czerniak and Piontek, 1980). Startin (1978) suggested that a group of only 50 would have been needed to provide adequate communal labour for the construction of each settlement, and Hammond (1981) proposed that new settlements were founded once the population had reached between 20 and 60. Estimates that these settlements contained 150 or more people, based on the amount of floor space available for each person, are probably unrealistically high. One reason why this may be so is that these long-houses probably served several functions, including the storage of grain and perhaps animals. One cannot thus assume that for every 6 m of each long-house, there was one extra nuclear family, as suggested by Soudsky and Pavlů (1972).

Population growth after areas were first colonized appears to have been low, and accomplished by a gradual process of infilling and the founding of daughter settlements near to parent ones. Turning again to the Middle Neckar region of Germany, the density of settlement increased from 1/1000 sq km to 1/120 sq km by the end of the fourth ceramic phase (Milisauskas, 1977), some four or five centuries later. Hammond (1981) has shown through a variety of simulation models that regional growth rates were probably far lower than the 3% *p.a.* suggested by Ammerman and Cavalli-Sforza (1971) for early farming communities. In the area of north-west Germany that Hammond studied, this rate of growth would have led to 40 new settlements within 200 years following initial colonization, 2500 after 400 years, and 6000 after only 450 years. At that rate of growth, the entire region would have been saturated with settlements after only five centuries. Even allowing for the burial and destruction of large numbers of settlements, there is no evidence that this rate of growth was ever approached, and the density of settlement even after a millennium appears to have been low. Consequently, there would have been little need for the occupation of different environments beyond the area of initial colonization until long after areas were first settled. This point is important in the context of arguments that areas such as Britain were colonized by agriculturalists in the fourth millennium b.c. because of continental population pressure (see next section).

The subsistence of these settlements has received much attention over the years, and its main features now seem reasonably clear. Wheat, barley and legumes were used, but the importance of each remains uncertain, as much depends upon the methods used to estimate crop importance (see e.g. Dennell, 1977 and Hubbard, 1976 for conflicting views). One important, and now reasonably certain, point is that these communities did *not* practise slash and burn cultivation, as was suggested many years ago largely as a way of explaining the rapidity with which these settlements were founded over a large area of central Europe. Settlement data indicate that land was cultivated continuously from the same settlements over several centuries, and botanical evidence (Willerding, 1980) suggests that fields and hedgerows were integral parts of the *Bandkeramik* landscape. Evidence that sites like Bylany were occupied periodically is highly ambiguous (see e.g. Modderman, 1970) and cannot be used to argue that their inhabitants practised shifting cultivation. In any case, it is most unlikely that the soils surrounding each settlement were ever over-exploited, given the low levels of population and the probability that some form of crop rotation with cereals and legumes was practised (see Hammond, 1981:215).

Discussions of the animal husbandry of *Bandkeramik* settlements encounter two problems. The first concerns the role of hunting. Müller (1964) showed that only 10% or less of the bones from several German *Bandkeramik* sites were of wild animals, and thus suggested that hunting was unimportant. However, if one considers the numbers of individual animals represented in each assemblage, the importance of wild animals then rises to 20 or 30% (see Milisauskas, 1978:71).

The second problem involves cattle, which are usually the commonest animals represented, but it is not clear whether they were wild or domestic. Most of the cattle bones are classed as domestic on the basis of their size but, unfortunately, one investigator's aurochs is often another one's cow. For example, almost all the cattle bones from Hungarian neolithic sites which Bökönyi (1971) classed as wild *Bos primigenius* are within the size range of those from German *Bandkeramik* sites identified as domestic *B. tauros*. Similarly, within Germany, the so-called wild cattle from Müddersheim are no larger than those called domestic from other *Bandkeramik* settlements (see Clason, 1972). In other words, most of the neolithic cattle in central Europe are probably *Bos tauros*; evidence of what may have been cattle pens further suggests that they may have been domesticated.

Contacts between widely separated *Bandkeramik* settlements is evidenced by the presence in several sites of *Spondylus* shells from the Aegean; by the finding at Müddersheim in West Germany of stone from Silesia, over 1000 km away in Poland; and of Hungarian ceramics and obsidian at Olszanica in Poland (Milisauskas, 1977). The social networks that enabled such materials to be distributed over such large areas must have operated through the territories of mesolithic communities, and may well have involved their participation. This point raises the question of the nature of the frontier between late mesolithic and early neolithic populations in Europe, a topic which we can now consider at greater length.

II. THE ASSIMILATION OF NOVEL RESOURCES INTO TRADITIONAL ECONOMIES

By 6000 radiocarbon years ago, cereals, legumes and sheep were used to a greater or lesser extent in south-east and central Europe, and perhaps in other areas such as southern France. There was thus a "frontier" between those societies using traditional resources (and possibly practising some form of food-production), and those which used novel ones, and were definitely food-producing (see Alexander, 1978). Three points are worth making about the societies that lived on either side of this frontier.

The first is that subsistence groups, irrespective of the type of economy that they practised, are likely to have minimized risks by remaining within the areas with which they were most familiar. This point should be kept in mind when considering distribution maps that show how specific pottery styles, or items such as pottery, cereals and sheep, reached new areas. It is all too easy to gain the impression from these that prehistoric groups—particularly early agriculturalists—moved around a great deal in their lifetimes. In fact, the opposite is likely to have occurred. Early farmers are likely to have remained in the areas they knew best as much as possible, if only because of the amount of time and effort they had to invest in tillage and storage. In addition, the times of year when they could have migrated into new areas would have been very tightly constrained by the sheer rigidity of their agrarian timetable (Case, 1969a). The lifetime territories of hunter-gatherers are also likely to have been fairly stable. Out of the many examples that could be cited to show the small-scale lifetime movements of hunter-gatherers, a neat example is provided by the fate of William Buckley, a convict who escaped from his penal settlement in South Australia in 1803 and joined a group of aborigines. When he gave himself up 32 years later, he was still in the local vicinity, and had spent the entire time there except for a few extended journeys for social gatherings with other groups (Morgan, 1979).

We should thus be very wary of arguments that the expansion of agriculture and/or neolithic culture over temperate Europe resulted from the movements of neolithic colonists. This caution is all the more justified by the weakness of many of the explanations for why such migrations should have occurred. We should, for example, reject vitalist explanations, whereby some neolithic peoples migrated because that was what they liked doing best. Case (1969a:183), for example, argued that the early farming communities along the coastal hinterland of northern Europe were "adaptable, sea-going and restless", and thus took up the challenge of colonizing Britain. In this instance, no explanation is given as to why these communities should have been so footloose, or so fascinated by marine travel when their lives were largely spent in cultivating crops and rearing livestock. Economic arguments have tended to be equally unconvincing. We have noted already the lack of evidence to sustain earlier views that *Bandkeramik* expansion was effected by slash and burn civilization. More recent arguments have been little more convincing, and often bizarre. One example is Bradley's (1978:99) proposal that early agriculture spread rapidly in northern Europe because "it might so easily lead to crop failure and renewed migration". Agriculturalists who were experiencing difficulties in producing a worthwhile crop in areas they knew well seem unlikely to have compounded their troubles by trying to cultivate crops in areas that were unfamiliar to them, and already occupied by people who are most unlikely to have appreciated having their lands appropriated by itinerant groups of experimental crop breeders. No less strange is the argument of Dolukhanov (1979:150), who argued that the eastward expansion of neolithic cultures into parts of western Russia occurred because the surplus population of agricultural societies migrated into new areas already occupied by hunter-gatherers, but then decided that they too were better off hunting and gathering.

The second point worth making about communities on both sides of the agricultural frontier is that they may have lived in worlds that were very circumscribed, but not in ones that were closed. This point is especially relevant to hunter-gatherers. As Wobst (1978) has pointed out, ethnographic studies can all too easily—and wrongly—give the impression that recent hunter-gatherers were unaware of, and unaffected by, the world outside their own mating networks. This view is all the more likely to be held when those aspects of their behaviour that result from contact with outside groups are regarded as a distortion of their "real" behaviour, filtered out, and the rest treated as exemplifying their "traditional" way of life. Instead, it is more realistic to assume that these people have always been meshed in a complex web of contacts that extended across different cultural, linguistic and, for that matter, economic boundaries. We should also be wary of the hypnotic effect of our own archaeological constructs. These can easily lure prehistorians into the illusion that all significant events in the lives of prehistoric subsistence groups occurred within a one or two hour's walk of their settlements, or that cultures enclosed people who were all the same (the "clonial" hypothesis), and who had no dealings with those in adjacent cultures except perhaps at their boundaries. (For a stimulating discussion of this problem, see Hodder, 1977.) So far as late mesolithic Europe is concerned, its inhabitants are likely to have been aware of the fact that groups elsewhere used cereals, legumes, sheep and pottery, just as early farming communities would have known of the existence of hunting-gathering groups.

The third point is that hunter-gatherers are no more conservative than agriculturalists, but equally open to change if it seems to their advantage to do so. As Schrire (1980) has elegantly shown, for at least the past 300 years the San bushman of the Kalahari have alternated between hunting-gathering and herding their own, and other people's, livestock as and when they have found fit; economies may end, but societies usually continue. In the context of prehistoric Europe, late mesolithic societies would certainly have been able to weigh the pros and cons of rearing cattle and pig if they were not doing so already, and of using sheep, cereals and pottery. In some cases, they may have seen little reason to abandon a viable way of life for one that involved a much greater expenditure of time and labour without producing a dramatic improvement in their diet. Instead, they may simply have incorporated into their own lives those aspects of neolithic culture that they found useful or convenient. The most obvious of these would have been pottery, which would have been useful for storage and culinary purposes, and perhaps also for expressing status and social affiliation. Knowledge of how it was made could easily have led to local production and to the rapid development of local styles, some of which may have been copied from other groups. In other cases, pottery could have been acquired by exchange with neighbouring pottery-making groups. If so, the apparent expansion of a "culture" into a new area need not imply that there had been any migration of one ethnic group into another's territory.

Other items that may have been useful to mesolithic groups were cereals and sheep. The value of these was that they provided solutions to problems of winter food supplies. In most areas of temperate Europe, traditional economies operated in environments that effectively closed down for the winter, not unlike the tourist industry. Although a wide variety of plant foods may well have been abundant when in season, there were probably very few that could be stored in large amounts for consumption in the winter. Hazel nuts provide a good example of this point. These are commonly represented in mesolithic sites, and are highly nutritious; their yields could also have been increased by forest clearance. However, it is most unlikely that groups would have stored several tons of these for winter usage in view of the amount of time it would have taken to gather such large amounts and then to crack each shell. In contrast, cereals grow in denser concentrations and can thus be more easily harvested; processing them is also easier because it is not necessary to dehusk each ear individually. The advantages of sheep over red deer are also readily apparent: sheep have lower feeding requirements, faster rate of growth and a higher reproductive rate. They may also be useful in maintaining open areas of woodlands for cereal production, as well as providing manure. Thus sheep and cereals could have been usefully incorporated into existing practices based on red deer and hazel nuts.

In my opinion, the "spread" of farming after 6000 b.p. over most of temperate Europe is best explained by the way that mesolithic societies assimilated new resources and techniques, rather than by the expansion of farming pioneers. Two examples that show this process in very different ways are western Russia and Britain.

A. Western Russia

The archaeological record for the Mesolithic and Neolithic in this area (Dolukhanov, 1979) shows very neatly both the durability of traditional

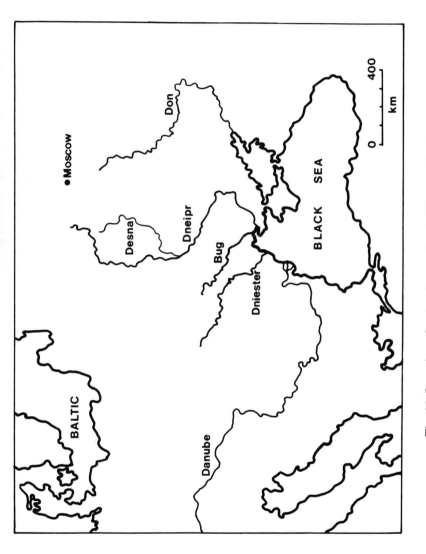

Fig. 28: Location of major river valleys in Western Russia.

economies, and the dangers of using the presence of pottery to create a major division between these two periods. We can look first at the group of sites at Soroki in the Dniester valley (Fig. 28).

These sites are all located on a narrow terrace 6 m above the present river in a steeply-sided valley, and were occupied from *ca.* 7500 to 6500 b.p. Soroki II has two aceramic levels, both dated to *ca.* 7500 b.p., the lower of which also contained evidence for two oval semi-subterranean structures. Three-quarters of the faunal assemblages from these two layers are composed of the remains of red and roe-deer. In the lower level, there were also 12 bones (14%) of "domestic" pig and two of "domestic" cattle; the remaining mammal bones were of "wild" pig. The identification of the cattle and pig as "domestic" appears to have been done on the basis of the size of bones, but is open to other interpretations: they could have been, for example, females or young adult males. Over 800 fish bones were also present in the lower level, and fishing appears to have been of some importance.

The same pattern emerges from Soroki I, dated to *ca.* 6800–6600 b.p. and containing pottery, but the same kind of lithic assemblage and structures as before. In both levels of this site, over half the faunal assemblage consists of red and roe-deer remains. The remainder are of pig and cattle, which are again classed as domestic, for reasons that appear arbitrary. Large numbers of fish bones were also recovered. The pottery contained impressions of emmer, einkorn and spelt, but could well have been imported from elsewhere. As Dolukhanov (1979:93) states, "The occurrence of domesticated animal bones and impressions of wheat grain may be attributed to the existence of economic contacts with agricultural tribes in other ecological zones". A further suggestion of such contacts is provided by the presence of some Linear-decorated pottery at Soroki V, which is dated to *ca.* 6400 b.p., and contains the same type of subsistence evidence as the other sites.

The evidence from the Bug valley is very similar. As at Soroki, these sites are located on the flood plains of deep valleys in areas quite unsuitable for crop cultivation or intensive stock-rearing. The earliest group of neolithic sites are dated to a short time-span between 6900 and 5500 b.p., and in Dolukhanov's (1979:98) opinion are the remains of seasonally occupied hunting camps. At sites like Baz'kov Island, Mitkov Island and Mikolina Broyarka, half to two-thirds of the animal remains are of red deer. Boar and roe-deer bones bring the total of these three animals to over 90% of the entire assemblages. The only "domestic" animal is cattle, again classed as such on the basis of its size. Fish bones are also very common. Although no plant remains were preserved, the presence of "hoe-like tools, querns and blades with a sickle gloss could all have been used for different kinds of gathering and preparing of vegetable foods" (Dolukhanov, 1979:95).

Later sites in the Bug and lower Dniester valleys contain pottery of the Tripolye culture, and have been dated to *ca.* 5500-4500 b.p. Most of these are located in the same type of environmental setting before, and contain similar faunal evidence. Only in the final stage are major differences seen in the location of sites and composition of faunal assemblages. Late Tripolye sites such as Kolomiiščina and Usatovo, for example, have large numbers of sheep and goat, and little evidence for red and roe-deer; they are also located on the edge of the loess plains away from river valleys. In view of the evidence for continuity between the early Tripolye sites in this area and preceding ones of the so-called Bug neolithic culture, it is likely that the same ethnic population was responsible for both, and that the presence of early Tripolye pottery resulted from exchange networks with areas further west.

Neolithic sites in the Desna and middle Dneipr valleys date from *ca.* 6500-5500 b.p., and are found in the same locations as mesolithic ones— on low river terraces, and on sand dunes of former flood plains. Apart from the addition of pottery, neolithic artefact inventories are identical to mesolithic ones, and contain large numbers of projectile points, microliths, core-axes and flake-axes. In Dolukhanov's (1979:141) opinion, most of these sites represent the camps of pottery-using hunters and gatherers. At the site of Pogorelovka in the Desna valley, the faunal assemblage is composed entirely of traditional resources, notably red and roe-deer, pig, wild ass, bear and elk. Those in the Dneipr valley are similar, but contain remains of small (?domestic) cattle and the occasional sheep. The latter vary considerably in their importance. At Igren 8 they are absent, and they form only 2% of the total assemblage of Buz'ki. At Sobacki and Sredni Stog, however, they form 27% and 39% of the total number of bones respectively. Unfortunately, the size of these assemblages is not stated, nor is it clear how many individual animals are represented. As rare animals can be over-represented in small faunal assemblages (Grayson, 1979), it is unclear if the commonness of sheep bones at these two sites was caused simply by the chance discovery of almost complete skeletons of one of two individual animals.

The only evidence for crop agriculture in the Dneipr valley consists of one grain impression of barley on a pot-sherd from the site of Vita Litovska, near Kiev. It is not stated whether the vessel to which this sherd belonged was made locally, or obtained from some distance away. As none of these sites in the Dneipr valley is located in areas suitable for crop agriculture, Dolukhanov's (1979:141) opinion that this evidence for cereals should be attributed to contacts with other groups seems entirely reasonable.

Within the area south and east of the Baltic, neolithic sites are usually found in lake basins. These sites date from *ca.* 5800 b.p. and are often large, have several phases and were probably occupied year-round. One example is the site of Usvyaty, dated to *ca.* 4000 b.p. Here, pile-dwellings were constructed at a time when broad-leaved forest had reached its maximum extent (and productivity). In all three layers at this site, over 85% of the faunal remains consisted of elk, bear, aurochs, boar, hare and beaver. Sheep were absent from the earliest level, but accounted for 1% of the total assemblage in the other two levels. Small types of cattle and pig formed between 5–8% each of the total in the last two levels. Bird bones were numerous, as were the remains of carp, pike, perch and bream. The main plant foods utilized appeared to have been acorns and chestnuts. Similar evidence was obtained from the settlement of Osovec I (*ca.* 5500 b.p.) near Minsk, where remains of berries, mushrooms and hazel nuts were also found. As elsewhere, Dolukhanov (1979:156) reasonably explains the occasional indication of sheep as the result of contacts across the agricultural frontier.

It would be tedious to repeat more of the evidence for the types of societies in western Russia that Dolukhanov characterizes as pottery-using hunters and gatherers who acquired as strays, or through exchange (or theft) small numbers of sheep and perhaps cattle. As Zvelebil (1978) has shown very clearly, this way of life continued with little basic alteration in the eastern Baltic until the first millennium A.D.

To summarize, the "Neolithic" of western Russia provides out-standing opportunities for investigating the types of economic systems that interest mesolithic prehistorians. Faunal material is well-preserved, and the fact that these sites contain pottery means that there are excellent means of tracing social territories and exchange networks, and of forming a sensitive chronological framework. An additional bonus of studying the Neolithic of this area is that the types of relationships between prehistoric hunter-gatherers and agriculturalists can be explored. Unfortunately, because these sites contain pottery, they have been called neolithic, and thus assumed to be of no interest to those interested in prehistoric hunter-gatherer behaviour.

B. Britain

The emergence in Britain of communities that used pottery, cereals, legumes and sheep has elicited an enormous amount of attention over the last century, and only the main features of this evidence need be summarized here.

From 6000 b.c. to the beginning of the fourth millennium b.c., mesolithic communities appear to have developed in isolation, and there is no evidence for any significant cross-Channel contacts (Jacobi, 1976). The Early Neolithic now dates from the early part of the fourth millennium b.c., but the events of most of this millennium still remain very shadowy indeed. One particularly important site is that of Ballynagilly in northern Ireland, where a hearth, some pits and some pottery sherds have been dated to *ca.* 3675-3800 b.c. (Smith *et al.*, 1971). A later occupation at this site is evidenced by a rectangular wooden structure and some pottery, dated to *ca.* 3200 b.c. A phase of clearance indicated in a pollen profile from a nearby bog is correlated with this structure, and both are assumed to have been the work of the same group. Other clearance horizons in England and Ireland are known that date from *ca.* 3400-3000 b.c. These are usually assumed to indicate the activities of neolithic communities, but are not associated with any artefacts and do not indicate any cereal cultivation, and so may have been done by either early neolithic or late mesolithic groups (see Bradley, 1978:9).

Evidence for the Middle Neolithic dates from the end of the fourth millennium b.c. and is much less ambiguous. One of the earliest pieces of evidence for crop cultivation is the find of spelt that was probably associated with the causewayed enclosure at Hembury, dated to *ca.* 3300-3150 b.c. The main evidence of cereals, however, is still the corpus of grain impressions on sherds from Windmill Hill, dating from the early third millennium b.c. Most of these were of emmer, and only a few were of barley. *Both* crops are likely to have been important, however, as most of the impressions of wheat were on sherds of vessels that had been made over 80 km away, probably in the Avon region to the north (Dennell, 1976b). Other evidence for crop cultivation comes from the set of furrows beneath the long barrow at South Street, near Windmill Hill, that were cut at some time before 2800 b.c., and then covered by a turf-line before the barrow was built. Other barrows, dating back to *ca.* 3400 b.c., were built on grassland, and all seem to have been constructed in open environments, presumed to result from neolithic clearance.

Evidence for early neolithic stock-rearing is still all too scarce. An additional problem is that most of the evidence for neolithic animal husbandry comes not from domestic settlements, but from the enigmatic and controversial causewayed enclosures. The scale of our ignorance on British animal husbandry after 4000 b.c. can be gauged from Legge's (1981:170) observation that the *earliest* domestic site with good data on the subsistence economy is at present Grimes Graves, *ca.* 1000 b.c. Neolithic evidence is thus confined largely to the causewayed enclosures of Windmill Hill and Hambledon Hill. The faunal collection from these shows a preponderance of cattle remains over those of sheep and pig. As in other British neolithic sites, the classification of cattle as (wild) *Bos primigenius* or (domestic) *B. tauros* is greatly complicated by problems of separating male from female animals (Grigson, 1978; Legge, 1981).

Evidence for settlements in the British Neolithic continues to be elusive. As indicated already, the function of causewayed enclosures remains conjectural, and the only hints of habitation structures (apart from Ballynagilly) are indeterminate clusters of pits and post-holes at sites such as Hurst Fen and Hazard Hill (Smith, 1974:105). Meanwhile, British prehistorians seem to be in an odd position of knowing more about the environment in which the dead were buried than about what the living did when not constructing enclosures, barrows, henges and trackways.

Two aspects of the mesolithic–neolithic transition have proved problematic, and these difficulties have grown rather than lessened with the years. The first is that it is hard to define when the Mesolithic ended and the Neolithic began. This is particularly true of the Early Neolithic of the fourth millennium b.c. As Bradley (1978:6) observed, "the actual onset of Neolithic clearance is not easy to define". Pennington (1975) noted that the effects of mesolithic populations on the vegetation in the Blea Tarn area of north-west England were hard to distinguish from those of neolithic groups. Spratt and Simmons (1976) encountered the same difficulties in distinguishing mesolithic from neolithic forest clearance in the North Yorkshire moors. These difficulties seem to stem from the way that both communities were attracted to the same kind of environments and resources. For example, the earliest sheep in Ireland are from coastal midden deposits at Dalkey Island, near Dublin, and dated to *ca.* 3400–3000 b.c. (Smith, 1974:120). Similarly, when noting that the earliest neolithic communities in Somerset were attracted to the marshy environment of the Levels where they built their trackways, Bradley (1978:99) commented that "the first Neolithic activity was not particularly different from Mesolithic practice".

The second problem that has bedevilled studies of the British Neolithic is that its origins have always remained enigmatic. There is no single area in northern Europe that can be considered to contain the cultural traditions that were directly ancestral to those seen in Britain by the end of the fourth millennium b.c. Instead, the British Neolithic seems to be a hotch-potch of different traits that can be derived from a large expanse of the coastal hinterland from Jutland to Brittany.

These conundrums have been explained in a variety of ways. We can take first the similarity of the activities undertaken by late mesolithic and early neolithic groups in the fourth millennium b.c. In Bradley's

(1978:100) opinion, "Both populations were undergoing a period of experiment and stress. This may account for a certain similarity between the environmental impacts of the two groups". We can return to the theme of mesolithic "stress" later, but meanwhile note that if both groups were under stress, their problems can hardly have been eased if both were competing for the same resources. This situation seems quite unlike that in central Europe, where, as already noted, *Bandkeramik* colonists occupied areas sparsely inhabited by local groups, and thus avoided competing for the local resources. The eclectic origin of the material culture of the Neolithic of the British Isles has been explained in ways that are often ingenious, if not a little strange. Case (1969a), for example, suggested that some of the donor cultures may have lived in coastal regions that are now submerged, and elsewhere (Case, 1969b) suggested that the earliest colonists were so preoccupied with survival that they had to lay aside some of their traditions and crafts until life became easier. Thus, when explaining the "baffling mixture" of local styles of early British ceramics, he suggested (1969b:8) that pottery is "likely to have been a luxury for early settlers; leather, wood and basketry will have served well as substitutes. When potting was resumed it too may be expected to show changes", and thus made differently from the types they had made on the continent. This argument was repeated by Bradley (1978:99), who particularly stressed the problems that early agricultural colonists would have encountered:

"It was necessary for a population which may have been essentially land-based to undertake the colonisation of these islands by sea, together with the introduction of staple resources, both plant and animal, which could not be found in the wild. For this reason, the difficulties of pioneer agriculture may have been exacerbated, and the cohesion of immigrant groups lost. It is not surprising that the mature Neolithic, as it emerges from this period of strain, should prove such an eclectic mixture of ideas".

Much the same line of reasoning is evident in Pitts and Jacobi (1979:171), who suggested that in the Early Neolithic of Britain:

"threatened group security, whether the result of factors inherent in emigration from the parent society, of strains in group identity in a relatively unknown landscape, or of confrontation with alien indigenous communities, could lead to a greater emphasis of symbolic aspects in material culture":

early neolithic immigrants thus symbolized their alienation from their homeland by making and decorating pottery in different ways from before, and built different types of monuments.

To my mind at least, these explanations lead us into a world stranger than that which Alice encountered once through the looking-glass. According to these explanations, we are supposed to believe that in the fourth millennium b.c. there were two groups in Britain, one local and mesolithic and the other intrusive and neolithic. The latter came to Britain from an area that is unknown but presumed to lie somewhere between Jutland and Brittany; did so because of population pressure, for which there is no evidence; and came as "essentially land-based" (Bradley, 1978:99) populations by sea-travel, of which they had no prior experience. Once they reached Britain, they used the same areas as mesolithic groups, and had the same impact on the environment; found conditions so difficult that, instead of returning to the continent, they were either forced to abandon their normal crafts and traditions, or experienced such strain that they symbolized their plight by forming new ones.

Such explanations are ingenious but incredible, and justify a search for an alternative and simpler explanation.

III. NEOLITHIC WITHOUT COLONIZATION?

It is worth remembering that the essential features of explanations for the British Neolithic were established long before most of the evidence cited in the previous few pages had been discovered. When discussing "the arrival of the prehistoric farmer, and the herdsmen — the Neolithic civilisation", Boyd-Dawkins (1880:247) wrote:

> "We have to chronicle in the Prehistoric period the changes wrought . . . by the invasion of new peoples, and the appearance of new civilisations — *changes similar to those which are now rapidly causing the hunters of the bison in the far west to disappear before the advance of the English colonist*" (italics mine).

Like most prehistorians of the last century, Boyd-Dawkins could not envisage hunter-gatherers even having the ability to develop agriculture of their own accord. The persistence of this view is evidenced by Case (1969b:5): "cereal cultivation with hand-tools demands not only knowledge but social effort and tradition: thus the possibilities are unlikely that it was . . . imitated by enterprising natives who had stolen or bartered for seed-corn overseas". Implicit in most discussions of the British Neolithic have been the assumptions that the mesolithic populations of Britain lacked the ability to develop either seafaring or food-production. Each can be taken in turn.

A. Mesolithic seafaring

An impressive body of evidence now indicates that early holocene communities were capable of undertaking return sea voyages on a regular basis. The collection of obsidian from Melos in the Aegean has already been mentioned (Chapter 7), as has the colonization of Crete in the late seventh millennium b.c. by people who presumably also took with them cattle, sheep and cereals. At around 7000 b.c., Ireland seems to have been colonized, again by sea; the island of Jura was reached by at least 6000 b.c., and the island of Oronsay was frequented throughout the year around the end of the fifth millennium b.c. Looking further afield, it is interesting to note the high proportion of Norwegian stone age sites dating from the seventh millennium b.c. that are on islands giving access to the fishing grounds of the Norwegian Sea. Further evidence for the use of boats in mesolithic northern Europe comes from the remains of paddles and dug-out canoes from lake and river deposits (Clark, 1975:124). It is important to note, however, that these simple craft were probably used in inland waters, and not in the open sea, where they would have been of little use. The vessels used offshore are likely to have been more substantial, and probably like the skin boats depicted in Norwegian rock-engraving of the Younger Stone Age (see Clark, 1975:213-215). One of the most eloquent pieces of evidence for the extent to which offshore voyages were commonplace in the Mesolithic of northern Europe comes from the remains of deep-water fish at middens such as Morton and Oronsay in Scotland, and at sites along the Norwegian coast. Rock-engravings are again informative: some Norwegian examples show people in boats line-fishing, or taking seal and porpoise.

In view of all this evidence, there is every reason to suppose that seafaring was an integral part of mesolithic life in the coastal regions of the British Isles and Scandinavia. It thus seems strange that it was the "essentially land-based" (Bradley, 1978:99) agriculturalists of northern Europe who invented the seafaring techniques that enabled sheep and cereals to be brought to Britain. This assumption seems bizarre; neolithic land-based agriculturalists who spent their lives tending sheep and growing cereals would have had as little reason to take up seafaring as the Swiss Navy had to invent battleships.

B. Mesolithic food-production

Evidence for food-production in late mesolithic Britain is now as impressive as that for seafaring. The clearance of woodlands has already been noted, as has the explanation that these activities represent attempts to increase the productivity and predictability of their environment. Bradley (1978:99) has also commented on the possibility that cattle and pig may have been as domesticated in the late Mesolithic as in the Neolithic of the third millennium b.c. Mesolithic societies who were already manipulating their environment to manage animals such as deer, cattle and pig, and plant resources such as hazel and acorn, would not thus have been completely unaware of the potential value of novel resources such as cereals, legumes and sheep.

These two points taken together would suggest that mesolithic populations in Britain could have acquired of their own accord cereals, sheep and knowledge of how to make pottery, and adapted these to their own needs. A corollary of this view is that the origin of British neolithic colonists lies not in northern Europe, but in the minds of nineteenth century prehistorians who assumed that prehistoric agricultural expansion could have occurred only through the expansion of prehistoric agriculturalists. The removal of these mythical beings in fact makes explanations of the development of the British Neolithic more straightforward and credible.

An alternative explanation is that mesolithic populations in Britain were experiencing population pressure by the early fourth millennium B.C. This may have been brought about by an increase in population and/or a continuing expansion of forest that reduced the amount of plant foods for both men and other animals, as well as making hunting more difficult. These problems were resolved in three ways. The first was by a more systematic use of inland resources. Particularly important in this context was the clearance of woodland to provide larger amounts of animal forage and human plant foods, and to make hunting more predictable. Cattle, pig and deer may also have been provided with fodder during the winter; the first two of these animals may also have been brought under close human control, so that their movements and breeding were regulated by man. The second method of increasing the supply of food concerned coastal areas, and involved a more intensive use of marine resources than before. As a result, seafaring techniques developed rapidly, and led to contacts between coastal populations in the British Isles with those along the coasts of mainland Europe. Consequently mesolithic populations in Britain became aware of the existence of new resources such as cereals and sheep, and new techniques such as pottery-making. These were gradually acquired, and incorporated into existing practices and traditions. Consequently, local ceramic styles developed at a very early stage of manufacture in this country. By the late fourth millennium b.c., the integration of sheep and cereals into prevailing patterns of resource management is unlikely to have presented any major difficulties. Much of the landscape, particularly on the chalk downlands of southern England, was already open, and thus provided adequate grazing for sheep; cereals would have been grown in grasslands, or in open woodlands that were already used for producing hazel and other edible plants. By the end of the fourth millennium b.c., mesolithic populations in Britain had accomplished their own economic and social transformation, and the distinctive features of the British Neolithic had already emerged.

IV. DISCUSSION

I have dwelt at some length on the Neolithic of western Russia and Britain because they represent to me the opposite ends of a single spectrum of processes that probably affected most of Europe. In the former area, new items—notably pottery, but also some sheep—were merely added to existing practices, but engendered little substantial change in the ways societies were organized and economies maintained. In the latter area, the adoption of these items by the local populations had far-reaching consequences, and within five centuries or so radically transformed their society and economy. The factors which led to the adoption of novel resources and techniques elsewhere in most of Europe (outside the Balkans and central Europe) were probably intermediate between those affecting these two areas, and resulted in changes more pronounced than in Russia but less than in Britain.

Areas where the assimilation of pottery and/or novel resources had broadly the same consequences as in Russia are the Iron Gates region of the Danube, coastal Yugoslavia, central Italy, southern France, coastal Norway, and central Sweden. In all these areas, the initial appearance of pottery, cereals, legumes or sheep resulted in little change in the location of settlements or in diet. At Lepenski Vir, the appearance of sheep and pottery in the final phase of occupation (see Table 9) caused little substantial change; in Tringham's (1973:562) view, the inhabitants "preferred . . . to continue the traditional diet and subsistence economy, since the alternative 'early neolithic' economy offered no overwhelming advantages". So too in western Yugoslavia, where the earliest neolithic sites contain impressed-ware pottery made in the same forms as those on Starcevo sites. These impressed-ware levels usually overlie "mesolithic" ones, most of the artefacts are similar, and there is no evidence that subsistence was "based on anything but hunting and gathering" (Tringham, 1971:103) for several centuries.

In much of central Italy, early neolithic sites tend to lie in the same type of setting as epipalaeolithic ones, and contain evidence that most of the meat was obtained from the same animal species as before. Evidence for intensive cereal cultivation is also slight, and this seems to have played only an ancillary role. In northern Italy, Jarman (1971) commented on how traditional resources — especially red deer and pig — continued to be important well after the appearance of pottery and the introduction of sheep and cereals. Barker (1975a) has dwelt at some length upon the ways the appearance of the neolithic can be explained in central Italy; as he pointed out, the hypothesis that it resulted entirely from an immigrant population of agriculturalists necessitates some means of then explaining why their behaviour was so similar to that of existing local populations.

The evidence from southern France shows a similar picture. Here, sheep were used in the early Holocene, so their presence in early neolithic contexts need not be attributed to outside influences (Courtin, 1978). Artefactual analysis indicates that the early neolithic impressed-ware assemblages are probably the outcome of local developments; as in coastal Yugoslavia, there was no major change in settlement location or subsistence patterns for long after the first usage of pottery; in this case, until the Chasséen culture of the fifth millennium b.c. (Guilaine, 1979; Phillips, 1975).

The archaeological record for the Neolithic of much of Sweden and Norway is very like that of western Russia. Welinder (1975), for example, characterizes the Neolithic of central Sweden as essentially that of pottery-using hunter-gatherers, who relied only very slightly upon sheep or cereals. Two Norwegian examples (Indrelid, 1978) show clearly the strength of the traditionally based economies long after novel resources had become available. The rock-shelter at Skipshelleren near Bergen was used from *ca.* 6000 to 4000 b.p. As might be expected for a site located near the shore of a fjord, fish and shellfish remains were common in all layers, and fish-hooks the commonest type of artefact. Half the mammal remains were of red deer; seal and boar provided another 12% each. The cave of Viste, near Stavanger, contained two mesolithic levels, but was used into the historic period. Half the mammalian fauna was of pig; moose and seal were also important. The remains of birds, fish and shellfish were also common. What is interesting here is that the only significant differences in the faunal remains from the historic-period layer was the presence of dog and a few bones of domestic cattle. Whilst the function of these sites may have changed between the Mesolithic and later periods, traditional resources still seem to have retained much of their importance for long after alternatives became available.

In conclusion, the processes that led to the use of cereals, legumes and sheep (as well as pottery) over much of prehistoric Europe are probably better described as a "wave of assimilation" than as one of "advance". This rephrasing embodies an important shift of emphasis in explanations of the mesolithic–neolithic interface. Instead of looking at how and why neolithic farming populations expanded, it is probably more useful to examine the factors that caused mesolithic groups to incorporate new techniques and resources, and the social and economic consequences that these innovations engendered. This point emphasizes the need for a much closer dialogue between mesolithic and neolithic prehistorians than has existed to date. Far from being a convenient point at which studies of prehistoric hunter-gatherers can end, and those of agriculturalists can begin, the early Neolithic over most of Europe probably embodies yet another instance of the adaptability of hunter-gatherers to changing opportunities and circumstances.

Summary

The differences between the prevailing framework for European prehistory up to and including the Neolithic and the one proposed in the course of this book are shown in Fig. 29. As can be seen, I have suggested four main periods, rather than six, the boundaries of which do not coincide with those drawn in the last century.

Period 1 lasted from the time when hominids diverged from the African apes some 6–8 Myr ago to around 250 000-500 000 years ago. Its main features were the development of bipedalism, evident 3·5 Myr ago; took-making between 2·0 and 2·5 Myr b.p.; and the use of home bases by at least 2 million years ago. Hominids were probably omnivorous, and obtained most of their (mobile) animal resources in the course of foraging (static) plant foods. During this long span, most of Europe was occupied only intermittently.

Period 2 is marked by the colonization of Europe on a permanent basis some 250 000-500 000 years ago, and lasted until *ca*. 30 000 years ago. Conceptual, rather than technological, developments distinguish this period from the previous one. In particular, I suggest that the ability to map landscapes in terms of *mobility*, both of resources and neighbouring groups in the same mating network, was the most crucial adaptation needed to colonize temperate latitudes where plant resources were scarce. This period also marks the time when hominid diet became largely carnivorous.

During both these periods, most hominid actions were *immediate*; that is to say, they comprised simple sequences of actions over short time-spans. For example, food—whether plant or animal—would have been consumed within a few hours after procurement; similarly, artefacts before 30 000 b.p. seem to have involved few stages of manufacture, little forward planning in their usage, and were probably discarded soon after they had been used for the task for which they were made.

190

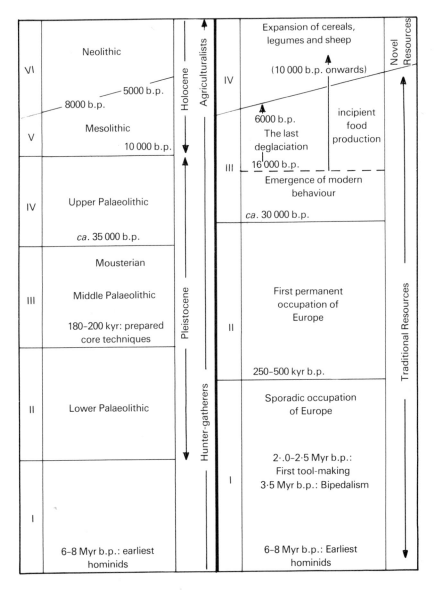

Fig. 29: The main periods of European prehistory: two views. The left hand side of the figure shows the traditional framework, drawn up in the nineteenth century primarily in terms of technological change. An alternative scheme is shown on the right-hand side.

The third phase marks the emergence of modern patterns of human behaviour. Where I suggest our behaviour differs most from that of earlier hominids (including Neanderthals) is the ability to retain concepts over long periods and through complicated sequences of actions. We can note in particular the development of *deferred* eating patterns involving food storage, and *deferred* usage of tools. Many of the actions evidenced after 30 000 b.p. were also considered more complicated than earlier ones, and involved several stages between the design and completion of tasks: bone-working and art provide the best examples. Technological evidence also suggests that a wider range of motor actions were used for tool-making after 30 000 years ago.

The fourth phase is characterized by the expansion of *novel* resources — notably emmer, bread-wheat, barley and sheep — over most of Europe after 8000 years ago. This expansion probably took place in three main ways. The first was through local developments in south-east Europe that led towards food-production, and the immigration (through natural means or exchange) of emmer and bread-wheat, rather than of agricultural colonists, from the Near East. Secondly, some small-scale colonization occurred, most notably in central Europe. Thirdly, societies reliant upon *traditional* resources (and perhaps obtaining some of these through methods of food-production) acquired sheep and cereals and assimilated these into existing patterns of food procurement. Unfortunately, the divide between the Mesolithic and Neolithic, between the last hunter-gatherers and the first farmers, has been greatly over-stated, to the detriment of our understanding of either.

References

Aaris-Sørensen, K. (1980). Depauperization of the mammalian fauna of the island of Zealand during the Atlantic period. *Vidensk. Meddr. dansk. naturh. Foren.* **142**, 131-148.

Agache, R. (1971). Informations archéologiques, circonscription de Nord-Picardie. *Gallia Préhist.* **14**, 271-310.

Alexander, J. (1978). Frontier studies and the earliest farmers in Europe. In *Social Organisation and Settlement* (ed. D. Green, C. Haselgrove and M. Spriggs). *Brit. Archaeol. Rep. Internat. Ser.* **47**, 13-29.

Allen, H. (1974). The Bagundji of the Darling basin: cereal gatherers in an uncertain environment. *World Archaeol.* **5 (3)**, 309-322.

Ammerman, A. J. and Cavalli-Sforza, L. L. (1971). Measuring the rate of spread of early farming in Europe. *Man (N.S.)* **6**, 674-688.

Andel, T. H. van *et al.* (1980). Late quaternary history of the coastal zone near Franchthi Cave, southern Argolid, Greece. *J. Field Archaeol.* **7 (4)**, 389-402.

Andersen, J. (1953). Analysis of a Danish roe-deer population. *Dan. Rev. Game Biol.* **2**, 127-155.

Andresen, J. M. *et al.* (1981). The deer hunters: Star Carr reconsidered, *World Archaeol.* **13 (1)**, 31-46.

Andrews, J. T. and Barry, R. G. (1978). Glacial inception and disintegration during the last glaciation. *Ann. Rev. Earth Planet. Sci.* **6**, 205-228.

Andrews, P. (1982). Hominoid evolution. *Nature* **295**, 185-186.

Andrews, P. and Tekkaya, I. (1980). A revision of the Turkish Miocene hominoid *Sivapithecus meteai. Palaeontology* **23 (1)**, 85-95.

ApSimon, A. M. (1980). The last Neanderthal in France? *Nature* **287**, 271-272.

Bahn, P. G. (1977). Seasonal migration in south-west France during the late glacial period. *J. Archaeol. Sci.* **4**, 245-257.

Bahn, P. G. (1978). The 'unacceptable face' of the West European Upper Palaeolithic. *Antiquity* **52**, 183-192.

Bahn, P. G. (1980). Crib-biting: tethered horses in the Palaeolithic? *World Archaeol.* **12 (2)**, 212-217.

Bailey, G. (1975). The role of molluscs in coastal economies: the results of midden analysis in coastal Australia. *J. Archaeol. Sci.* **2**, 45-62.

Bailey, G. (1978). Shell middens as indicators of postglacial economies: a territorial perspective. In *The Early Post-Glacial Settlement of Northern Europe* (ed. P. Mellars), pp.37-63. London: Duckworth.

Bakels, C. C. (1978). Four Linearbandkeramik settlements and their environments. *Analecta Praehist. Leidensia* **11**, 1-248.

Baker, R. R. (1978). *The Evolutionary Ecology of Animal Migrations.* London: Hodder and Stoughton.

Banning, E. B. and Pavlish, L. A. (1979). A revolution in radio-carbon dating. *Antiquity* **53**, 226-228.

Barbetti, M. and Flude, K. (1979). Geomagnetic variation during the late pleistocene period and changes in the radio-carbon time scale. *Nature* **279**, 202-205.

Barker, G. W. (1975a). Prehistoric territories and economies in Central Italy. In *Palaeoeconomy* (ed. E. S. Higgs), pp.111-175. Cambridge: Cambridge University Press.

Barker, G. W. (1975b). Early neolithic land use in Yugoslavia. *Proc. Prehist. Soc.* **41**, 85-104.

Becker, C. J. (1971). Late palaeolithic finds from Denmark. *Proc. Prehist. Soc.* **37**, 131-139.

Behrensmeyer, A. K. (1978). Taphonomic and ecologic information from bone weathering. *Palaeobiology* **4 (2)**, 150-162.

Behrensmeyer, A. K. and Hill, A. (1979). *Fossils in the Making.* Chicago: University of Chicago Press.

Benač, A. and Brodar, M. (1958). Crvena Stijena, 1956. *Glasnilo Zemaljskog Muzeja u Sarajevu* **13**, 21-42.

Berger, A. L. (1978). Long term variations of caloric insolation resulting from the earth's orbital elements. *Quat. Res.* **9**, 139-167.

Berglund, B. E., Hakansson, S. and Lagerlund, E. (1976). Radio-carbon-dated mammoth (*Mammuthus primigenius* Blumenbach) finds in South Sweden. *Boreas* **5**, 177-191.

Bibikov, S. N. (1978). Mezin "Prazdinchiii dom" i kostjaoj muzikalnij kompleks. *Sov. Archaeol. (Moscow)* **3**, 29-46.

Bidduttu, I. *et al.* (1979). Anagni, a K-Ar dated lower and middle Pleistocene site, Central Italy: Preliminary report. *Quaternaria* **21**, 53-71.

Bilsborough, A. (1976). Patterns of evolution in Middle Pleistocene hominids. *J. Hum. Evol.* **5**, 423-439.

Binford, L. R. (1965). Archaeological systematics and the study of culture process. *Am. Antiq.* **31 (2)**, 203-210.

Binford, L. R. (1973). Inter-assemblage variability—the Mousterian and the 'functional' argument. In *Explanations of Culture Change* (ed. C. Renfrew), pp.227-254. London: Duckworth.

Binford, L. R. (1977). Olorgesailie deserves more than the usual book review. *J. Anthropol. Res.* **33**, 493-502.

Binford, L. R. (1978a). *Nunamiut Ethnoarchaeology.* London: Academic Press.

Binford, L. R. (1978b). Dimensional analysis of behaviour and site structure: learning from an Eskimo hunting stand. *Am. Antiq.* **43**, 330-361.

Binford, L. R. (1979). Organisation and formation processes: looking at curated technologies. *J. Anthropol. Res.* **35 (3)**, 255-273.

Binford, L. R. (1980a). Willow smoke and dogs' tails: hunter-gatherer settlement systems and archaeological site formation. *Am. Antiq.* **45 (1)**, 4-20.

Binford, L. R. (1980b). Review of *Reindeer and Caribou Hunters*, by A. E. Spiess. *Am. Anthropol.* **82**, 628-631.

Binford, L. R. (1981). Behavioural archaeology and the "Pompeii premise". *J. Anthropol. Res.* **37 (3)**, 195-208.

Binford, L. R. and Binford, S. R. (1966). A preliminary analysis of functional variability in the Mousterian of Levallois facies. *Am. Anthropol.* **68 (2)**, 238-295.

Binford, S. R. (1970). Late middle palaeolithic adaptations and their possible consequences. *BioScience* **20 (5)**, 280-283.

Black, E. C. (1969). Can one cook in a skin? *Antiquity* **43**, 217-218.

Boaz, N. T. (1977). Paleoecology of early hominidae in Africa. *Kroeber Anthropol. Soc. Pap.* **50**, 37-62.

Boaz, N. T. (1979a). Hominid evolution in eastern Africa during the Pliocene and early Pleistocene. *Ann. Rev. Anthropol.* **8**, 71-85.

Boaz, N. T. (1979b). Early hominid population densities: new estimates. *Science* **206**, 592-595.

Boaz, N. T. and Behrensmeyer, A. K. (1976). Hominid taphonomy: transport of human skeletal parts in an artificial fluviatile environment. *Am. J. Phys. Anthropol.* **45**, 53-60.

Bogucki, P. J. (1979). Tactical and strategic settlements in the early neolithic of lowland Poland. *J. Anthropol. Res.* **35**, 238-246.

Bökönyi, S. (1970). Animal remains from Lepenski Vir. *Science* **167**, 1702-1704.

Bökönyi, S. (1971). The development and history of domestic animals in Hungary: the Neolithic through the Middle Ages. *Am. Anthropol.* **73**, 640-674.

Bökönyi, S. (1975). Vlasac: an early site of dog domestication. In *Archaeozoological Studies* (ed. A. T. Clason), pp.167-178. Amsterdam: North Holland Publishing Co.

Bolomey, A. (1973a). An outline of the late epipalaeolithic economy at the "Iron Gates": the evidence on bones. *Dacia* **17**, 41-52.

Bolomey, A. (1973b). The present stage of knowledge of mammal exploitation during the epipalaeolithic and the earliest neolithic of the territory of Roumania. In *Domestikationsforschung und Geschichte der Haustiere* (ed. J. Matolcsi), pp. 197-203. Budapest: Academai Kiado.

Bonifay, E. (1975). Stratigraphie du quaternaire et âge des gisements préhistoriques de la zone littorale des Alpes-Maritimes. *Bull. Soc. Préhist. Fr.* **72 (7)**, 197-208.

Bonifay, M.-F. (1980). Relations entre les données isotopiques océaniques et l'histoire des grandes faunes européennes plio-pleistocenes. *Quat. Res.* **14 (2)**, 251-262.

Bordes, F. (1973). On the chronology and contemporaneity of different palaeolithic cultures in France. In *Explanations of Culture Change* (ed. C. Renfrew), pp.217-226, London: Duckworth.

Bordes, F. (1978). Typologial variability in the Mousterian layers at Pech de l'Azé I, II and IV. *J. Anthropol. Res.* **34**, 181-193.

Bordes, F. (1979). Comments on the Clactonian: an independent complex or an integral part of the Acheulean? by M. Y. Ohel. *Current Anthropol.* **20 (4)**, 714.

Bordes, F., Laville, H. and Paquereau, M-M. (1966). Observations sur le Pleistocène supérieur du gisement de Combe-Grenal (Dordogne). *Actes Soc. Linnéenne Bordeaux B* **103**, 3-19.

Bordes, F. and Prat, F. (1965). Observations sur les faunes du Riss et du Würm I. *L'Anthropologie* **69 (1-2)**, 31-46.

Bordes, F. and Sonneville-Bordes, D. (1970). The significance of variability in palaeolithic assemblages. *World Archaeol.* **2**, 61-73.

Bordes, F. and Thibault, C. (1977). Thoughts on the initial adaptation of hominids to European glacial climates. *Quat. Res.* **8**, 115-127.

Boroneant, V. (1970). La période épipaléolithique sur la rive roumaine des Portes de Fer du Danube. *Praehist. Z.* **45**, 1-25.

Bottema, S. (1974). *Late Quaternary Vegetation of North-western Greece.* Groningen: University of Groningen Press.

Bottema, S. (1978). The late glacial in the eastern Mediterranean and the Near East. In *The Environmental History of the Near and Middle East* (ed. W. C. Brice), pp.15-28. London and New York: Academic Press.

Bouchud, J. (1956). La faune épimagdalenienne et romanello-azilienne en Dauphine. *Bull. Mus. Anthropol. & Préhist. Monaco* **3**, 177-187.

Bouchud, J. (1965). Le *Cervus megaceros* dans le sud et le sud-ouest de la France. *Israel J. Zool.* **14**, 24-37.

Bouchud, J. (1966). *Essai sur la renne et la climatologie du paléolithique moyen et supérieur.* Périgeaux: Magne.

Bouchud, J. (1974). Étude de la faune ahrensbourgienne de Remouchamps. *Bull. Soc. R. Belg. Anthropol. & Préhist.* **85**, 118-127.

Bouchud, J. and Desbrosse, R. (1973). La faune de la grotte des Freydières à Saint-Agnan-en-Vercors (Drôme). *Bull. Soc. Préhist. Fr.* **70**, 330-336.

Boulton, G. S. (1979). A model of Weichselian glacier variation in the North Atlantic region. *Boreas* **8 (3)**, 373-395.

Bowen, D. Q. (1980). Antarctic ice surges and theories of glaciation. *Nature* **283**, 619-620.

Boyd-Dawkins, W. (1880). *Early Man in Britain.* London: MacMillan and Co.

Brace, C. L. (1979). Krapina, "Classic" Neanderthals, and the evolution of the European face. *J. Hum. Evol.* **8**, 527-550.

Bradley, R. (1978). *The Prehistoric Settlement of Britain.* London: Routledge and Kegan Paul.

Braidwood, R. J. and Howe, B. (1960). Prehistoric investigations in Iraqi Kurdistan. *Studies in Ancient Oriental Civilisation* **31**.

Brain, C. K. (1981). *The Hunters or the Hunted? An Introduction to African Cave Taphonomy.* Chicago: University of Chicago Press.

Bricker, H. M. (1976). Upper palaeolithic archaeology. *Ann. Rev. Anthropol.* **5**, 133-148.

Brinch-Petersen, E. (1973). A survey of the late palaeolithic and the mesolithic of Denmark. In *The Mesolithic in Europe* (ed. S. K. Kozlowski), pp.77-129. Warsaw.

Broadbent, N. D. (1978). Prehistoric settlement in northern Sweden: a brief survey and a case study. In *The Early Post-Glacial Settlement of Northern Europe* (ed. P. Mellars), pp. 177-204. London: Duckworth.

Brose, D. S. and Wolpoff, M. H. (1971). Early Upper Palaeolithic man and late Middle Palaeolithic tools. *Am. Anthropol.* **73**, 1156-1194.

Brothwell, D. R. (1975). Salvaging the term "domestication" for certain types of man-animal relationship: the possible value of an eight-point scoring system. *J. Archaeol. Sci.* **2**, 397-400.

Bunn, H. *et al.*, (1980). FxJj50: an early Pleistocene site in northern Kenya. *World Archaeol.* **12 (2)**, 109-136.

Bunn, H. T. (1981). Archaeological evidence for meat-eating by Plio-Pleistocene hominids from Koobi Fora and Olduvai Gorge. *Nature* **291**, 574-577.

Burch, E. S. (1972). The caribou/wild reindeer as a human resource. *Am. Antiq.* **37 (3)**, 339-368.

Burr, D. (1976). Further evidence concerning speech in Neanderthal Man. *Man (N. S.)* **11**, 104-110.

Butzer, K. W. (1965). Acheulian occupation sites at Torralba and Ambrona, Spain: their geology. *Science* **150**, 1718-1722.

Butzer, K. W. (1974). Paleoecology of South African Australopithecines: Taung revisited. *Curr. Anthropol.* **15**, 367-382.

Butzer, K. W. (1975). Pleistocene littoral-sedimentary cycles of the Mediterranean basin: a Mallorquin view. In *After the Australopithecines* (ed. K. W. Butzer and G. L. Isaac), pp. 25-71. The Hague: Mouton.

Butzer, K. W. (1981). Cave sediments, upper pleistocene stratigraphy and Mousterian facies in Cantabrian Spain. *J. Archaeol. Sci.* **8**, 133-183.

Butzer, K. W. and Isaac, G. L. (1975). *After the Australopithecines.* The Hague: Mouton.

Butzer, K. W. *et al.* (1978). Lithostratigraphy of Border Cave, KwaZulu, South Africa: a middle stone age sequence beginning *c.* 195,000 B.P. *J. Archaeol. Sci.* **5**, 317-341.

Cachel, S. (1979). A paleoecological model for the origin of higher primates. *J. Hum. Evol.* **8**, 351-359.

Cahen, D. and Keeley, L. H. (1980). Not less than two, not more than three. *World Archaeol.* **12 (2)**, 166-180.

Campbell, B. G. and Bernor, R. L. (1976). The origin of the Hominidae: Africa or Asia? *J. Hum. Evol.* **5**, 441-454.

Campbell, J. M. (1978). Aboriginal human overkill of game populations: examples from interior North Alaska. In *Archaeological Essays in Honour of Irving B. Rouse* (ed. R. C. Dunnell and E. S. Hall), pp.179-208. The Hague: Mouton.

Cârciumaru, M. (1973a). Analiza polinică a coprolitelor din statiunea arheologică de la Icoana (defileul Dunării). *Stud. Cerc. Ist. Verche* **24 (1)**, 5-14.

Cârciumaru, M. (1973b). Analyse pollinique des coprolites livrés par quelques stations archéologiques des deux bords du Danube dans la zone des "Portes de Far". *Dacia* **17**, 53-60.

Carlisle, R. C. and Siegel, M. I. (1974). Some problems in the interpretation of Neanderthal speech capabilities: a reply to Lieberman. *Am. Anthropol.* **76**, 318-322.

Carney, J. *et al.* (1971). Late Australopithecine from Baringo District, Kenya. *Nature* **230**, 509-514.

Carter, H. H. (1975). Fauna of an area of mesolithic occupation in the Kennett Valley considered in relation to eating habits. *Berks. Archaeol. J.* **68**, 1-3.

Case, H. (1969a). Neolithic explanations. *Antiquity* **43**, 176-186.

Case, H. (1969b). Settlement-patterns in the North Irish Neolithic. *Ulster J. Archaeol.* **32**, 3-27.

Charteris, J., Wall, J. C. and Nottrodt, J. W. (1981). Functional reconstruction of gait from the Pliocene hominid footprints at Laetoli, northern Tanzania. *Nature* **290**, 496-498.

Cherry, J. F. (1981). Pattern and process in the earliest colonisation of the Greek islands. *Proc. Prehist. Soc.* **47**, 41-68.

Childe, V. G. (1929). *The Danube in Prehistory*. Oxford: Clarendon Press.

Childe, V. G. (1958). *The Prehistory of European Society*. London: Penguin Ltd.

Clark, J. D. and Haynes, C. V. (1970). An elephant butchery site at Mwanganda's village, Karonga, Malawi, and its relevance for Palaeolithic archaeology. *World Archaeol.* **1**, 390-409.

Clark, J. D. and Kurashina, H. (1979). Hominid occupation of the East-Central Highlands of Ethiopia in the Plio-Pleistocene. *Nature* **282**, 33-39.

Clark, J. G. D. (1954). *Star Carr*. Cambridge: Cambridge University Press.

Clark, J. G. D. (1972). Star Carr: a case study in bioarchaeology. *Addison Wesley Modular Publs.* **10**, 1-42.

Clark, J. G. D. (1975). *The Earlier Stone Age Settlement of Scandinavia*. Cambridge: Cambridge University Press.

Clark, J. G. D. (1978). Neothermal orientations. In *The Early Post-Glacial Settlement of Northern Europe* (ed. P. Mellars), pp.1-10. London: Duckworth.

Clark, J. G. D. and Piggott, S. (1965). *Prehistoric Societies*. London: Hutchinson.

Clarke, D. L. (1968). *Analytical Archaeology*. London: Methuen.

Clarke, D. L. (1976). Mesolithic Europe: the economic basis. In *Problems in Economic and Social Archaeology* (ed. G. de G. Sieveking, I. H. Longworth and K. E. Wilson), pp.449-481. London: Duckworth.

Clason, A. T. (1972). Some remarks on the use and presentation of archaeozoological data. *Helinium* **12**, 139-153.

CLIMAP Project Members (1976). The surface of the ice-age Earth. *Science* **191**, 1131-1137.

Close, A. E. (1978). The identification of style in lithic artefacts. *World Archaeol.* **10 (2)**, 223-237.

Clottes, J. (1976). Les civilisations du Paléolithique supérieure dans les Pyrénées. In *La Préhistoire Française* (ed. H. de Lumley), pp.1214-1231. Paris: CRNS.

Cohen, M. N. (1977). *The Food Crisis in Prehistory.* New Haven and London: Yale University Press.

Coles, J. M. (1971). The early settlement of Scotland: excavations at Morton, Fife. *Proc. Prehist. Soc.* **37 (2)**, 284-366.

Coles, J. M. (1979). *Experimental Archaeology.* London: Academic Press.

Conchon, O. (1976). The human settlement of Corsica: palaeogeographic and tectonic considerations. *J. Hum. Evol.* **5**, 241-248.

Conkey, M. W. (1980). The identification of prehistoric hunter-gatherer aggregation sites: the case of Altamira. *Curr. Anthropol.* **21 (5)**, 609-630.

Coope, G. R. and Pennington, W. (1977). The Windermere interstadial of the last Devensian. *Phil. Trans. R. Soc. London B* **280**, 337-339.

Coope, G. R., Morgan, A. and Osborne, P. J. (1971). Fossil coleoptera as indicators of climatic fluctuations during the last glaciation in Britain. *Palaeogeog., Palaeoclimatol & Palaeoecol.* **10**, 87-101.

Courtin, J. (1978). Les animaux domestiques du néolithique provençal: la faune sauvage et les débuts de l'élevage dans le sud-est de la France. *Bull. Mus. Nat. Hist. Marseilles* **38**, 187-194.

Courtin, J. and Erroux, J. (1974). Aperçu sur l'agriculture préhistorique dans le Sud-Est de la France. *Bull. Soc. Préhist. Fr.* **71**, 321-334.

Cronin, J. E. *et al.* (1981). Tempo and mode in hominid evolution. *Nature* **292**, 113-122.

Czerniak, L. and Piontek, J. (1980). The socioeconomic system of Europe neolithic populations. *Curr. Anthropol.* **21 (1)**, 97-100.

Dams, M. and Dams, L. (1977). Spanish rock art depicting honey gathering during the Mesolithic. *Nature* **268**, 228-230.

David, N. (1973). On upper palaeolithic society, ecology and technological change: the Noaillian case. In *The Explanation of Culture Change* (ed. C. Renfrew), pp.277-303. London: Duckworth.

Davidson, I. (1974). Radiocarbon dates for the Spanish solutrean. *Antiquity* **48**, 63-65.

Davidson, I. (1976). Les Mallaetes and Mondùver: the economy of a human group in prehistoric Spain. In *Problems in Economic and Social Archaeology* (eds. G. de G. Sieveking, I. H. Longworth and K. E. Wilson), pp.484-499. London: Duckworth.

Davis, R. S., Ranov, V. S. and Dodonov, A. E. (1980). Early man in Soviet Central Asia. *Sci. Am.* **243 (6)**, 130-137.

Davis, S. J. M. (1981). The effects of temperature change and domestication on the body size of Late Pleistocene to Holocene mammals of Israel. *Palaeobiology* **7 (1)**, 101-114.

Davis, S. J. M. and Valla, F. R. (1978). Evidence for domestication of the dog 12,000 years ago in the Natufian of Israel. *Nature* **276**, 608-610.

Day, M. H. (1977). *Guide to Fossil Man* (3rd edition). London: Cassell.

Day, M. H., Leakey, M. D. and Magori, C. (1980). A new hominid fossil skull (L.H. 18) from the Ngaloba Beds, Laetoli, northern Tanzania. *Nature* **284**, 55-56.

Delpech, F. (1968). Faunes du Magdalénien VI et de l'Azilien du gisement de Duruthy, commune de Sorde-l'Abbaye (Landes). *Actes Soc. Linn. Bordeaux* **105 (B.6)**, 3-19.

Delpech, F. (1970). Faune du magdalénien IV du gisement de Duruthy, commune de Sorde-l'Abbaye (Landes). *Bull. Assoc. Fr. Étud. Quatern.* **28**, 13-26.

Delpech, F. (1972). Étude paléoclimatique des faunes aurignaciennes et périgordiennes du gisement du Roc de Combe (Payrignac, Lot). *Quaternaria* **16**, 247-254.

Delporte, H. (1976). Les premières industries humaines en Auvergne. In *La Préhistoire Française* (ed. H. de Lumley), pp. 801-803. Paris: CRNS.

Dennell, R. W. (1973). The phylogenesis of *T. dicoccum*: a reconsideration. *Econ. Bot.* **27 (3)**, 329-331.

Dennell, R. W. (1976a). The economic importance of plant resources represented on archaeological sites. *J. Archaeol. Sci.* **3**, 229-247.

Dennell, R. W. (1976b). Prehistoric crop cultivation in southern England: a reconsideration. *Antiq. J.* **56 (1)**, 11-23.

Dennell, R. W. (1977). On the problems of studying prehistoric climate and crop agriculture. *Proc. Prehist. Soc.* **43**, 361-369.

Dennell, R. W. (1978). Early farming in South Bulgaria from the VIth to the IIIrd millennia B.C. *Brit. Archaeol. Rep. Internat. Ser.* **45**, 1-304.

Dennell, R. W. and Webley, D. (1975). Prehistoric land use and settlement in southern Bulgaria. In *Palaeoeconomy* (ed. E. S. Higgs), pp.97-109. Cambridge: Cambridge University Press.

Desbrosse, R. (1976). Les civilisation du Paléolithique supérieur dans le Jura méridional et dans les Alpes du Nord. In *La Préhistoire Française* (ed. H. de Lumley), pp.1196-1213. Paris: CRNS.

Desbrosse, R. and Mourer-Chauviré, C. (1973). Les oiseaux magdaléniens de Pierre-Châtel (Ain). *Quartär* **23-24**, 149-164.

Diamant, S. (1979). A short history of archaeological sieving at Franchthi Cave, Greece. *J. Field Archaeol.* **6**, 203-217.

Dobosi, V. T. and Vörös, I. (1979). Data to an evaluation of the finds assemblage of the palaeolithic paint mine at Lovas. *Folia Archaeol. (Budapest)* **30**, 7-26.

Dolhinow, P. J. (ed.) (1972). *Primate Patterns*. New York: Holt, Rinehart and Winston.

Dolukhanov, P. (1979). *Ecology and Economy in Neolithic Eastern Europe*. London: Duckworth.

Duplessy, J. C. *et al.* (1981). Deglacial warming of the north-eastern Atlantic Ocean: correlation with the paleo-climatic evolution of the European continent. *Palaeogeogr., Palaeoclimatol. & Palaeoecol.* **35**, 121-144.

Edwards, K. J. (1979). Palynological and temporal inference in the context of prehistory, with special reference to the evidence from lake and peat deposits. *J. Archaeol. Sci.* **6 (3)**, 255-270.

Eicher, U., Siegenthaler, U. and Wegmüller, S. (1981). Pollen and oxygen isotope analyses on late- and post-glacial sediments of the Tourbière de Chirens (Dauphiné, France). *Quat. Res.* **15 (2)**, 160-170.

Elias, M. (1980). The feasibility of dental strontium analysis for diet-assessment of human populations, *Am. J. Phys. Anthropol.* **53**, 1-4.

Elton, C. R. (1972). *The Ecology of Invasions by Animals and Plants*. London: Chapman and Hall.

Ericson, J. E., Sullivan, C. H. and Boaz, N. T. (1981). Diets of Pliocene mammals from Omo, Ethiopia, deduced from carbon isotope ratios in tooth apatite. *Palaeogeogr., Palaeoclimatol. & Palaeoecol.* **36**, 69-73.

Evans, J. D. (1964). Excavations in the neolithic settlement of Knossos, 1957-60, Part I. *Ann, Brit. Sch. Archaeol. Athens* **59**, 132-240.

Fejfar, O. (1969). Human remains from the early Pleistocene in Czechoslovakia. *Curr. Anthropol.* **10 (2-3)**, 170-173.

Fink, J. and Kukla, G. J. (1977). Pleistocene climates in Central Europe: at least 17 interglacials after the Olduvai event. *Quat. Res.* **7**, 363-371.

Flohn, H. (1979). On time-scales and causes of abrupt palaeo-climatic events. *Quat. Res.* **12 (1)**, 135-149.

Florschütz, F., Menendez-Amor, J. F. and Wijmstra, T. A. (1971). Palynology of a thick Quaternary succession in southern Spain. *Palaeogeogr., Palaeoclimatol. & Palaeoecol.* **10**, 233-264.

Foley, R. (1981). Off-site archaeology: an alternative approach for the short-sited. In *Pattern of the Past: Studies in Honour of David Clarke* (ed. I. Hodder, G. Isaac and N. Hammond), pp.157-183. Cambridge: Cambridge Univ. Press.

Fredén, C. (1975). Subfossil finds of arctic whales and seals in Sweden. *Sver. Geol. Unders.* **69 (2)**, 3-62.

Freeman, L. G. (1973). The significance of mammalian faunas from palaeolithic occupations in Cantabrian Spain. *Am. Antiq.* **38 (1)**, 3-41.

Freeman, L. G. (1981). The fat of the land: notes on palaeolithic diet in Iberia. In *Omnivorous Primates: Gathering and Hunting in Human Evolution* (ed. R. S. O. Harding and G. Teleki), pp.104-165. New York: Columbia University Press.

Freeman, L. G. and Butzer, K. W. (1966). The acheulean station of Torralba (Spain): a progress report. *Quaternaria* **8**, 9-21.

French, D. H. (1970). Notes on site distribution in the Çumra area. *Anatolian Studies* **20**, 139-148.

Frenzel, B. (1973). *Climatic Fluctuations of the Ice Age*. Cleveland and London: The Press of Case Western Reserve.

Frost, G. H. (1980). Tool behavior and the origins of laterality. *J. Hum. Evol.* **9**, 447-459.

Gábori-Csánk, V. (1968). *La Station du Paléolithique Moyen d'Érd-Hongrie*. Budapest: Akadémiai Kiadó.

Gábori-Csánk, V. (1970). C-14 dates of the Hungarian palaeolithic. *Acta Archaeol. Acad. Sci. Hung.* **22**, 3-11.

Gage, T. B. (1979). The competitive interactions of man and deer in prehistoric California. *J. Hum. Ecol.* **7 (3)**, 253-268.

Gamble, C. (1978). Resource exploitation and the spatial patterning of hunter-gatherers: a case study. In *Social Organisation and Settlement* (ed. D. Green, C. Haselgrove and M. Spriggs), pp.153-185. *Brit. Archaeol. Rep. (Internat. Ser.)* **47**.

Gamble, C. (1979). Hunting strategies in the Central European Palaeolithic. *Proc. Prehist. Soc.* **45**, 35-52.

Gamble, C. (1980). Information exchange in the palaeolithic. *Nature* **283**, 522-523.

Gamble, C. (1981). Scratches on the palaeolithic record. *Nature* **291**, 533-534.

Gascoyne, M., Currant, A. P. and Lord, T. C. (1981). Ipswichian fauna of Victoria cave and the marine palaeoclimatic record. *Nature* **294**, 652-654.

Gates, W. L. (1976). Modelling the ice-age climate. *Science* **191**, 1138-1144.

Geist, V. (1979). *Life Strategies, Human Evolution, Environmental Design*. New York: Springer Verlag.

Gifford, D. P. and Behrensmeyer, A. K. (1977). Observed formation and burial of a recent human occupation site in Kenya. *Quat. Res.* **8**, 245-266.

Gillespie, R. *et al.* (1978). Lancefield Swamp and the extinct Australian megafauna. *Science* **200**, 1044-1048.

Godwin, Sir H. (1975). *The History of the British Flora* (2nd ed.). Cambridge: Cambridge University Press.

Godwin, Sir H. (1978). *Fenland: Its Ancient Past and Uncertain Future*. Cambridge: Cambridge University Press.

Goudie, A. S. (1977). *Environmental Change*. Oxford: Clarendon Press.

Gould, R. A. (1971). Uses and effects of fire among the Western Desert Aborigines of Australia. *Mankind* **8**, 14-24.

Gould, S. J. (1980). The misnamed, mistreated and misunderstood Irish elk. In *Ever Since Darwin* (ed. S. J. Gould), pp.79-90. London: Penguin.

Gowlett, J. A. J. *et al.* (1981). Early archaeological sites, hominid remains and traces of fire from Chesowanja, Kenya. *Nature* **294**, 125-129.

Grayson, D. K. (1977). Pleistocene avifaunas and the overkill hypothesis. *Science* **195**, 691-693.

Grayson, D. K. (1979). On the quantification of vertebrate archaeofaunas. In *Advances in Archaeological Method and Theory, Vol. 2* (ed. M. Schiffer), pp.199-237. London and New York: Academic Press.

Green, H. S. *et al.* (1981). Pontnewydd Cave in Wales—a new Middle Pleistocene hominid site. *Nature* **294**, 707-713.

Greenfield, L. O. (1979). On the adaptive pattern of *Ramapithecus*. *Am. J. Phys. Anthropol.* **50**, 527-548.

Greig, J. (1981). The investigation of a medieval barrel-latrine from Worcester. *J. Archaeol. Sci.* **8**, 265-282.

Grigson, C. (1978). The craniology and relationships of four species of *Bos*: 4. The relationships between *Bos primigenius* Boj. and *Bos tauros* L. and its implications for the phylogeny of the domestic breeds. *J. Archaeol. Sci.* **5**, 123-162.

Grosswald, M. G. (1980). Late Weichselian ice sheets of northern Eurasia. *Quat. Res.* **13 (1)**, 1-32.

Grote, K. (1978). Die Grabung 1977 in der mittelpaläolithischen Freilandstation Salzgitter-Lebenstedt. *Archäol. Korresp.* **8**, 155-162.

Grüger, E. (1977). Pollenanalytische Untersuchung zur würmzeitlichen Vegetationsgeschichte von Kalabrien (Süditalien). *Flora* **166**, 475-489.

Guilaine, J. (1979). The earliest neolithic in the West Mediterranean: a new appraisal. *Antiquity* **53**, 22-30.

Hahn, J. (1978). New aspects of the Magdalenian in Central Europe. *Rev. Anthropol.* **5 (3)**, 313-331.

Hall, A. D. (1917). *The Book of the Rothamsted Experiments*. London: Murray.

Hallam, J. S. *et al.* (1973). A late glacial elk with associated barbed points from High Furlong, Lancashire. *Proc. Prehist. Soc.* **39**, 100-128.

Halstead, P. L. J. (1981). From determinism to uncertainty: social storage and the rise of the Minoan palace. In *Economic Archaeology* (ed. A. Sheridan and G. Bailey), pp.187-213. *Brit. Archaeol. Rep. Internat. Ser.* **96**.

Hammond, F. (1981). The colonisation of Europe: the analysis of settlement process. In *Pattern of the Past: studies in honour of David Clarke* (ed. I. Hodder, G. Isaac and N. Hammond), pp.211-248. Cambridge: Cambridge Univ. Press.

Hansen, J. and Renfrew, J. M. (1978). Palaeolithic-neolithic seed remains at Franchthi Cave, Greece. *Nature* **271**, 349-352.

Harlan, J. R. (1967). A wild wheat harvest in Turkey. *Archaeology* **20 (3)**, 197-201.

Harlan, J. R. (1971). Agricultural origins: centers and noncenters. *Science* **174**, 468-474.

Harmon, R. S., Glazek, J. and Nowak, K. (1980). ^{230}Th/^{234}U dating of travertine from the Bilzingsleben archaeological site, *Nature* 284, 132-135.

Harrold, F. B. (1980). A comparative analysis of Eurasian Palaeolithic burials. *World Archaeol.* **12 (2)**, 195-211.

Hatley, T. and Kappelman, J. (1980). Bears, pigs, and Plio-Pleistocene hominids: a case for exploitation of belowground food resources. *Hum. Ecol.* **8 (4)**, 371-387.

Hawkes, K. and O'Connell, J. F. (1981). Affluent hunters? Some comments in the light of the Alyawara case, *Am. Anthropol.* **83**, 622-626.

Hay, R. L. (1980). The KBS tuff controversy may be ended. *Nature* **284**, 401.

Haynes, G. (1980). Evidence of carnivore gnawing on Pleistocene and Recent mammalian bones. *Paleobiology* **6 (3)**, 341-351.

Hays, J. D., Imbrie, J. and Shackleton, N. J. (1976). Variations in the earth's orbit: pacemaker of the Ice Ages. *Science* **194**, 1121-1132.

Helbaek, H. (1960). The palaeoethnobotany of the Near East and Europe. In *Prehistoric Investigations in Iraqi Kurdistan* (by R. J. Braidwood and B. Howe), pp.99-118. *Studies in Ancient Oriental Civilisation* **31**.

Helbaek, H. (1969). Plant collecting, dry-farming, and irrigation agriculture in prehistoric Deh Luran. In *Prehistory and human ecology of the Deh Luran Plain* (by F. Hole, K. V. Flannery and J. A. Neely), pp.383-426. *Mem. Mus. Anthrop. Univ. Mich.* **1**.

Helbaek, H. (1970). The plant husbandry of Haçilar. In *Excavations at Haçilar (1)* (by J. Mellaart), pp.189-244. Edinburgh: Edinburgh University Press.

Hemingway, M. F. (1980). The initial Magdalenian in France, *Brit. Archaeol. Rep. Internat. Ser.* **90**.

Hennig, G. J. *et al.* (1981). ESR-dating of the fossil hominid cranium from Petralona Cave, Greece. *Nature* **292**, 533-536.

Henschel, J. R., Tilson, R. and Blottnitz, F. F. von (1979). Implications of a spotted hyaena bone assemblage in the Namib Desert. *S. Afr. Archaeol. Bull.* **34**, 127-131.

Herman, Y. and Hopkins, D. M. (1980). Arctic oceanic climate in late Cenozoic time. *Science* **209**, 557-562.

Heusser, L. E. and Shackleton, N. J. (1979). Direct marine-continental correlation: 150,000-year oxygen isotope — pollen record from the North Pacific. *Science* **204**, 837-839.

Higgs, E. S. and Jarman, M. R. (1972). The origins of animal and plant husbandry. In *Papers in Economic Prehistoric* (ed. E. S. Higgs), pp.3-13. Cambridge: Cambridge University Press.

Hillman, G. (1972). Excavations at Can Hasan III: The plant remains. In *Papers in Economic Prehistory* (ed. E. S. Higgs), pp.182-188. Cambridge: Cambridge University Press.

Hillman, G. (1975). The plant remains from Tell Abu Hureyra: a preliminary report. *Proc. Prehist. Soc.* **41**, 70-73.

Hjort, C. (1979). Glaciation in northern East Greenland during the Late Weichselian and Early Flandrian. *Boreas* **8 (3)**, 281-296.

Hodder, I. (1977). The distribution of material culture items in the Baringo district, western Kenya. *Man N.S.* **12**, 239-269.

Hole, F. and Flannery, K. V. (1967). The prehistory of south-western Iran: a preliminary report. *Proc. Prehist. Soc.* **33**, 147-206.

Holloway, R. L. (1973). Endocranial volumes of early African hominids, and the role of the brain in human mosaic evolution. *J. Hum. Evol.* **2**, 449-459.

Hooker, P. J. and Miller, J. A. (1979). K-Ar dating of the Pleistocene hominid site at Chesowanja, North Kenya. *Nature* **282**, 710-712.

Hopf, M. (1969). Plant remains and early farming in Jericho. In *The Domestication and Exploitation of Plants and Animals* (ed. P. J. Ucko and G. W. Dimbleby), pp.355-360. London: Duckworth.

Howell, N. (1980). *Demography of the Dobe Area !Kung.* New York: Academic Press.

Hubbard, R.N.L.B. (1976). Crops and climate in prehistoric Europe. *World Archaeol.* **8 (2)**, 159-168.

Hughes, T. *et al.* (1977). Was there a late-Würm Arctic ice sheet? *Nature* **266**, 596-602.

Ikeya, M. (1978). Electron spin resonance as a method of dating. *Archaeometry* **20 (2)**, 147-158.

Imbrie, J. and Imbrie, J. Z. (1980). Modelling the climatic response to orbital variations. *Science* **207**, 943-953.

Indrelid, S. (1975). Problems relating to the early mesolithic settlement of southern Norway. *Norw. Archaeol. Rev.* **8**, 1-18.

Indrelid, S. (1978). Mesolithic economy and settlement patterns in Norway. In *The Early Post-Glacial Settlement of Northern Europe* (ed. P. Mellars), pp.147-176. London: Duckworth.

Ingold, T. (1980). *Hunters, Pastoralists and Ranchers.* Cambridge: Cambridge University Press.

Isaac, G. L. (1971). The diet of early man: aspects of archaeological evidence from lower and middle Pleistocene sites in Africa. *World Archaeol.* **1**, 1-28.

Isaac, G. L. (1972). Chronology and the tempo of cultural change during the Pleistocene. In *Calibration of Hominid Evolution* (eds W. W. Bishop and J. A. Miller), pp.381-430. Edinburgh: Scottish Academic Press.

Isaac, G. L. (1977). *Olorgesailie.* Chicago: University of Chicago Press.

Isaac, G. L. (1978). Food sharing and human evolution: archaeological evidence from the Plio-Pleistocene of East Africa. *J. Anthropol. Res.* **34**, 311-325.

Isaac, G. L. (1980). Casting the net wide: a review of archaeological evidence for early hominid land-use and ecological relations. In *Current Arguments on Early Man* (ed. L-K. Konigsson), pp.226-251. Roy. Swedish Acad. Sci: Pergamon Press.

Isaac, G. L. (1981). Stone Age visiting cards: approaches to the study of early land use patterns. In *Pattern of the Past: studies in honour of David Clarke* (ed. I. Hodder, G. Isaac, and N. Hammond), pp.131-155. Cambridge: Cambridge University Press.

Isaac, G. L. and Crader, D. C. (1981). To what extent were early hominids carnivorous? In *Omnivorous Primates: Gathering and Hunting in Human Evolution* (ed. R. S. O. Harding and G. Teleki), pp.37-103. New York: Columbia University Press.

Ivanova, I. K. and Chernysh, A. P. (1965). The palaeolithic site of Molodova V on the Middle Dneistr (USSR). *Quaternaria* **7**, 197-217.

Jacobi, R. M. (1976). Britain inside and outside Mesolithic Europe. *Proc. Prehist. Soc.* **42**, 67-84.

Jacobi, R. M. (1978). Northern England in the eighth millennium b.c.: an essay. In *The Early Post-Glacial Settlement of Northern Europe* (ed. P. Mellars), pp.295-332. London: Duckworth.

Jacobi, R. M. (1980). The Upper Palaeolithic in Britain, with special reference to Wales. In *Culture and environment in prehistoric Wales* (ed. J. A. Taylor), pp.15-99. *Brit. Archaeol. Rep.* **76**.

Jacobs, L. L. and Pilbeam, D. (1980). Of mice and men: fossil-based divergence dates and molecular "clocks". *J. Hum. Evol.* **9**, 551-555.

Jacobsen, T. W. (1976). 17,000 years of Greek prehistory. *Sci. Am.* **234 (6)**, 76-87.

Jarman, H. N. (1972). The origins of wheat and barley cultivation. In *Papers in Economic Prehistory* (ed. E. S. Higgs), pp.15-26. Cambridge: Cambridge Univ. Press.

Jarman, M. R. (1971). Culture and economy in the north Italian Neolithic, *World Archaeol.* **2 (3)**, 255-265.

Jarman, M. R. (1972). European deer economies and the advent of the Neolithic. In *Papers in Economic Prehistory* (ed. E. S. Higgs), pp.125-148. Cambridge: Cambridge University Press.

Jarman, M. R. and Wilkinson, P. F. (1972). Criteria of animal domestication. In *Papers in Economic Prehistory* (ed. E. S. Higgs), pp.83-96. Cambridge: Cambridge University Press.

Jelinek, J. (1980). European *Homo erectus* and the origin of *Homo sapiens.* In *Current Argument on Early Man* (ed. L-K. Konigsson), pp.137-143. Roy. Swedish Acad. Sci: Pergamon Press.

Jennings, J. N. (1979). Man and other animals in Australian caves and shelters: a review, *Trans. Brit. Cave. Res. Assoc.* **6 (3)**, 91-130.

Jequier, J-P. (1975). Le Mousterien alpin. *Eborodunum* **2**.

Jochim, M. A. (1976). *Hunting-Gathering Subsistence and Settlement: A Predictive Model.* New York: Academic Press.

Johanson, D. C. and Edey, M. A. (1981). *Lucy: The Beginnings of Mankind.* New York: Simon and Schuster.

Johanson, D. C. and Taieb, M. (1976). Plio-Pleistocene hominid discoveries in Hadar, Ethiopia. *Nature* **260**, 293-297.

Johanson, D. C. and White, T. D. (1979). A systematic assessment of early African hominids. *Science* **203**, 321-330.

Johanson, D. C., White, T. D. and Coppens, Y. (1978). A new species of the genus *Australopithecus* (Primates: Hominidae) from the Pliocene of eastern Africa. *Kirtlandia* **28**, 1-14.

Jolly, C. J. (1970). The seed-eaters: a new model of hominid differentiation based on a baboon analogy. *Man. (N.S.)* **5**, 5-26.

Jones, P. R. (1979). Effects of raw materials on biface manufacture. *Science* **204**, 835-836.

Jones, R. (1979). The Fifth Continent: problems concerning the human colonisation of Australia. *Ann. Rev. Anthropol.* **8**, 445-466.

Keeley, L. H. (1980). *Experimental Determination of Stone Tool Uses: A Microwear Analysis.* Chicago: Chicago Univ. Press.

Keeley, L. H. and Toth, N. (1981). Microwear polishes on early stone tools from Koobi Fora, Kenya, *Nature* **293**, 464-465.

Kennedy, G. (1980). The emergence of modern man, *Nature* **284**, 11-12.

Kennett, J. P. (1980). Paleooceanographic and biogeographic evolution of the southern ocean during the Cenozoic, and Cenozoic microfossil datums. *Paleogeogr., Paleoclimatol., Paleoecol.* **31**, 123-152.

Kerr, R. A. (1981). Staggered Antarctic ice formation supported. *Science* **213**, 427-428.

Klein, R. G. (1969a). The Mousterian of Europe Russia. *Proc. Prehist. Soc.* **35**, 77-111.

Klein, R. G. (1969b). *Man and Culture in the Late Pleistocene: A Case Study.* San Francisco. Chandler Publishing Co.

Klein, R. G. (1973). *Ice-Age Hunters of the Ukraine.* Chicago and London: University of Chicago Press.

Klein, R. G. (1975). A preliminary report on the 'middle stone age' open-air site of Duinefontein 2 (Melkbosstrand, south-western Cape Province, South Africa). *S. Afr. Archaeol. Bull.* **31**, 12-20.

Klein, R. G. (1976). The mammalian fauna of the Klasies River Mouth sites, southern Cape Province, south Africa. *S. Afr. Archaeol. Bull.* **31**, 75-98.

Klein, R. G. (1977). The mammalian fauna from the middle and later stone age (later pleistocene) levels of Border Cave, Natal Province, South Africa. *S. Afr. Archaeol. Bull.* **32**, 14-27.

Klein, R. G. (1978a). The fauna and overall interpretation of the "Cutting 10" Acheulean site at Elandsfontein (Hopefield), Southwestern Cape Province, South Africa. *Quat. Res.* **10**, 69-83.

Klein, R. G. (1978b). Stone age predation on large African bovids. *J. Archaeol. Sci.* **5**, 195-217.

Kleindienst, M. R. and Keller, C. M. (1976). Towards a functional analysis of handaxes and cleavers: the evidence from eastern Africa. *Man* **11**, 176-187.

Korobitsyna, K. V. *et al.* (1974). Chromosomes of the Siberian snow sheep, *Ovis nivicola*, and implications concerning the origin of Amphiberingian wild sheep (subgenus *Pachyceros*). *Quat. Res.* **4**, 235-245.

Kozlowski, J. (1974). Upper palaeolithic site with dwellings of mammoth bones — Cracow, Spadzista Street B. *Folia Quatern.* **44**, 1-103.

Kretzoi, M. (1975). New ramapithecines and *Pliopithecus* from the Lower Pliocene of Rudabánya in north-eastern Hungary. *Nature* **257**, 578-581.

Kretzoi, M. and Vertes, L. (1965). Upper Biharian (Intermindel) pebble industry occupation site in western Hungary. *Curr. Anthropol.* **6 (1)**, 74-87.

Kruuk, H. (1972). *The Spotted Hyaena: a study of predation and social behaviour.* Chicago: University of Chicago Press.

Kurtén, B. (1968). *Pleistocene Mammals of Europe.* London: Weidenfeld and Nicolson.

Lacaille, A. D. (1954). *The Stone Age of Scotland.* London: Oxford University Press.

Lallo, J. W. and Rose, J. C. (1979). Patterns of stress, disease and mortality in two prehistoric populations from North America. *J. Hum Evol.* **8**, 323-335.

Lambert, J. B., Szpunar, C. B. and Buikstra, J. E. (1979). Chemical analysis of excavated human bone from Middle and Late Woodland sites. *Archaeometry* **21 (2)**, 115-129.

Lamprecht, J. (1981). The function of social hunting in larger terrestrial carnivores. *Mammal. Rev.* **11 (4)**, 169-179.

Laville, H. (1973). The relative position of Mousterian industries in the climatic chronology of the Early Würm in the Perigord. *World Archaeol.* **4 (3)**, 323-329.

Laville, H., Rigaud, J.-P. and Sackett, J. (1980). *Rock Shelters of the Perigord: Geological Stratigraphy and Archaeological Succession.* New York: Academic Press.

Leakey, M. D. (1971). *Olduvai Gorge, Vol III.* Cambridge: Cambridge University Press.

Leakey, M. D. and Hay, R. L. (1979). Pliocene footprints in the Laetolil Beds at Laetoli, northern Tanzania. *Nature* **278**, 317-323.

Leakey, M. D. *et al.* (1976). Fossil hominids from the Laetolil Beds. *Nature* **262**, 460-466.

Leavy, C. (1979). *The Naturalised Animals of the British Isles.* London: Granada.

Lee, R. B. and DeVore, I. (1968). *Man the Hunter.* Chicago: Aldine.

Legge, A. J. (1981). Aspects of cattle husbandry. In *Farming Practice in British Prehistory* (ed. R. Mercer), pp.169-181. Edinburgh: Edinburgh University Press.

Leroi-Gourhan, A. and Allain, J. (1979). Lascaux inconnu. *Gallia Préhist., Suppl.* **12**.

Leroi-Gourhan, A. and Brezillon, M. (1972). Fouilles de Pincevent. *Gallia Préhist., Suppl.* **7**.

Lévêque, F. and Vandermeersch, B. (1980). Découverte de restes humains dans un niveau castelperronian à Saint-Césaire (Charente-Maritime). *C. r. Séanc. Acad. Sci. Paris* (D) **291**, 187-189.

Levine, L. D. and McDonald, M. M. A. (1976). The neolithic and chalcolithic periods in the Mahidasht. *Iran* **15**, 39-50.

Lewin, R. (1981). Ethiopian stone tools are world's oldest *Science* **211**, 806-807.

Lieberman, P. and Crelin, E. S. (1971). On the speech of Neanderthal Man. *Ling. Inq.* **2 (2)**, 203-222.

Lindsay, E. H., Opdyke, N. D. and Johnson, N. M. (1980). Pliocene dispersal of the horse *Equus* and late Cenozoic mammalian dispersal events. *Nature* **287**, 135-138.

Littauer, M. A. (1980). Horse sense, or nonsense? *Antiquity* **54**, 139-140.

Lourandos, H. (1980). Change or stability?: hydraulics, hunter-gatherers and population in temperate Australia. *World Archaeol.* **11 (3)**, 245-264.

Lovejoy, C. O. (1981). The origin of man. *Science* **211**, 341-351.

Lumley, H. de (1969). A palaeolithic camp at Nice. *Sci. Am.* **220 (5)**, 42-50.

Lumley, H. de (1976). Les civilisations du Paléolithique inférieur en Provence. In *La Préhistoire Française* (ed. H. de Lumley), pp.819-851. Paris: CRNS.

Lumley, H. de *et al.* (1963). La grotte du Vallonnet Roquebrune-Cap-Martin (A.-M.). *Bull. Mus. Anthropol. & Préhist. Monaco* **10**, 5-20.

Lumley, M.-A. de and Garcia-Sanchez, M. (1971). L'enfant néandertalien de Carigüela a Piñar (Andalousie). *L'Anthropologie* **75 (1)**, 29-56.

Lyman, R. L. (1979). Available meat from faunal remains: a consideration of techniques. *Am. Antiq.* **44 (3)**, 532-546.

McBurney, C. B. M. (1968). *The Haua Fteah.* Cambridge: Cambridge University Press.

McDonald, M. M. A. (1979). An examination of mid-Holocene settlement patterns in the Central Zagros region of western Iran. University of Toronto: Ph.D. dissertation.

McGovern, T. H. (1980). Cows, harp seals, and church bells: adaptation and extinction in Norse Greenland. *Hum. Ecol.* **8 (3)**, 245-275.

McGrew, W. C., Tutin, C. E. G. and Baldwin, P. J. (1979). Chimpanzees, tools, and termites: cross-cultural comparisons of Senegal, Tanzania and Rio Muni. *Man (N.S.)* **14**, 185-214.

McHenry, H. M. (1976). Early hominid body weight and encephalization. *Am. J. Phys. Anthropol.* **45**, 77-84.

McHenry, H. M. and Corruccini, R. S. (1980). Late Tertiary hominoids and human origins. *Nature* **285**, 397-398.

Malez, M. *et al.* (1980). Upper Pleistocene hominids from Vindija, Croatia, Yugoslavia. *Curr. Anthropol.* **21 (3)**, 365-367.

Mangerud, J., Sønstegaard, E. and Sejrup, H-P. (1979). Correlation of the Eemian (interglacial) stage and the deep-sea oxygen-isotope stratigraphy. *Nature* **277**, 189-192.

Mania, D. (1979a). *"Homo erectus"*—seine Kultur und Umwelt: 2nd Bilzingsleben-Kolloquium. *Ethnogr.-Archäol. Z.* **20**.

Mania, D. (1979b). Zur Technologie der Knochen- und Geweihartefakte von Bilzingsleben. *Ethnogr.-Archäol. Z.* **20**, 708-722.

Mania, D. (1979c). Quellen, Quellenforschung und Quellenauswertung in der Pleisto-zänarchäologie. *Wissensch. Beitr. Martin Luther Univ. Halle-Wittenburg 1979*, 29-58.

Mania, D. and Töpfer, V. (1973). Gliederung, Ökologie und der Mittelpaläolithische Funde der letzten Eiszeit. *Veröff. Landesmus. Vorgesch. Halle* **26**.

Margolis, S. V. and Herman, Y. (1980). Northern Hemisphere sea-ice and glacial development in the late Cenozoic, *Nature* **286**, 145-149.

Marshack, A. (1972a). Upper palaeolithic notation and symbol. *Science* **178**, 817-828.

Marshack, A. (1972b). Cognitive aspects of upper palaeolithic engravings. *Curr. Anthropol.* **13 (3-4)**, 445-461.

Matson, M. and Wiesnet, D. R. (1981). New data base for climate studies. *Nature* **289**, 451-456.

Mech, L. D. (1970). *The Wolf: the Ecology and Behaviour of an Endangered Species.* New York: The Natural History Press.

Mellars, P. A. (1969). The chronology of Mousterian industries in the Perigord region. *Proc. Prehist. Soc.* **35**, 134-171.

Mellars, P. A. (1973). The character of the middle-upper palaeolithic transition in southwest France. In *Explanations of Culture Change* (ed. C. Renfrew), pp.255-276. London: Duckworth.

Mellars, P. A. (1976). Fire ecology, animal populations and man: a study of some ecological relationships in prehistory. *Proc. Prehist. Soc.* **42**, 15-46.

Mellars, P. A. (1978). Excavation and economic analysis of Mesolithic shell middens on the island of Oronsay (Inner Hebrides). In *The Early Post-Glacial Settlement of Northern Europe.* (ed. P. Mellars), pp.371-396. London: Duckworth.

Mellars, P. A. and Wilkinson, M. R. (1980). Fish otoliths as evidence of seasonality in prehistoric shell middens: the evidence from Oronsay (Inner Hebrides). *Proc. Prehist. Soc.* **46**, 19-44.

Mercer, J. (1974). New C[14] dates from the Isle of Jura, Argyll. *Antiquity* **48**, 65-66.

Merwe, N. J. van der, Roosevelt, A. C. and Vogel, J. C. (1981). Isotopic evidence for prehistoric subsistence change at Parmana, Venezuela. *Nature* **292**, 536-538.

Milisauskas, S. (1977). Adaptations of the early neolithic farmers in Central Europe. *Anthropol. Pap. USA* **61**, 295-316.

Milisauskas, S. (1978). *European Prehistory.* London: Academic Press.

Modderman, P. J. R. (1970). Linearbandkeramik aus Elsloo und Stein. *Analecta Praehis. Leidensia* **3**.

Møhl, U. (1970). Fangstdyrene ved de Danske strande. *Kuml* **1970**, 297-329.

Møhl-Hansen, U. (1964). Marrow-split bones in interglacial deposits in Jutland. *Aarbøger* **1964**, 121-126.

Morgan, J. (1979). *The Life and Adventures of William Buckley.* Canberra: Australian National University Press.

Mosimann, J. E. and Martin, P. S. (1975). Simulating overkill by Paleoindians, *Am. Sci.* **45**, 304-313.

Movius, H. L. (1950). A wooden spear of third interglacial age from lower Saxony. *Southwestern J. Anthropol.* **6** (2), 139-142.

Movius, H. L. (1974). The Abri Pataud orogram of the French Upper Palaeolithic in retrospect. In *Archaeological Researches in Retrospect* (ed. G. R. Willey), pp.87-116. Cambridge (Mass.): Winthrop.

Movius, H. L. (1975). Excavation of the Abri Pataud, les Eyzies (Dordogne). *Bull. Am. School Prehist. Res.* **30**, 1-305.

Moynahan, E. J. (1979). Trace elements in man. *Phil. Trans. R. Soc. London B* **288**, 65-79.

Müller, H. H. (1964). Die Haustiere der Mitteldeutschen Bandkeramiker. *Deutsch. Akad. Wissensch. Berlin* **17**.

Müller-Beck, H. (1978). New light on the Pleistocene period of Central Europe. *Rev. Anthropol.* (USA) **5** (3), 291-312.

Mulvaney, J. (1975). *The Prehistory of Australia* (revised ed.). London: Pelican.

Musil, R. (1970). Domestication of the dog already in the Magdalenian? *Anthropologie* (Brno) **8** (1), 87-88.

Niklewski, J. and Zeist, W. van (1970). A late Quaternary pollen diagram from north-western Syria. *Acta Bet. Neerl.* **19** (5), 737-754.

Ninkovich, D. and Burckle, L. H. (1978). Absolute age of the base of the hominid-bearing beds in eastern Java. *Nature* **275**, 306-308.

Oakley, K. P. (1980). Relative dating of the fossil hominids of Europe. *Bull. Br. Mus. Nat. Hist. (Geol.)* **34** (1), 1-63.

Odner, K. (1966). Komsakulturen i Nesseby og Sør-Varanger. *Tromsø Univ. Skr.* **12**.

Oerlemans, J. (1980). Model experiments on the 100,000-yr glacial cycle. *Nature* **287**, 430-432.

Ohel, M. Y. (1979). The Clactonian: an independent complex or an integral part of the Acheulean? *Curr. Anthropol.* **20** (4), 685-726.

Osborne, P. J. (1974). An insect assemblage of early flandrian age from Lea Marston, Warwickshire, and its bearing on the contemporary climate and ecology. *Quat. Res.* **4**, 471-486.

Palmer, S. (1976). The Mesolithic habitation site at Culver Well, Portland, Dorset: interim note. *Proc. Prehist. Soc.* **42**, 324-327.

Partridge, T. C. (1973). Geomorphological dating of cave openings at Makapansgat, Sterkfontein, Swartkrans and Taung. *Nature* **246**, 75-79.

Payne, S. (1975). Faunal change at Franchthi Cave from 20,000 B.C. to 3,000 B.C. In *Archaeozoological Studies* (ed. A. T. Clason), pp.120-131. Amsterdam: North Holland Publishing Co.

Pennington, W. (1975). The effect of Neolithic man on the environment in northwest England: the use of absolute pollen diagrams. *Council for Brit. Archaeol. Res. Rep.* **11**, 74-86.

Perkins, D. (1964). Prehistoric fauna from Shanidar, Iraq. *Science* **144**, 1565-1566.

Peters, C. R. (1979). Toward an ecological model of African Plio-Pleistocene hominid adaptations. *Am. Anthropol.* **81 (2)**, 261-278.

Peterson, G. M. *et al.* (1979). The continental record of environmental conditions at 18,000 B.P.: an initial evaluation. *Quat. Res.* **12**, 47-82.

Phillips, P. (1975). *Early Farmers of West Mediterranean Europe.* London: Hutchinson.

Phillips, P. (1980). *The Prehistory of Europe.* London: Allen Lane.

Pilbeam, D. (1979). Recent finds and interpretations of Miocene Hominoids. *Ann. Rev. Anthropol.* **8**, 333-352.

Pilbeam, D. R. (1980). Major trends in human evolution. In *Current Arguments on Early Man* (ed. L.-K. Konigsson), pp.261-285. Roy. Swedish Acad. Sci.: Pergamon Press.

Pilbeam, D. (1982). New hominoid skull material from the Miocene of Pakistan. *Nature* **295**, 232-234.

Pilbeam, D. and Gould, S. J. (1974). Size and scaling in human evolution. *Science* **186**, 892-901.

Pilbeam, D. *et al.* (1977). New hominoid primates from the Siwaliks of Pakistan and their bearing on hominoid evolution. *Nature* **270**, 689-695.

Pirie, N. W. (1969). *Food Resources Conventional and Novel.* London: Penguin.

Pitts, M. W. (1979). Hides and antlers: a new look at the gatherer-hunter site at Star Carr, North Yorkshire, England. *World Archaeol.* **11 (1)**, 32-42.

Pitts, M. W. and Jacobi, R. M. (1979). Some aspects of change in flaked stone industries of the Mesolithic and Neolithic in southern Britain. *J. Archaeol. Sci.* **6 (2)**, 163-177.

Planchais, N. (1970). Tardiglacaire et postglacaire à Mur-de-Sologne (Loire-et-Cher) (1). *Pollen et Spores* **12 (3)**, 381-428.

Potts, R. and Shipman, P. (1981). Cutmarks made by stone tools on bones from Olduvai Gorge, Tanzania. *Nature* **291**, 577-590.

Poulain, T. (1971). Le camp mésolithique de Gramari à Methamis (Vaucluse). III: Étude de la faune. *Gallia Préhist.* **14 (1)**, 121-131.

Radulesco, P. C. and Samson, P. (1962). Sur un centre de domestication du Mouton dans le Mésolithique de la grotte "La Adam" en Dobrogea. *Z. Tierz. Züchtungsbiol.* **76**, 282-320.

Ranov, V. A. and Davis, R. S. (1979). Toward a new outline of the Soviet Central Asian palaeolithic. *Curr. Anthropol.* **20 (2)**, 249-262.

Rak, Y. and Clarke, R. J. (1979). Ear ossicle of *Australopithecus robustus. Nature* **279**, 62-63.

Reimers, E. and Klein, D. R. (1979). Reindeer and caribou. *Nature* **282**, 558-559.

Renfrew, C. (1978). Trajectory discontinuity and morphogenesis: the implications of Catastrophe Theory for archaeology. *Am. Antiq.* **43 (2)**, 203-222.

Renfrew, C., Dixon, J. E. and Cann, J. R. (1968). Further analysis of Near Eastern obsidians. *Proc. Prehist. Soc.* **34**, 319-331.

Rightmire, G. P. (1979a). Cranial remains of *Homo erectus* from Beds II and IV, Olduvai Gorge, Tanzania. *Am. J. Phys. Anthropol.* **51**, 99-116.

Rightmire, G. P. (1979b). Implications of Border Cave skeletal remains for later Pleistocene human evolution. *Curr. Anthropol.* **20 (1)**, 23-35.

Rightmire, G. P. (1980). Middle Pleistocene hominids from Olduvai Gorge, Northern Tanzania. *Am. J. Phys. Anthropol.* **53**, 225-241.

Rightmire, G. P. (1981). Patterns in the evolution of *Homo erectus. Paleobiology* **7 (2)**, 241-246.

Roe, D. (1981). *The Lower and Middle Palaeolithic Ages in Britain.* London: RKP.

Rolland, N. (1981). The interpretation of middle palaeolithic variability. *Man (N.S.)* **16**, 15-42.

Rowley-Conwy, P. (1981). Mesolithic Danish bacon: permanent and temporary sites in the Danish Mesolithic. In *Economic Archaeology* (ed. A. Sheridan and G. Bailey), pp.51-55. *Brit. Archaeol. Rep. Internat. Ser.* **96**.

Ruddiman, W. F. (1977). North Atlantic ice-rafting: a major change at 75,000 years before the present. *Science* **196**, 1208-1211.

Ruddiman, W. F. and McIntyre, A. (1981). The North Atlantic Ocean during the last deglaciation. *Palaeogeogr., Palaeoclimatol., Palaeoecol.* **35**, 145-214.

Ruddiman, W. F., Sancetta, C. D. and McIntyre, A. F. (1977). Glacial/interglacial response rate of subpolar North Atlantic waters to climatic change: the record in oceanic sediments. *Phil. Trans. R. Soc. London B.* **280**, 119-142.

Ryan, M. (1980). An early mesolithic site in the Irish highlands. *Antiquity* **54**, 46-47.

Ryder, M. L. (1974). Hair of the mammoth. *Nature* **249**, 190-192.

Sabater, J. (1974). An elementary industry of the chimpanzees in the Okorobiko Mountains, Rio Muni (Republic of Equatorial Guinea), West Africa. *Primates* **15 (4)**, 351-364.

Sackett, J. R. (1981). From de Mortillet to Bordes: a century of French Palaeolithic research. In *Towards a History of Archaeology* (ed. G. Daniel), pp.85-99. London: Thames and Hudson.

Sahlins, M. (1974). *Stone Age Economics.* London: Tavistock Publications.

Salinger, M. J. (1981). Palaeoclimates north and south. *Nature* **291**, 106-107.

Salisbury, Sir E. (1964). *Weeds and Aliens.* London: Collins.

Sarich, V. W. and Cronin, J. E. (1977). Generation length and rates of hominoid molecular evolution. *Nature* **269**, 354-355.

Schaller, G. B. (1972). *The Serengeti Lion: a study of predator-prey relations.* Chicago: Univ. of Chicago Press.

Schaller, G. B. and Lowther, G. (1969). The relevance of carnivore behaviour to the study of early hominids. *Southwestern J. Anthropol.* **25 (4)**, 307-341.

Schild, R. (1976). The final palaeolithic settlements of the European plain. *Sci. Am.* **234 (2)**, 88-99.

Schrire, C. (1980). An inquiry into the evolutionary status and apparent identity of San hunter-gatherers. *Hum. Ecol.* **8 (1)**, 9-32.

Schwarcz, H. P. (1980). Absolute age determination of archaeological sites by uranium series dating of travertines. *Archaeometry* **22 (1)**, 3-24.

Schwarcz, H. P. and Skoflek, I. (1982). New dates for the Tata, Hungary, archaeological site. *Nature* **295**, 590-591.

Scott, K. (1980). Two hunting episodes of Middle Palaeolithic age at La Cotte de Saint-Brelade, Jersey (Channel Islands). *World Archaeol.* **12 (2)**, 137-152.

Service, E. (1962). *Primitive Social Organisation: An Evolutionary Perspective.* New York: Random House.

Sevink, J. *et al.*, (1981). A note on an approximately 730,000 year old mammal fauna and associated human activity sites near Isernia, Central Italy. *J. Archaeol. Sci.* **8 (1)**, 105-106.

Shackleton, J. C. and Andel, T. H. van (1980). Prehistoric shell assemblages from Franchthi Cave and evolution of the adjacent coastal zone. *Nature* **288**, 357-359.

Shackleton, N. J. (1973). Oxygen isotope analysis as a means of determining season of occupation of prehistoric midden sites. *Archaeometry* **15 (1)**, 133-141.

Shackleton, N. J. (1975). The stratigraphic record of deep-sea cores, and its implications for the assessment of glacials, interglacials, stadials and interstadials in the Middle

Pleistocene. In *After the Australopithecines* (ed. K. W. Butzer and G. L. Isaac), pp.1-24. The Hague: Mouton.

Shackleton, N. J. and Opdyke, N. D. (1973). Oxygen isotope and palaeomagnetic stratigraphy of equatorial Pacific core V28-238: oxygen isotope temperatures and ice volumes on a 10^5 year and 10^6 year scale. *Quat. Res.* **3**, 39-55.

Shackleton, N. J. and Opdyke, N. D. (1976). Oxygen-isotope and paleomagnetic stratigraphy of Pacific core V28-239, Late Pliocene to latest Pleistocene. *Geol. Soc. Am. Mem.* **145**, 449-464.

Shackleton, N. J. and Opdyke, N. D. (1977). Oxygen isotope and palaeomagnetic evidence for early Northern Hemisphere glaciation. *Nature* **270**, 216-219.

Shackley, M. L. (1978). The behaviour of artefacts as sedimentary particles in a fluviatile environment. *Archaeometry* **20 (1)**, 55-61.

Shackley, M. (1980). An Acheulean industry with *Elephas recki* fauna from Namib IV, South West Africa (Namibia). *Nature* **284**, 340-341.

Sheets, J. W. and Gavan, J. A. (1977). Dental reduction from *Homo erectus* to Neanderthal. *Curr. Anthropol.* **18 (3)**, 587-588.

Shimkin, E. M. (1978). The Upper Palaeolithic in North-Central Eurasia: evidence and problems. In *Views of the Past* (ed. L. G. Freeman), pp.193-316. The Hague: Mouton.

Shipman, P. (1981). *Life History of a Fossil.* Cambridge (Mass.): Harvard University Press.

Shipman, P., Bosler, W. and Davis, K. L. (1981). Butchering of giant geladas at an Acheulean site. *Curr. Anthropol.* **22 (3)**, 257-268.

Simmons, I. G. (1979). Late mesolithic societies and the environment of the uplands of England and Wales. *Bull. Inst. Archaeol. London* **16**, 111-129.

Simmons, I. G. and Dimbleby, G. W. (1974). The possible role of ivy (*Hedera helix* L.) in the mesolithic economy of western Europe. *J. Archaeol. Sci.* **1**, 291-296.

Simmons, I. G. and Innes, J. B. (1981). Tree remains in a North York Moors peat profile. *Nature* **294**, 76-78.

Simons, E. L. (1969). Late Miocene hominid from Fort Ternan, Kenya. *Nature* **221**, 448-452.

Simons, E. L. (1977). *Ramapithecus. Sci. Am.* **236 (5)**, 28-35.

Slicher van Bath, B. H. (1963). *The Agrarian History of Western Europe A.D. 500-1850.* London: Edward Arnold.

Smith, A. G., Pilcher, J. R. and Pearson, G. W. (1971). New radiocarbon dates from Ireland. *Antiquity* **45**, 97-102.

Smith, F. H. (1976). A fossil hominid frontal from Velika Pecina (Croatia) and a consideration of Upper Pleistocene hominids from Yugoslavia. *Am. J. Phys. Anthropol.* **44**, 127-134.

Smith, F. H. and Ranyard, G. C. (1980). Evolution of the supraorbital region in Upper Pleistocene fossil hominids from South-Central Europe. *Am. J. Phys. Anthropol.* **53 (4)**, 589-610.

Smith, I. F. (1974). The neolithic. In *British Prehistory* (ed. C. Renfrew), pp.100-136. London: Duckworth.

Soffer, O. (1981). Social intensification among hunter-gatherers: the case of the Upper Palaeolithic on the Russian plain. Paper presented at meeting of Society for American Archaeology, San Diego. Unpublished.

Sonneville-Bordes, D. de (1963). Le palaeolithique en Suisse. *L'Anthropologie* **67 (3-4)**, 205-268.

Soudsky, B. and Pavlů, I. (1972). The Linear Pottery Culture settlement patterns of Central Europe. In *Man, Settlement and Urbanism* (ed. P. J. Ucko, R. Tringham and G. W. Dimbleby), pp.317-328. London: Duckworth.

Spiess, A. E. (1979). *Reindeer and Caribou Hunters.* London: Academic Press.

Spratt, D. A. and Simmons, I. G. (1976). Prehistoric activity and environment on the North York Moors. *J. Archaeol. Sci.* **3 (3)**, 193-210.

Srejović, D. (1969a). The roots of the Lepenski Vir culture, *Archaeol. Iugosl.* **10**, 13-21.

Srejović, D. (1969b). Lepenski Vir: protoneolithic and early neolithic settlements, *Archaeology* **22 (1)**, 26-35.

Srejović, D. and Letica, Z. (1969). Epipalaeolithic settlements at Vlasac, *Starinar* **5**, 1-32.

Stanley, D. J. and Blanpied, C. (1980). Late Quaternary water exchange between the eastern Mediterranean and the Black Sea. *Nature* **285**, 537-541.

Stanley, V. (1980). Paleoecology of the arctic-steppe mammoth biome. *Curr. Anthropol.* **21 (5)**, 663-666.

Startin, W. (1978). Linear Pottery Culture houses: reconstruction and manpower. *Proc. Prehist. Soc.* **44**, 143-159.

Steudel, K. (1980). New estimates of early hominid body size. *Am. J. Phys. Anthropol.* **52 (1)**, 63-70.

Stordeur-Yedid, D. (1979). Les aiguilles à chas au paléolithique. *Gallia Préhist. Suppl.* **13**.

Straus, L. G. (1977). Of deerslayers and mountain men: palaeolithic faunal exploitation in Cantabrian Spain. In *For Theory Building in Archaeology* (ed. L. R. Binford), pp.41-75. London and New York: Academic Press.

Straus, L. G. *et al.* (1980). Ice-age subsistence in northern Spain. *Sci. Am.* **242 (6)**, 120-129.

Streeter, S. S. and Shackleton, N. J. (1979). Paleocirculation of the deep North Atlantic: 150,000-year record of benthic foraminifera and oxygen-18. *Science* **203**, 168-170.

Stringer, C. B. (1974). Population estimates of later Pleistocene hominids: a multivariate study of available crania. *J. Archaeol. Sci.* **1**, 317-342.

Stringer, C. B. (1978). Some problems in Middle and Upper Pleistocene hominid relationships. *Recent Adv. Primatol.* **3**, 395-418.

Stringer, C. B. and Burleigh, R. (1981). The Neanderthal problem and the prospect for direct dating of Neanderthal remains. *Bull. Br. Mus. Nat. Hist. (Geol).* **35 (3)**, 225-341.

Stringer, C. B., Howell, F. C. and Melentis, J. K. (1979). The significance of the fossil hominid skull from Petralona, Greece. *J. Archaeol. Sci.* **6**, 235-253.

Stuart, A. J. (1977). The vertebrates of the last cold stage in Britain and Ireland. *Phil. Trans. R. Soc. London B.* **280**, 295-312.

Stuiver, M. (1978). Radiocarbon timescale tested against magnetic and other dating methods. *Nature* **273**, 271-274.

Sturdy, D. A. (1972). The exploitation patterns of a modern reindeer economy in west Greenland. In *Papers in Economic Prehistory* (ed. E. S. Higgs), pp.161-168. Cambridge: Cambridge University Press.

Sturdy, D. A. (1975). Some reindeer economies in prehistoric Europe. In *Palaeoeconomy* (ed. E. S. Higgs), pp.55-95. Cambridge: Cambridge University Press.

Sutcliffe, A. J. (1970). Spotted hyaena: crusher, gnawer, digester and collector of bones. *Nature* **227**, 1110-1113.

Swardt, A. M. J. de (1974). Geomorphological dating of cave openings in South Africa. *Nature* **250**, 683-684.

Swedlund, A. C. (1974). The use of ecological hypotheses in Australopithecine taxonomy. *Am. Anthropol.* **76**, 515-529.

Szabo, B. J. and Collins, D. (1975). Age of fossil bones from British interglacial sites. *Nature* **254**, 680-681.

Szalay, F. S. (1975). Hunting-scavenging protohominids: a model for hominid origins. *Man (N.S.)* **10**, 420-429.

Tauber, H. (1981). ^{13}C evidence for dietary habits of prehistoric man in Denmark. *Nature* **292**, 332-333.

Tauxe, L. (1979). A new date for *Ramapithecus. Nature* **282**, 399-401.

Teleki, G. (1975). Primate subsistence patterns: collector-predators and gatherer-hunters. *J. Hum. Evol.* **4**, 125-184.

Thiede, J. (1978). A glacial Mediterranean. *Nature* **276**, 680-683.

Thunell, R. C. (1979a). Climatic evolution of the Mediterranean Sea during the last 5.0 million years. *Sediment. Geol.* **23**, 67-79.

Thunell, R. C. (1979b). Eastern Mediterranean Sea during the last glacial maximum; an 18,000 years B.P. reconstruction. *Quat. Res.* **11**, 353-372.

Tobias, P. V. (1973). Implications of the new age determination of the early South African hominids. *Nature* **246**, 79-83.

Tobias, P. V. (1980). A survey and synthesis of the African hominids of the late Tertiary and early Quaternary periods. In *Current Arguments on Early Man* (ed. L. -K. Konigsson); pp.86-113. Royal Swedish Acad. Sci.: Pergamon Press.

Todaro, G. J. (1980). Evidence using viral gene sequences suggesting an Asian origin of man. In *Current Arguments on Early Man* (ed. L.-K. Konigsson), pp.252-260. Royal Swedish Acad. Sci.: Pergamon Press.

Tode, A. F. *et al.* (1963). Die Untersuchung der paläolithischen Freilandstation von Salzgitter-Lebenstedt. *Eiszeitalter & Gegenw.* **3**, 144-220.

Tratman, E. K. (1976). A late upper palaeolithic calculator (?), Gough's Cave, Cheddar, Somerset. *Proc. Univ. Bristol Speleol. Soc.* **14 (2)**, 123-129.

Trevor-Deutsch, B. and Bryant, V. M. (1978). Analysis of suspected human coprolites from Terra Amata, Nice, France. *J. Archaeol. Sci.* **5 (4)**, 387-390.

Tringham, R. (1971). *Hunters, Fishers and Farmers of Eastern Europe, 6000-3000 B.C.* London: Hutchinson and Co.

Tringham, R. (1973). The Mesolithic of southeastern Europe. In *The Mesolithic in Europe* (ed. S. K. Kozlowski), pp.551-569. Warsaw: Warsaw Univ. Press.

Trinkhaus, E. and Howells, W. W. (1979). The Neanderthals. *Sci. Am.* **241 (6)**, 94-105.

Tudge, C. (1981). 'Exaptation': a term is born. *New Scientist* **92**, 912.

Valen, L. van (1969). Late Pleistocene extinctions. *Proc. North Am. Palaeontol. Congr.* Part E, 469-485.

Valoch, K. (1975). Neue Primaten- und Hominidenfunde in Jugoslawien. *Anthropologie* (Czech) **13 (1-2)**, 159-160.

Valoch, K. (1976). Aperçu de premiers industries en Europe. IXe Congr. UISPP Nice, Coll. X, 86-91. Paris: CRNS.

Valoch, K. (1980). La fin des temps glaciaires en Moravie (Tchécoslovaquie). *L'Anthropologie* **84 (3)**, 380-390.

Valoch, K., Smoliková, L. and Zeman, A. (1978). The Middle Pleistocene site Pribice I in South Moravia (Czechoslovakia). *Anthropologie* (Czech) **16 (3)**, 229-241.

Vita-Finzi, C. (1973). Palaeolithic finds from Cyprus? *Proc. Prehist. Soc.* **39**, 453-454.

Vita-Finzi, C. and Higgs, E. S. (1970). Prehistoric economy in the Mount Carmel area of Palestine: site catchment analysis. *Proc. Prehist. Soc.* **36**, 1-37.

Vlček, E. (1978). A new discovery of *Homo erectus* in Central Europe. *J. Hum. Ecol.* **7**, 239-251.

Vogel, J. C. and Merwe, N. J. van der (1977). Isotopic evidence for early maize cultivation in New York State. *Am. Antiq.* **42**.

Vogel, J. C. and Waterbolk, H. T. (1964). Groningen radiocarbon dates V. *Radiocarbon* **6**, 349-369.

Vogel, J. C. and Waterbolk, H. T. (1972). Groningen radiocarbon dates X. *Radiocarbon* **14**, 59-66.

Vogel, J. C. and Zagwijn, W. H. (1967). Groningen radiocarbon dates VI. *Radiocarbon* **9**, 63-106.

Voorhies, M. R. (1969). Taphonomy and population dynamics of an early Pliocene vertebrate fauna, Knox County, Nebraska. *Univ. Wyoming Spec. Contrib. Geol.* **1**, 1-69.

Vrba, E. S. (1974). Chronological and ecological implications of the fossil Bovidae at the Sterkfontein Australopithecine site. *Nature* **250**, 19-23.

Walker, A. and Leakey, R. E. F. (1978). The hominids of East Turkana. *Sci. Am.* **239 (2)**, 44-56.

Welinder, S. (1975). Agriculture, inland hunting, and sea hunting in the western and northern region of the Baltic, 6000-2000 B.C. In *Prehistoric Maritime Adaptations of the Circumpolar Zone* (ed. W. Fitzhugh), pp.21-39. The Hague — Paris: Mouton.

Welinder, S. (1978). The concept of 'ecology' in Mesolithic research. In *The Early Post-Glacial Settlement of Northern Europe* (ed. P. Mellars), pp.11-25. London: Duckworth.

Wendorf, F. *et al.* (1975). Dates for the Middle Stone Age of East Africa. *Science* **187**, 740-742.

Wendorf, F. *et al.* (1979). Use of barley in the Egyptian late palaeolithic. *Science* **205**, 1341-1347.

Wendt, W. E. (1976). "Art mobilier" from the Apollo II cave, South-West Africa: Africa's oldest dated works of art. *S. Afr. Archaeol. Bull.* **31**, 5-11.

Westropp, H. M. (1872). *Prehistoric phases.* London: Bell and Daldy.

Wheat, J. B. (1973). A paleo-Indian kill. In *Early Man in America* (ed. R. S. McNeish), pp.80-88. San Francisco: Freeman and Co.

Wheeler, A. C. (1969). *The Fishes of the British Isles and North-West Europe.* London: Macmillan.

Wheeler, A. C. (1978). Why were there no fish remains at Star Carr? *J. Archaeol. Sci.* **5 (1)**, 85-90.

White, J. P. and Thomas, D. H. (1972). What mean these stones? Ethno-taxonomic models and archaeological interpretations in the New Guinea Highlands. In *Models in Archaeology* (ed. D. L. Clarke), pp.275-308. London: Methuen.

White, T. D. (1980). Evolutionary implications of Pliocene hominid footprints. *Science* **208**, 175-176.

Wilkinson, P. F. (1972). Current experimental domestication and its relevance to pre-history. In *Papers in Economic Prehistory* (ed. E. S. Higgs), pp.107-118. Cambridge: Cambridge University Press.

Wilkinson, P. F. (1975). The relevance of musk ox exploitation to the study of prehistoric animal economies. In *Palaeoeconomy* (ed. E. S. Higgs), pp.9-53. Cambridge: Cambridge University Press.

Wilkinson, P. F. (1976). "Random" hunting and the composition of faunal samples from archaeological excavations: a modern example from New Zealand. *J. Archaeol. Sci.* **3**, 321-328.

Willerding, U. (1980). Zum Ackerbau der Bandkeramiker. *Materialhefte Ur- & Fruhgesch. Niedersachsens* **16**, 421-456.

Wilmsen, E. N. (1973). Interaction, spacing behaviour, and the organisation of hunting bands. *J. Anthropol. Res.* **29 (1)**, 1-31.

Wintle, A. G. and Aitken, M. J. (1977). Thermoluminescence dating of burnt flint: application to a lower palaeolithic site, Terra Amata. *Archaeometry* **19 (2)**, 111-130.

Wobst, M. (1974). Boundary conditions for paleolithic social systems: a simulation approach. *Am. Antiq.* **39**, 147-178.

Wobst, M. (1978). The archaeoethnology of hunter-gatherers or the tyranny of the ethno-graphic record in archaeology. *Am. Antiq.* **43 (2)**, 303-309.

Woillard, G. M. (1978). Grande Pile peat bog: continuous pollen record for the last 140,000 years. *Quat. Res.* **9**, 1-21.

Woillard, G. M. (1979). Abrupt end of the last interglacial s.s. in North-East France. *Nature* **281**, 558-562.

Woillard, G. M. and Mook, W. G. (1982). Carbon-14 dates at Grande Pile: correlation of land and sea chronologies. *Science* **215**, 159-161.

Wolff, R. G. (1973). Hydrodynamic sorting and ecology of a pleistocene mammalian assemblage from California (U.S.A.). *Palaeogeogr., Palaeoclimatol., Palaeoecol.* **13**, 91-101.

Wolpoff, M. H. (1976). Primate models for Australopithecine sexual dimorphism. *Am. J. Phys. Anthropol.* **45**, 497-510.

Wolpoff, M. H. (1980). Cranial remains of Middle Pleistocene European hominids. *J. Hum. Evol.* **9**, 339-358.

Wolpoff, M. H. (1981). Allez Neanderthal. *Nature* **289**, 823.

Woodman, P. C. (1978). The chronology and economy of the Irish mesolithic: some working hypotheses. In *The Early Post-Glacial Settlement of Northern Europe* (ed. P. Mellars), pp.333-369. London: Duckworth.

Wright, R. V. S. (1972). Imitative learning of a flaked stone technology—the case of an orangutan. *Mankind* **8**, 296-306.

Wynn, T. (1979). The intelligence of later Acheulean hominids. *Man (N.S.)* **14**, 371-391.

Wynn, T. (1981). The intelligence of Oldowan hominids. *J. Hum. Evol.* **10**, 529-541.

Y'Edynak, G. (1978). Culture, diet, and dental reduction in mesolithic forager-fishers of Yugoslavia. *Curr. Anthropol.* **19 (3)**, 616-618.

Zagwijn, W. H. (1974). The Plio-Pleistocene boundary in western and southern Europe. *Boreas* **3**, 75-97.

Zeist, W. van (1969). Reflections on prehistoric environments in the Near East. In *The Domestication and Exploitation of Plants and Animals* (ed. P. J. Ucko and G. W. Dimbleby), pp.35-46. London: Duckworth.

Zeist, W. van (1972). Palaeobotanical results of the 1970 season at Çayönü, Turkey. *Helinium* **12**, 3-19.

Zeist, W. van (1976). On macroscopic traces of food plants in southwestern Asia (with some reference to pollen data). *Phil. Trans. R. Soc. London B* **275**, 27-41.

Zeist, W. van, Woldring, H. and Stapert, D. (1975). Late Quaternary vegetation and climate of southwestern Turkey. *Palaeohistoria* **17**, 53-143.

Zivonovic, S. (1975). A note on the anthropological characteristics of the Padina population. *Z. Morphol. Anthropol.* **66 (2)**, 161-175.

Zohary, D. (1969). The progenitors of wheat and barley in relation to domestication and dispersal in the Old World. In *The Domestication and Exploitation of Plants and Animals* (ed. P. J. Ucko and G. W. Dimbleby), pp.47-66. London: Duckworth.

Zvelebil, M. (1978). Subsistence and settlement in the north-eastern Baltic. In *The Early Post-Glacial Settlement of Northern Europe* (ed. P. M. Mellars), 205-241. London: Duckworth.

Site Index

215